INDIAN PUBLIC ADMINISTRATION

Indian
Public Administration

*[According to the UGC Syllabus
For UGC-NET]*

By
NASEEM AHMAD

ANMOL PUBLICATIONS PVT. LTD.
NEW DELHI - 110 002 (INDIA)

ANMOL PUBLICATIONS PVT. LTD.
4374/4B, Ansari Road, Daryaganj
New Delhi - 110 002
Ph.: 23261597, 23278000
Visit us at: www.anmolpublications.com

First Published, 2005

PRINTED IN INDIA

Published by J.L. Kumar for Anmol Publications Pvt. Ltd., New Delhi - 110 002 and Printed at Mehra Offset Press, Delhi.

Contents

Preface

Public Administration in India has been cultivated , nursed and polished over the years. It's mature now. Originally, Indian Public Administration is based on British system. In fact, it were the Englishmen only, who introduced, developed and established modern administration in this country. Although, Mughal Administration was perfect and well oiled, as per contemporary standards and initially, East India Company laid the foundation of its administrative setup on the remainders of Mughal system, yet, they made necessary alterations and renovations, in accordance with the changing trends and, of course, their own strategies of governance.

After Independence, Indian Public Administration was moulded by new custodian, according to indigenous requirement and national standards.

Indian Public Administration has come a long way. It has evolved and developed over the decades. This book covers all the milestones in the journey of Indian Public Administration and discusses in detail the basic philosophy, functioning and further prospects of the system.

In order to make this book beneficial for the students, it has been prepared in accordance with the syllabi of various universities in general and UGC-NET in particular.

Hopefully, this comprehensive book would prove to be useful for the teachers, students and aspirants, appearing at various tests.

Editor

1

Introduction

The study of Public Administration as an independent discipline emerged in the recent past. In the earliest stages of society the rudiments of administrative activity were discernible but no adequate attention was paid to develop an independent science of public administration.

Administrative process is as old as human society, whereas, public administration as a process is as old as government. Public Administration as a separate branch of knowledge is, however, of recent origin. As an academic subject, it is taught in most of the countries, though in many instances since the end of the World War II only.

A lot of literature on Public Administration can be found in ancient writings such as Plato's Laws, Aristotle's Politics, Kautilya's Arthasastra, Machiavelli's 'Prince' and also in the maximum approaches of philosopher king Confucious. Conscious training arrangements made for the administrators can also be traced in the ancient as well as medieval period. This was mainly due to the reason what the nature of state was undergoing somewhat change with its activities increasing from merely the maintenance of law and order and collection of revenue to social welfare, public works, and also some interference in business and economy.

In the modern period, pure administration began to develop as a university study during the eleventh century. As Dimock and Dimock write, "Economists, political scientists and sociologists in the USA gave their main attention during the later part of the nineteenth century to public policy and social engineering providing the ingredients out of which the future university discipline of public administration was to be fashioned".

It is now an established fact that public administration is not only an art but also a science—a body of systematised knowledge, and therefore, it must be possible to sum up 'principles' some leading truths of administration having general application. Though it cannot be claimed that these principles approach scientific laws in precision or serve as a means of prediction, yet they do serve the practical purpose of providing an essentially conceptual framework to facilitate the study of the subject. Our principles are the headings-labels, we can call them, if we like, for the drawers of filling cabinets in which material for the comprehensive study of the subject may be sorted or arranged.

Richard Warner, enumerates following principles of public administration :

(i) Principle of political direction, (ii) Principle of public responsibility, (iii) Principle of social necessity, (iv) Principle of efficiency, (v) Principle of organization, (vi) Principle of public relations, (vii) Principle of evolution and progress, (viii) Principle of research.

The study of public administration has been approached from various angles. A brief survey of various important approaches to its study is as under :

Various Approaches

One peculiar feature regarding the rise of public administration as a discipline was that almost without exception those, who might be called the founding fathers of public administration, were trained as political scientists (rather than say, jurists or economists) and tended to view public administration as a part of sub-discipline of political science. Their writings, however, analytically divided the government into two different functions, or types of action : first to decide and second, to carry out decision. These two types of action are identified with and by the words—politics and administration. Making of decisicns is the realm of politics and policy making; whereas execution of decision is the realm of administration.

This can be regarded as the first (or original approach to study public administration and can be named as ·Non-Political or Efficiency Oriented Approach). The earliest writers on the subject concentrated their attention on the question of achievement of efficiency and economy in public administration. This non-political stress got intellectual encouragement by the view that policy making and policy implementation are two different things; the first is the function of popularly elected legislatures and the second is the function of technically skilled and politically 'neutral' civil servants.

A line of distinction was drawn between 'politics' and 'administration' on the assumption that whereas 'administration involves how to do things, the field of policies admits of 'deciding what is to be done'. Policy-determining was considered to be the field of politics, and 'policy-implementation' the field of administration. "It was almost as if the two elements, though both clearly related to the common goal of the public interest, operated in separate vacuum chambers. The policy 'cake' was baked in the legislative chamber, and was then delivered to the administrative chamber for slicing and distribution. But the bakers and the slicers did not really consult or communicate with each other except at arm's length".

This 'politics-administration dichotomy' has been criticized and has now been rejected by students of public administration. Administration is involved in policy formulation also. It is absolutely wrong to say that policies can be formulated without the advice or assistance of administrative staff. There is hardly a minister who is not influenced by the advice and opinion of civil servants while framing policies for administration. Many bills are introduced by ministers in the legislature at the initiative of administrators. Many bills are passed by the legislature in outlines, and the details are filled in by the civil servants. The whole theory of 'delegated legislation' disproves the distinction between policies and administration.

No policy can be framed successfully without proper knowledge of facts and figures. These facts are supplied by the civil servants. Many laws are amended or withdrawn because of the difficulties experienced by the civil servants in implementing those laws. At every step there is an intermingling of politics and administration, at every step administrators influence policy makers. A policy which is divorced from official experience is very likely to have disastrous consequences. Since the civil servants are experienced administrators, they have great knowledge about the facts of the problem, and as such they play a vital role in policy formulation.

How can the advice and opinion of these intelligent civil servants be ignored at the time of policy making? Thus the old distinction between 'Politics' and 'administration' of you-go-your-way and I 'will-go mine' has been rejected as out of date and an impracticable concept. Appleby observed. "Public administration is policy making. But it is not autonomous, exclusive or isolated policy making. It is policy making on a filed where mighty forces contend, forces engendered in and by society". Public Administration cannot be separated from policy formulation. Further, public administration cannot be fruitully studied apart from its political and social setting.

Scientific Management

As public administration was beginning to differentiate from political science during the early twentieth century, business administration began in its turn to break away from the aegis of economics to become a specialization in its own right. Under the influence of developing technology and the leadership of Frederick W. Taylor, engineer and business managers started the search for greater efficiency and effectiveness in organisation functioning giving rise to classical theory of administration which was also called Scientific Management, approach to the study of organisation. According to this approach man is viewed as motivated by economic incentives and the organisation was characterized by a clearly defined division of labour with highly specialized personnel and by a distinct hierarchy or authority.

The assumptions of this approach were as follows :

(i) An individual is primarily motivated by economic incentives i.e., the monetary rewards he gets in return of his labour. This is the biggest force which induces the labour to produce more or to maximize the production.

(ii) There incentives being under the control of organisation, man is essentially a passive agent to be manipulated, motivated and controlled by the organisation.

(iii) Human feelings are essentially irrational and must be prevented from his interfering with his rational calculation of self interest.

(iv) Organisation controls man's feelings and his unpredictable behaviour, because man basically lazy and incapable of self-discipline and self-control.

(v) Individual goals and organisational goals contradict each other. Man, therefore must be controlled by external forces to ensure his working towards organisational goals i.e., individuals goals are subordinate to organisation and man must work for the achievement of organisational goals even at the cost of sacrificing his own goals.

(vi) Organisation was to protect itself and employees from the irrational side of his nature by a system of authority and control.

(vii) Authority rested in designated offices or positions and employee was expected to obey who so ever occupied the position of authority regardless of his expertise or personality. Management ideology had been authoritarian and undemocratic even antidemocratic. Orders always went downward, policies were formulated at the top and communication was one way, i.e., upwards reporting of results.

The scientific management approach, thus views organisation as machine and human beings or workers as cogs in the machine to run it towards the achievement of the organisational goals. This approach has also been known as "machine model" because it views workers as automations. The human beings in the organisation must adjust to the job and the task. It is the job and the task which form the basis of organisational structure. The human being in the job should be ignored and they should adopt or adjust themselves to the needs the jobs or organisation and those who can not fulfil the needs or requirements of the job should be retrenched or discarded.

In short, the organisational structure, according to this approach, is viewed as position and task oriented and not man oriented. The production workers are to obey the leader without talking back to him i.e., to obey the authority without any questioning. Orders from the higher executives run downward and reports of accomplishment go upward.

Besides Taylor, the chief thinkers who contributed to scientific management approach were Fayol, Luther Gulick and Urwic. Under this approach emphasis is laid on the actual operation of management. Management may be seen as consisting of POSDCORB, a device used by Luther Gulick. Here 'P' stands for planning, '0' for organising 'S' for Staffing 'D' for directing, 'CO for co-ordinating, 'R' for reporting and 'B' for budgeting.

The chief object under this approach is to find out how the working of organisation can be improved. In this sense this approach has a normative or clinical emphasis. Improvement of management is seen to be possible by bringing about changes in the planning process (for example by having five years plans instead of one year plans), changing the organisation, reforming the number of levels, decentralization, changed field organisation, and reforming the financial management (for example, by introducing a performance budget) and similarly by improving personnel (for example, through advertising of posts) and so on. The foundations of this approach are the so-called principles of administration, enunciated by Gulick and Urwick in their 'famous "Papers on the Science of Administration" 1937. These so-called principles were, derived from the experience of managers and acute observation of thinkers.

The approach rests firmly on the assumption that the more a particular job can be broken down into its simplest component parts, the more specialized and skilled a worker can become in carrying out his part of the job. The more skilled a worker, the more efficient the whole production system would be. The theory, further pointed out that the division of labour has to be balanced by unity of command, which means that the tasks have to be broken up into small work units by a central authority in line with a central plan of action. The work efforts of each unit have to be co-ordinated to achieve the ultimate goal of the organisation. Each supervisor can supervise or control the work of limited number of workers effectively. The number of subordinates controlled by one supervisor defines his, 'Span of Control'. One supervisor was supposed to control not more than, five to ten subordinates. The whole chain of supervisors formed a pyramid of control leading up to one top executive with a centre of authority.

Thus, the scientific management or classical organisational approach concentrates on the formal structural principles which can be categorised in the following broad categories.

The Co-ordinate Principle : It provides unity of command for the achievement of common organisational goal. It includes the need for authority and leadership i.e., some one should have the ultimate responsibility for co-ordinating all administrative units in the organisation.

Hierarchical Conformation : This principle is also called 'scalar principle' which moans that channels of administrative authority would follow the hierarchical pattern by making every one in the pyramid administratively answerable to the chief executive.

The Functional Principle : It is really a concept of specialization. Classical theory treats specialization as the basis of efficiency. Consequently it places emphasis on the most effective grouping of specialist functions for management purposes. This purposal grouping of functions should be based on four principles such as specialization by purposes process clientele and geographical area.

Staff and Line Principle : Staff agencies are to advise the chief executive in the specific field the line agencies represent authority, i.e., persons in the administrative hierarchy who have the authority to command.

Span of Control : The number of subordinates reporting to the ,chief executive should be small enough so that he can supervise the work of his subordinates effectively.

Unity of Command : The term means that an employee should not receive orders from more than one superior. In other words a subordinate should report only to one superior office and he should receive instructions only from him. Fayol says, "If this principal should be violated, authority is undermined, discipline is jeopardize, order disturbed and stability threatened".

All the classical writers accepted the principles and paid considerable attention to formal structure of organization. However, later Herbert A. Simon in his "Administrative Behaviour" 1945 criticised these so called principles. The application of the classical approach has by no means died out. It is still being applied in its modified from

The Criticism

Dehumanization of Organisation : The assumption of the approach that man is separable form the job and it is the task that is important than the job holder is to miss the substance. The concept that labour had always been in surplus supply and due to fear of hunger and scarcity of jobs and for economic benefits man had to adjust himself with the job, is not correct because man is very complex in his nature and it is not only fear of hunger and economic benefits which motivated him to produce more. He has his socio-psychological needs which must be satisfied to get the best out of him. The idea that man is mere commodity is wrong in this age of more human industrial relations. The positive view is that workers are human beings who have right to work and live in social groups with dignity.

Job Task Hierarchy : The concept of job task hierarchy visualizes people as working at specialized tasks or, in administrative term playing different roles. It embodies the concepts such as unity of command, superior subordinate relations, limited span of control, staff and line distinctions, and downward control from the top. The classical theory emphasised this dimension of the organisation much. This approach is authoritarian and undemocratic in the sense that it recognises only job task relationships, authoritarian control, and orders from top to bottom. In the whole jargon of hierarchical relations, it fails to recognise the human beings who fulfil the various jobs. Thus the concept is not in tune with democratic political and social institutions.

Division of Work : As stated earlier the principal objective of the Scientific Management Theory was the division of work into so small component units and tasks that the workers would spend the whole day on one repetitive operation. It means that man in the organisation was just a cog which rotates automatically. But the truth is otherwise. Man on the job wants to create something new and finds pleasure in completing the whole operation instead of minute repetitive part of it. Repetition makes him fed up his job and he finds no self actualization in the task. The principles of departmentalisation by functions, process, clientele and geographical area and allied to this concept the span of control have been the greatest forgets of criticism by the theorist of Human Relations Approach to the study of organisation.

Productivity, a Single Standard of Value : The traditional organisational theory recognised only the single value system of productive efficiency and maximization of financial returns. Financial incentive was the only philosophy of human motivation. The behaviour of the managers towards the employees was not that of brotherhood, but as of authoritarian dictator who considered the workers as commodity and made them to adjust within the law of the organisation. This type of behaviour insulated the organisation from the board problems of human welfare.

Anti-Democratic Bias : As has already been stated that according to this theory the administrative or management ideology has been traditionally authoritarian and undemocratic, rather anti-democratic because orders always went downwards. The chief executive was the repository of all wisdom, therefore, policies were always generated at the top and communication was always one way i.e., superiors were to send orders to the subordinates and the latter were expected to obey the orders of their superiors without any complaint and grudge.

Thus, the essence of the controversy centres round the fact that classical or Scientific Management approach dehumanises the organisation and glorifies the management principles. These principle have been termed as mere proverbs which had never been scientifically tested particularly the 'span control' principle. According to Pfiffner and Sherwood, "The revolt against the principles by the more theoretical students of administration had emotional roots in the social philosophers, distrust of techniques. The behavioural scientists thus, challenged the traditional classical approach by emphasising the role of human beings in the organisation."

Moreover, the scientific management approach separated politics from administration which was not acceptable to the students of public administration. It was claimed that administrators take part in policy making which is a political function.

Thus the two classical approaches—the non-political approach and the scientific management approach cannot be treated as distinct from each other but the two aspects of the same approach emphasising mechanical aspect of public administration.

Human Relations Approach

The resentment shown against the scientific management approach led to the growth of human relations approach. It is generally agreed that the human relations movement began as a result of a study undertaken at Western Electric Company's

Hawthorne works in Chicago between 1927 and 1932, conducted under the direction of Harward psychologist Elton Mayo. It began as an examination of physical environment and productivity and some other things. The findings contradicted the anticipated results. Mayo's conclusions were that human behaviour and sentiments were closely related, which effect the output. All this led to a new emphasis of the human factor in the functioning of organisations .and their attainment of goals.

Other important thinkers of this school of thought are ' F.J. Roethilisberger, Robert K. Merton, Keith Davis, A. H. Maslow, Chris Argyris, etc. They viewed administration as a complex of inter-personal relationship, and thus laid emphasis on human behaviour and motivation.

Under human relations approach, great emphasis is laid on the major psychological processes such as perception, learning personality and motivation. It also laid emphasis on social psychology, which should be understood and practised by the administrators for enriching their knowledge in group behaviour, motivation and inter personal relations.

The thinkers of this school criticised earlier approaches for ignoring human factor in organisations. They say that scientific management school treat human beings as machines which lack feelings, sentiments or willingness. They stressed that every individual has a separate personality, which should not be allowed to be suppressed in any organisational environment, so that there should not be any conflict between the individual's goals and the organisational goals.

Legal Approach

This approach is entirely different from earlier approaches and has a stress on the legal framework of an organisation. Exponents of this approach would like to study public administration as part of law and concentrate on the formal legal structure and organisation of public bodies. Its chief concern has been with power, its structure and functions. It stresses the formal organisation of offices, official duties, limitations of power and discretionary authority of administrators. Its main sources are constitutions, codes of law, office manuals of rules and regulations and judicial decisions.

Many countries of Europe like Germany, Belgium and France have particularly applied the legal approach to the study of public administration. In these countries there are two principal divisions of law-constitutional and administrative. Whereas constitutional law deals with the three organisations of the government their interrelations and the distribution of power among them, administrative law is mainly concerned with the structure and functions of public bodies, departments and authorities. The legal approach is valuable for the understanding of the legal framework within which the administrative system has to operate.

Frank Goodnow is prominent among those who adopted this approach to study public administration. However, it has been criticised on the ground that it stops at the legal framework and does not go to the actual operations. It has also been pointed out that it goes into dry aspect and ignores human aspect or human behaviour in administration. Thus by neglecting the informal aspects of the organisation it remains to a great extent an incomplete approach to the study of public administration.

Historical Approach

It is one of the traditional approaches. To the political scientists it has long been familiar and it has had its followers even in the study of administration in a number of countries. Like all history administrative history seeks to illuminate the administrative institution land arrangements of today with the light of the experience of the past. Thus, the historical approach is essentially based on the belief that knowledge of history is absolutely essential for an in-depth study of any subject. For a proper understanding of the subject the study of public administration of the past in particular periods is necessary of link up with the present administrative systems. For example, for a proper understanding of the background and growth of administration in India, a historical perspective is essential. To understand the evolution of the administrative system of India, the characteristics of British Indian Administration and also the pre-British period have to be studied. White's two volumes 'The Federalists' (1948) and 'The Jaffersonians' (1951) are important studies of the federal administration of the USA during the early years of the Republic.

In public administration the early thinkers did not seek much reliance on the historical approach as the effort has towards evolving a science of management or administration. But, of late, there is a revival of interest in the historical studies of the public administration. In Europe and America eminent administrators and ex-administrators are induced to record their reminiscences, of the outstanding events and decisions of the administration of their days. To take a recent example, Richard Milhaus Nixon, the former president of USA, has put down on paper his reminiscences of his days in power. Some call it a history in a hurry. In India too, a number of books by writers, administrators and journalists according what in their view went on in the recent-past have generated a lot of argument. Though none of the works provides an in-depth analysis of the administrative process, quite a few of these throw light on the functioning of policy makers and top administration.

Institutional Approach

Another traditional approach to study public administration is the institutional or descriptive approach. In point of time, it is the oldest and in point of number, it has the largest following. But it is the least homogeneous of all the approaches of public administration as it includes among its protagonists teachers and researchers with varied training ranging from political scientists to specialists in scientific management techniques. Nevertheless, there are some common features of this approach which distinguish it from others. These are :

(a) The followers of this approach took the policy administration dichotomy quite seriously. They defined the task of the administrator as non-political or technical which lay merely in carrying out the will of the political authority by ethically neutral means. Thus, they directed all their efforts to discover 'principles' of public administration.

(b) The early work of this school is characterized by the empirical and pragmatic approach. Their sole aim was to describe a set of facts and not to build any theory. This view prevailed particularly in the United States in between the two World Wars and its greatest exponents were Leonard D. White and Luther Gulick.

Since the nineteen fifties, there has been a shift in this approach. Although the study has retained its descriptive and institutional character, yet the policy administration dichotomy has been qualified after having been found too hasty. More attention is now being given to the normative aspects of public administration and administration is being viewed as an element in political theory and the accepted political values. For instance, the old time concept of efficiency and economy as the sole objectives of public administration has been dubbed as "sterile, scholastic and to be avoided". It is insisted that good administration is no substitute for self government and that therefore, good administration must not conflict with the requirements. Problems of organisation management, etc., must, therefore, be considered in the larger context of the democratic purpose. John M. Gaus, Paul Appleby and other of this school have frankly given up the technical view of public administration and they approach administration from the broad political standpoint. They and some later writers tried to make improvements where necessary and possible.

Bureaucratic Approach

Another way of portraying and rigorously testing administrative reality is by assuming that since professionalized bureaucracies exist in most countries of the world and as well as in varying degree in all institutions, therefore, bureaucracy itself provides the most useful model of administration. Here the emphasis is more on people and professionalization than on organisation, which is said to be largely only structural until animated by human behaviour.

Max Weber, the exponent of bureaucratic approach, was very much concerned with the distribution of power among the organisational positions in the bureaucratic structure, and this represents the formal' element of his work. At the same time, in his exploration of legitimation, he opened up a whole new perspective on the study of satisfaction derived from participation in the organisation. His insight on the interplay between the power to control and the ability to justify (legitimize) its use set the context for a great deal of the following work on the central organisational question : how to control the participants so as to maximize effectiveness and efficiency and minimize unhappiness. This very need to control produces, Weber spelled out in considerable detail the features of the bureaucratic structure, all of which specify what makes a highly rational structure.

In Weberian formulation, bureaucracy refers to the socio-legal concept of rationalisation of collective activities. It constructs a form or design organisation that assures predictability of behaviour of the organizational members. The bureaucratic form according to Weber, 'is the most efficient organisational form for large scale, complex administration that has been developed in the modern, world so far. To achieve the maximum benefits of the bureaucratic form an organization, according to Weber, has to have the following characteristics :

1. Division of labour and specialization. All tasks necessary for the accomplishment of goals are divided into highly specialised jobs.
2. Each task is performed according to a consistent system of abstract rules, ensuring uniformity and coordination of different tasks.
3. Each member is accountable to a superior for his and subordinates, actions. The principle of hierarchy is thus expansions.
4. Each official conducts the business of his in an impersonal, formalistic manner.
5. Employment is based on technical qualifications and is protected against arbitrary dismissal. Promotions are based on seniority and achievement.

These are fairly straightforward characteristics that immediately bring to mind some of the organisational features emphasised in Taylorism. To the extent these characteristics are highly articulated in an organisation, it approaches the ideal types of bureaucracy.

There are a number of other writers too who have contributed to bureaucratic approach; some have adopted Webreian model while some others have severely criticised Weberian model. Among the chief critics of weber are Robert Merton, Philip Selznick, Robert Blau, etc. The critics point out that the Weberian model is subject to the dysfunctional consequences of failing to consider the individual or behavioural aspects of his people in the organisation.

Advantages claimed for the bureaucratic approach over the institutional and other approaches include the fact that since the former is human focused, it is more dynamic. Nor does the bureaucratic approach involve a dichotomy between organisation as the organisation model does 'for administration is firmly lodged in bureaucracy as its unifying process. Moreover, from the standpoint of methodology and testing, bureaucracy is a better instrument than organisation because fewer factors are involved. And finally, development administration which is public administration modified to meet the special needs of developing countries has an urgent need for trained bureaucrats, and the bureaucracy model seems best suited to meet the requirements.

However, scientists like 'Warren Bennis' predict that bureaucracy is likely to go out of use in the wake of new special systems better suited to the 20th century demands of industrialization. Besides this prediction, the bureaucratic approach is suitable to study the public administration of the contemporary developing countries.

Case Study Approach

It was during the thirties, that case method was first used in the study of public administration. The case method and technique arose out of a dissatisfaction with the public administration of the twenties and thirties. In the mid forties a new type of case report was developed in the Graduate School of Public Administration at Harward University. The new type was judged to be rewarding the promising. It represented a search for "reality", a desire to view the administrative world afresh, in its wholeness and without a fire theory of over simplified, assumptions.

The case study method consists in the study of single-unit such as a department, a programme or an office. In public administration generally refers to one decisions such as the setting up of an agency, the transfer of an officer or the budget allocation for a project. Such case studies can be used for three purposes i.e., teaching, research and administrative improvement.

The function of case studies in teaching is to provide vicarious or second hand experience of administration. They are in the nature of stories Which give the., student, an understanding of the administrative process. As used originally at the Harward Business School, these were only half stories. Students were asked to read such a story and were then asked to analyse the situation and indicate what decision they would take under the circumstances. A discussion followed and gave the students an opportunity to understand the pros and cons of alternative courses of action.

In the field of theoretical and applied research, case studies are used for exploratory purposes. They provide useful branches, or hypotheses, which can later be tested. In theoretical research they are valuable because they present the working of an organisation in its totality. They thus provide deep and meaningful understanding of the factors at work within and around the organisation. Once these factors have been identified they can be measured through more extensive studies, called surveys. In a survey one studies a large number of cases to test a theory. These stories, if upheld, take the shape of universal laws. Case studies, thus constitute only the first step in the process' of research.

In applied research, that is research for purpose of improvement, the object is not to build universal law but to know what is ailing a particular organisation. Here also the study of one administrative unit or decision can indicate broad problem areas. The tools of survey and work study can now be used to find the exact nature, location and extent of the problem. Thus low production may be due to bad machines, or lack of communication, or low morale among employees. If a case study of one small workshop indicates low morale, a survey of employees can be made to identify the nature of their difficulties and grievances.

Thus the case study approach went beyond the old public administration both in content and in objective. In the recent years, many scholars have developed case literature from real administrative episodes. However, the application of case method was effective in so far as this approach rejected the old public administration maxim of a separation between politics and administration.

Decision Making Approach

This approach also has a mixed parentage. The starting point is Herbert Simon's book "Administrative Behaviour : A study of Decision Making Process in Administrative Organisation." Other contributors are William J. Gore, March, Russell Ackoff, Martin Starr, Jay Forrester and Kenneth. This approach has probably been influenced more by economics than by any other academic discipline. Thus, calculations of price and value in theoretical economics are equated with input output calculations in public administration. In addition, however, this model is also influenced by the philosophical system known as logical positivism, which seeks exactitude and simple logical constructs. Additional influence comes from some aspects of political science for a main responsibility of judges and lawyers is making decisions, legislators also make decisions in formulating statutes, and administrators make more decision than either.

The principal advantage claimed for the decision-making approach is that a decision involves a clear series of steps resembling those familiar in the physical sciences :, analyse the problem, identify alternative solutions, choose the solution most likely to produce favourable results, take action accordingly, and then test the result, modify the procedure necessary, and finally validate, the course chosen.

How to include all aspects of public administration within the boundaries of this approach presents something of a problem.

The usual rational is to say that the decision-making model helps to define problems and goals by devising alternative solutions through research, and then making a choice among them according to the decision-making formula. Once the goals are set, then instrumentation still according to the formula because largely a material of securing teamwork, which involves organisation, personnel, process, delegation and control. According to this line of reasoning, the setting of goals and the winning of compliance are the most important aspects of public administration.

Those who support the decision-making model acknowledge, however, that administration also, involves values, but it is argued that from the standpoint of the models in practice, the administrator as "citizen" can and will supply his own values.

From all of this it may be concluded that no more in public administration than in "pure" economics, is any single theory wholly 'sufficient. The decision-making approach in public administration does not necessarily, nor is it even likely, to constitute a completely realistic description of how programmes are actually carried out.

Modern Approaches

Earlier approaches to study administration had a number of shortcomings and failed to provide realist position. One of the earliest attempts to examine organizations, at the beginning of the twentieth century, took 'efficiency, as its problem and concentrated on explaining why organizations were or were not satisfying their goals. At about the same period, Max Weber's sociological ideal type of bureaucracy stressed the contribution to efficiency of the rational, formally instituted aspects of organisation. Although Weber was more concerned to offer a clear cut tool for analysis than to deny the empirical importance of informal behaviour, later social scientists grew dissatisfied with what appeared to be concentration upon formal structures and organizational goals. It followed that most attention should be paid to informal activities and to the factors influencing the formation and character of work groups.

To the later students of organization, it seemed illogical however, to replace one distorted emphasis with another. Neither the formal nor the informal aspects of organisation appeared to demand prior attention. A dilemma about the future course of research was eventually resolved by referring to the modern behavioural approach and to parallel tendencies in social thought structure functionalism and general systems approach. These approaches were adopted in public administration also.

Behavioural Approach

Just as the human relations movement was a reaction to scientific management, so the behavioural approach to organization is a reaction to the human relations movement. Some members of the human relations movement were very much concerned with normative propositions about what should and should not be done by administrators. They had a missionary-like zeal to convert administrators from what they considered the human view of human nature implicit in scientific management.

The behavioural scientists, while sharing many of the same values of those in the human relations movement believe that their, duty is to reasons for descriptive, rather than normative, propositions. Human relations, was based on some very simplistic assumptions about human behaviour and offered equally simplistic perspective solutions for managing people. The behavioural approach on the other hand, assumes that humans are extremely complex, and that there is need for theoretical understanding backed by rigorous empirical researches before applications can be made for managing people effectively.

The behavioural scientists, thus, want to determine by scientific means how administrators actually behave rather than how they should behave. What is achieved, how it is achieved and why it is achieved is viewed in relation to its impact and influence upon people who, it is believed, are the really important entity of administration.

Among the originators of the behavioural approach are Hugo Munsterberg, Watson and E. Durkheim; and among the other contributors are Herbert Simon, Chester Barnard and others. The behavioural scientists interested in organization and management were bothered by the lack of scientific rigour of much of the traditional theorists and human relationists. They thought that academicians and practitioners had accepted the theory that had not been validated through accepted scientific procedures. Simon observed that 'administrative behaviour is a part of the behavioural sciences and the study of public administration should involve the study of individual and collective human behaviour in administrative situations. It brings to bear upon administrative problems, an interdisciplinary approach which included sociology, social psychology and cultural anthropology.

The behavioural approach in public administration has given up additional impetus to scientific research and systematic theory construction. The scholars in the field of public administration have made, cross-structural cross-national and cross-cultural" studies of administrative behaviour. This helped the development of knowledge of public administration in the comparative context in the field of comparative public -administration Robert Presthus and, Michael Crozier have conducted empirical; studies of bureaucratic behaviour in different social and cultural perspectives. In India also a number of scholars have used behavioural techniques in research like sh Panandikar, Kuldip Mathur, Ramathrary Roy, Shanti Kothari, C.P. Bhambari. Contemporary research in administrative behaviour has been classified by Herbert Simon as follows :

(i) The study of bureaucracy.; (Robert Merton, Peter Blau and others using and extending upon the Weberian Model);

(ii) Human relations pertaining to motivation and increasing job satisfaction (Chris Argyris, Warren Bennis and others);

(iii) Motivation and studies using the Barnard Simon Equilibrium Model; and

(iv) Decision-making studies emphasizing primarily cognitive processes and the rational components of administrative behaviour.

Major Features : *First,* this approach chooses a frame of reference that is shared by the behavioural sciences, notably, Anthropology, Sociology and Psychology. In other words, this approach is interdisciplinary. It considers the possible effects of cultural, social, and personal factors of behaviour in the organisation.

Second, this type of, analysis takes the individual person's behaviour, including not only his acts but also his identifications demands expectations and evaluations, as the proposition unit of analysis. Thus if we wish to study personnel administration in an organization, it should examine the information, beliefs attitudes (such as morale) individual civil servants. This gives us an idea of the working of the organisation.

Third, this approach chooses theoretical proposition that lend themselves in principle at least, to operational formulation of purpose of empirical research. The effort is to formulate a theoretical frame work which can be tested by gathering data. The frame work consists of abstract universal propositions so that they apply to all cases. These hypotheses can be-tested by going to actual organisation getting relevant facts. An effort is thus made to build up a scientific theory. It is the hope of students of public administration that in this way some scientific principles will discovered, which will be tell us more about behaviour in organisations. If such scientific principle are once discovered, they can no doubt be applied in practice. However every applied science uses a number of pure sciences. Thus the applied science of medicine uses the pure sciences of Anatomy, Physiology, Pathology, Physics, Chemistry and so on. Similarly the applied science of management makes use of the pure sciences of Anthropology, Psychology, Sociology, Mathematics, Statistics so on.

Fourth, this approach, chooses rigorous method and, technique of enquiry for purposes of description and testing of hypotheses. Collection of data, its processing and drawing of inferences, all require the use of method and techniques such as those of survey research, computer programming and multifarious analysis (a statistical technique).

Critical Evaluation

The behavioural approach focuses upon the theory and research concerning human behaviour in organizations developed by behavioural scientists. A number of writers have claimed outstanding and significant contributions by the behavioural school, at the same time a number of other authors have criticised it on certain grounds. The advocates of behavioural approach, claim it to be very useful to managers as well as academicians. They say it all to the managers what to do in problem situations, provide them with a description of their environment, or provide them with a conceptual frame work on which to rely in problem solving situations to help them explain their organisational environment. In other words, it provides them with guides for defining a problem correctly, problem solving, explanation behaviour and control of variables.

Thus it helps to solve problems in area of marketing, public relations, personnel management and industrial relations. For example, the emphasis upon the use of participation and the ways to handle conflict arising from strong differences of opinion and of conduct within an organisation. This school has also led to fruitful discoveries regarding the needs and motivations of people at work, the use of authority, the importance of irrationality in people's behaviour and the informal relationship existing within a work environment. Further in the area of personnel management, recruitment, training, morale and motivation and other aspects are heavily dependent upon the behavioural methods. For instance, despite their limitations, the psychological tests for recruitment are the best. In a client oriented administration (essentially public administration) it is essential to know the cultural factors, personality attributes, beliefs and values of those who are subjects of administrative action.

Those who criticise the behavioural approach point out that the idea of building a science of human behaviours a gross error since human behaviour cannot be the subject of scientific study. Another criticism is that this approach has achieved very little. Thus it is said that most of the findings made through it were already known. The third criticism of this approach is that it requires highly sophisticated tools techniques and skills. The content of research is guided more by the subject-matter. The fourth criticism is that, the approach involves a lot of expenditure, time and effort, and the results are not commensurate with these.

Besides, there are observational dilemmas. Aeinz Evalu writes, "Behaviour is a series of acts through which man moves in time and space. It is datum of observations but a datum that does not constitute a self-evident fact. Instead, it is a fact that is given meaning by observer in the very process of observation. Otherwise observation itself would be meaningless. And if observation had no meaning, it would not occur. Observation is itself a form of behaviour that involves giving certain types of meaning to the object of observation, depending on who the observer is? Error in observation means that the observed act or behavioural pattern has 'been given false meaning".

Eulau and others say that the social scientists ate prone to overestimate the significance of small projects, to over magnify their affects and thus confuse immediate with ultimate ends. As regards to theories, it has been said that it would be foolish to deny that theories occasionally fail to work. In the "real world" it is not difficult to find examples that have failed to produce expected results and consequently cost the organisation considerable sums of money. The theories are likely to fail because,: sometimes it is not properly understood by the individual applying them; the theory is designed for the general case and not specific; all relevant variables are not accounted for, no consideration is giving for system's effect or the theory itself is wrong.

Systems' Approach

Systems approach, a fast developing trend in modern science and technology, is a general scientific and methodological conception. If one considers contemporary science on the whole, it is hard to find a word that is used more frequently than the term 'system'. Biologist, physicists, sociologists, psychologists, managers and others argue about systems and instigate systems of various kinds.

Broadening the spectrum of organisational and administrative issues even further than previous approaches, this stream of thought sees the organisation as a total system of interconnected and interacting sub systems, all dependent upon one another. Thus systems are the essentials of this approach and are basis to most activities. Analysis reveals that an activity is in reality the result of many other sub activities, and in turn, these sub activities of many sub-activities. To illustrate the activities of the human body can be considered a system and a result of many subsystems, including the digestive system, the circulatory system and the nervous system. Thinking in terms of systems simplifies, to some degree, the conception of multitudinous activities with which an administrator must work and, it also enables the administrator to see better the nature of the complex problems to be solved. An enterprise is looked upon as an artificial system, the internal parts of which work together to achieve established goals, the external parts to achieve interplay with its environment, including customers the general public, suppliers and government. The administrator integrates available facilities towards goal achievement by means of systems which relate needed activities required for the end result.

The origin of general systems is traced to the thinking of the biologist Von Bertalanffy in the twenties. But it was only due to the quest of a number of post World War II scholars for a body of concepts leading unity to studies, undertaken in various disciplines, that the concept of 'system' was developed. In short, general systems theory originated in a movement aimed at the unification of science and scientific analysis.

Among the major contributors to the systems approach are Boulding Barnard, Kenneth Bounding, Katz and Khan, Forrester, Stafford Beer Meloskey, Blauberg and others. Besides, David Easton adopted systems approach to politics and Herbert Simon and James Mar viewed organisation as a total system.

An Organisation is an open system. It depends upon its environment for the resources that it needs to operate. An organisation is composed of a set of interdependent parts. Each part of an organisation contributes and receives something from the whole. The process through which the parts are related should be the main area of study. In this process, both resources and problems are exchanged. This will become clearer if we take a hypothetical example the relations between personnel and a production department in an industrial enterprise. Of course, in actual systems, analysis one may often examine relationships between analytically separable parts of the organisation, rather than parts defined by the organisation itself.

Organisations as social systems, are governed by a series of needs which they must satisfy if they are to survive. Only one of the needs is goal attainment. Erzioni argues that by being goal oriented an organisation may fail to meet other functional requirements such as securing the support of its membership. Thus, organisation as a system has multiple objectives. Further, an organisation in, interaction with its environment can be understood as input-output model.

It means that various elements, although possessing their own distinct objectives, contribute to the overall goals of the system through the process of mutual reinforcement. Consequently, the systems approach requires that the 'whole' be investigated from the standpoint of the totality of the elements that compose it.

The flow of input and outputs considered the basic starting point in the description of the organisation. In simplest terms, the organisation takes resources (its inputs) from the larger system (its environment); processes these resources and returns them in changed form its output).

Basically, inputs include men, money and material. The nature of material differs from our organisation to other depending upon the basic objects of the organisation. Similarly, the process and output depends upon the nature and objects of an organisation.

The organisation has also been conceived by many administrative thinkers as a socio-technical system comprising both the social and technical variables. It is not merely an assembly of buildings, money, machines and processes. The system consists in the organisation of these around various technologies, whose motivation, behaviour and relationships determine both the quality and quantity of its inputs and outputs.

The major contribution of systems approach lies in the fact that it helps to build a model which facilitates the better visualizing of the organisation. The systems approach permits a method of examining the enterprise as a whole than as a chaotic arrangement of unrelated parts. Systems approach has, thus, proved useful in studying complex public organisations with social, political and economic environments.

The problem with the systems approach is that the basic concepts of the systems approach are formulated in -terms so abstract that the researchers concerned are "walking on the knife edge falling in danger of mouthing trivialities rather than making original conclusions, should they side step just a bit."

Structural–Functional Approach

This approach envisages that in every society certain important functions have to be carried out by a number of structure with the application of certain specified methods. Social structure is considered as any pattern of behaviour which has become a standard feature of a social system.

The structural functional approach as an analytical tool in the social sciences developed from the work of the anthropologists, Malinowaski and Radcliffe Brown in the early years of the present century. The important followers of this approach are Gabriel Almond, David Apter, M. Lery, F.X. Sutton, Talcott Parsons, Robert Merton and Freud Riggs.

In 1959, Gaberial Almond (with Coleman) in his book entitled "Politics of Developing Countries" gave first application of structural functionalism.

According to Almond, all political systems have four main structures which may be called as legitimate patterns of interaction. His structural functional approaches lay emphasis on functional aspects of the political structures. If a political systems is to continue or to remain in working order, it must perform certain functions.

In different political systems however, the functions may differ. Some may perform more, while others only a few. Within the political systems, many types of political structures or machines develop to complete certain types of functions. These structures with the passage of time become an important part of the political system. If they stop functioning, there is every danger that the system may disintegrate. Either same other structures will have to replace them or the political system will not remain workable.

Davies and Lewis remark about Almond's structural-functional approach that it attempts to shift the focus of analysis from the observable institutional political mechanism to many areas where the actual performance of the functional requirements of the system are located. This approach is inclined to emphasize the search for processes that maintain the, stability of the system.

Riggs makes a distinction between "structure" and "function". He accepts the definition of 'structure' as any pattern of behaviour which has become a standard feature of a social system. Thus a government bureau is a 'structure' or rather a whole set of structures consisting of the many things the officials in the bureau do regularly : the decisions they make, the people they see and paper they sign. The structure is not composed of the people and things themselves, but of their action by 'function' we mean any consequences of a structure in so far as they affect other structures or the total system of which they are a part. A function is a pattern of interdependence between two or more structures, a relationship between variables.

The traditional study of government and of public administration has been primarily concerned with structures. It has developed itself to the analysis of behaviour in legislatures, political parties, government departments, personnel officers, field stations, etc. Such concepts as "line and staff", "headquarters field", "span of control", "position classification" etc., relate chiefly to institutionalized patterns of behaviour to structures.

Structural analysis, of course, leads to an examination of the functions performed by the structures examined, their impact upon related structures. An analysis of the requisite functions (e.g., for the survival of any society) gives us categories to identify structures which, though different, are analytically comparable.

Whenever a structure performs a large number of functions, we may say it is "functionally diffuse", when it performs a limited number it is "functionally specific". This distinction was originally used by Talcott Persons (he gave five pattern variables between functional specifically and functional diffuseness). Riggs used three of persons' variables : the less number of functions a structure performs, the more "diffracted" it is; conversely, the more functions a structure performs, the more "fused" it is; and a mixture of "diffracted" and "fused" structures creates "prismatic" structures.

The structural-functional approach facilitates to analyse different social processes. The experts can locate the structures they want to analyse and their functions, e.g., to analyse the working of bureaucracy in any society it is first defined and identified in structural functional terms. Structurally bureaucracy is viewed as an administrative system possessing features such as hierarchy, specialisation, system of rules, and role specifically. The set of behavioural characteristics identified with bureaucracy are rationality, impersonality, rule orientation and neutrality. However, it may be clarified at the outset that there is no clear and direct relationship between structures and functions. All similar structures do not necessarily perform similar functions. A social structure may perform multiple functions and similarly one function may be performed by more than one structure. Structural-functionalists have helped to clarify the general misconception that similar structure in diverse environments perform similar functions or that absence of certain structure implies that particular functions are not being performed in particular social systems.

According to Riggs, "In every society five important types of functions are discharged viz., economic, social, communication, symbolic and political functions". The same set of functional requisites apply to an administrative sub-system in which various structures carry out a number of functions in a specified manner. A study of these structures, function and methods to understand the phenomena in the structural- function approach.

In the field of public administration, it was first suggested in 1955 by Dwight Waldo that structural-functional analysis might provide some guidance in the construction of a model of ' what an administrative system is like as a general type. Waldo's suggestion was first followed by Fred W. Riggs when he came out with his agrarian industrial typology two years later. Since then, Riggs has been the prime user of the approach in comparative public administration. Various other scholars were also influenced by this approach in comparative public administration. This approach has helped to prove the vital points of difference between the administrative culture and process of the developing and developed societies.

Basically the approach has brought a consciousness that the institutions and practices of the administrative systems of the Western nations are not necessarily the best in all cases. These various indigenous structures in non-Western nations, though seemingly dysfunctional from Western views, may prove "functional" for their own particular social settings.

Comparative Approach

The comparative approach to public administration has become dominant today. The cultural setting in which administration operates has long been recognised as a major determinant of the pattern of administration that evolves. Consequently, in each nation and in and in most institutions, the pattern of administration that evolves is in some degree distinctive., There are some theoretical assumptions too, for the comparative study of public administration. Robert Jackson has outlined four such assumptions:

1. A science of public administration, if not fully achievable, is at least worthy of seeking. Obviously not all the scholars share this view. However, there seems to be a broad agreement on the proposition that there are patterns of administrative behaviour which are susceptible to rigorous systematic analysis and thus capable of being, drawn together into a body of theory.

2. The scientific study of public administration requires exploration of administrative patterns in the cross-cultural and cross-national contexts.

3. The empirical findings resulting from such cross-cultural studies should be subjected to rigorous systematic comparative analysis.

4. Such a comparative analysis will hopefully lead to the derivation of hypothesis about administrative patterns on various levels of generality, having different degrees of applicability and universality. Such propositions could then be integrated into a general theory of public administration.

Though the comparative approach got impetus in the late fifties and early sixties there were a number of comparative studies even much earlier than that. The traditional literature on comparative government focused on foreign relations, political parties, election machinery, pressure groups, constitutions or institutions in their formal aspects. Comparative administration on the other hand concentrated on central administrative machinery, decentralisation patterns, civil service structures, public finance, financial administration, etc. Post World War II studies abound with criticism of the traditional literature in comparative government and administration. A few of these criticism are : the traditional literature was culture bound limiting itself to the study of Western nations and institutions; it was normative in character because of its commitments to the values of constitutionalism and Western liberal democracy; it was parochial in character since it seemed to believe in a unidirectional development of political and administrative systems, in the Western patterns; it was essentially legalistic and formalistic; it was not ecological in perspective and it overlooked the multi-functional character of governmental institutions. Further, it has also been observed that the traditional comparative administration literature was primarily descriptive rather than analytical, explanatory and problem oriented.

Modern comparative study of public administration has grown up with the comparative study of political system, i.e., comparative politics. Both movements have been characterized by the comparative youth of their participants, by a general commitment to the outlook identified with behaviouralism, by an effort to be interdisciplinary in interests and techniques and by an effort to arrive at concepts formulas and theories that are truly universal, bridging and embracing all culture.

The American Society for Public Administration's "Comparative Administration Group" in a draft statement in 1961 described comparative public administration as "the theory of public administration applied to diverse cultures and national setting and the body of factual data, by which it can be examined and tested". Fred W. Riggs however, in the annual meeting at the ASPA in 1961 expressed his personal opinion that term 'Comparative' should be used only for empirical, nomothetic studies. In his paper on "Trends in the Comparative Study of Public Administration", he outlined three trends in the Comparative Study of Public Administration. The first being a trend from normative towards more empirical approaches (characterized by a growing interest in descriptive and analytic information for its, own sake). The second is a shift from Ideographic toward ' Nomothetic (any approach which concentrates on the unique case the historical episode or "Case Study", the single agency or country, the biography or cultural area is basically ideographic. By contrast, an approach which seeks generalizations "laws or hypotheses that assert regularities of behaviour, and correlations between variables, may be called nomothetic). The third is a shift from a predominantly non-ecological to an ecological basis for the study of public administration. The ecology implies not just a characterization of environments but rather an analysis of the patterns of interaction between the subject study and its environment. Riggs described the first trend as fairly well established and the second and third as "perhaps only fast emerging".

Presently, comparative administrative analysing has developed for the most part, on the macro and 'middle range levels. A collection of broad generalizations and hypotheses is developing while the empirical testing of these propositions is being left for the future.

Thus, in the area of empirical analysis, comparative public administration is far behind American public administration. Nevertheless in some other areas the comparative theory, can contribute to the American administrative theory, for example by way of proving certain propositions like those dealing with prismatic elements in a diffracted society and with positive formalism. Likewise comparative public administration can use the rich collection of propositions developed in recent years by American administrative theory and test the extent to which such propositions are culture bound.

However, a comparative study to be meaningful depends upon the availability of reliable data. Another problem with comparative studies, is regarding the social phenomenon which presents numerous problems varying from system to system. Similarly, since the political system varies from country to country and that political structure or political parties interest groups, legislatures, etc., are performing different functions, comparisons are of little use.

The critics also point out that the models of comparative approach such as bureaucratic and structural functional models, are not comprehensive enough to explain the social phenomenon which varies from country to country and the comparative administration does not offer consensus over its future growth.

Ecological Approach

The term ecology was derived from the ancient Greek work 'Oikos' meaning living place and was used extensively by nineteenth century Darwinian botanists and zoologists to describe how organism live and adapt to their environments. Biologists during the 1920's borrowed the ideas of plant and animal ecology and applied the concept to human life. Ecology was introduced into public administration vocabulary primarily through the writings of the late Harvard Professor John Gaus, one of the early pioneers of public administration. He elaborated on ecology in a series of famous lectures at the university of Allabama in 1945, later published as 'Reflections on Public Administration'.

In his writings, Gaus was peculiarly adapt at weaving the patterns and ideas of public administration into the total fabric of the issues and events of American society. Better than most observers, he showed how public administration, its development, and its activities were influenced by its setting, or its ecology. In his words, loan ecological approach to public administration build quite literally from the ground up from the elements of a place-soils climate, location, for example to the people who live there, their numbers, ages, and knowledge, and the ways of physical and social technology by which from the place and in relationships with one another, they gel their living. For John Gaus, the term ecology was not only relevant to cloistered scholars of administration at work on universal theories of the administrative process, but also to on-the-line practitioners of administration. A conscious awareness of ecological factors permits administrators to respond more wisely to the demands and challenges of the external environment of their organisations. Thus in the hands of the practitioner, ecology can become a diagnostic tool; it can help him to visualize the major elements in the administrative processes and provide a yardstick for measuring their impact upon an organisation.

Besides, J. M. Gaus, the ecological approach to study public administration was adopted by Robert, A Dahl, Robert Merton and Fred Riggs. The approach is further based on the idea that an administrative system may not act as an independent variable in all circumstances. It acts and reacts under the influence of various sub-systems surrounding it. There is a great degree of interdependence between all social organisations and their ecological settings-which include among others topography, population, level of physical and social technology and the interrelationships and interactions between people and organisations. Organisations, structures, procedures and goals are largely created and changed as a result of the interaction between an organisation and its environment. Thus, if an organisation is to survive it must adapt itself to the changing needs and conditions of its external environment which is continuously changing. In a highly industrialised and developed society like the USA the system of government and administration must not only cater to public needs and demands, but also to the compulsions of all

American economy. The level of production and consumption of material goods is the highest in the USA compared to any other country in the world. Therefore, the administrative framework most favoured in that country is a free market system through, which Americans are able to make free choices in production and consumption. A capitalistic economy with a democratic system of minimum state intervention and controls is what the Americans have found suitable and that has existed in the country with only minor variations from time to time.

Robert Dahl's advocacy of an ecological approach was based on what he stated were three problematic issues :

(i) Administrative generalizations based on the experience of one nation-state cannot be universally applied to administrative systems in all kinds of diverse environmental settings.

(ii) Before formulating theories and concepts of administration, it is necessary to empirically test their validity in all types of social settings to see what is universal.

(iii) This implies that public administration must be truly interdisciplinary and ecological in character, -not only to widen its horizon but to make its study more scientific and, relevant to all types of societies.

Fred Riggs made a distinctive contribution to this approach. Developing the approach further, he analysed the relationship between the administration and economic, social, technological, political and communication factors, in a large perspective. He explained, illustratively how environmental conditions influence administrative system, on the basis of his studies in Thailand and Philippines. On the basis of certain functional prerequisites of a social system, he attempted a variety of models and typologies such as the "agrariatransitia-industria " and "Fused prismatic-diffracted "' societies. Riggs, thus, made cross cultural studies of public administration with the application of ecological approach.

The basic assumption of this approach is that administration and its environment influence each other; therefore, understanding of the dynamics of this process is necessary to understand the administration. Besides administration, this approach helps us to understand the people in relation to their environment and the relationship of people, society, culture, economy and polity with administration It helps to understand various problems of administration in a particular society and the solutions to which may be found in its environment.

However, the ecological approach is not as simple as it appears to be. In the words of Gaus such an approach as this to our study of public administration is difficult, in that it makes demands upon our powers to observe, upon a sensitive awareness of changes and maladjustment.

Summary : After reviewing the various approaches employed in the study of public administration, the inescapable conclusion seems to be that none of them can be adequate by itself In view of the complexity of its public administration needs to be approached from all possible points of view to obtain a real insight into its problems and discover their possible solutions. The various approaches should not, therefore, be viewed as rivals contending for mastery, but as the necessary complements of one another.

With the increase in the subject-matter of Administration, it has become all that necessary to use all types of methods to simplify its studies. Since modern state is a welfare state, so Public Administration thinkers will have to develop to realize the set objectives.

2

Development and Growth

Public Administration has been one of the most serious problems in India. One of our earliest treaties on public administration was written by Kautilya. In his Arthsastra, he has tried to give a very detailed description of how the administration of a State should be run. We come to know from available records that in ancient India same standard for running public administration was maintained. It was more or less a personal rule in which King was the pivot. The whole administrative set-up moved to suit our convenience and wishes of the rulers rather than looking after the welfare of the masses.

The shape of Indian administration, as it exists today, is not just the result of administrative law enacted by the British Parliament during the British rule or by the Parliament of free India since independence. Its roots go deep in the administrative history of the country from the ancient times.

There has not been keen interest among scholars in Public Administration to understand the ancient administration. Thus an eminent scholar writes: "To the early Eastern mind, the fact that a thing existed was sufficient of itself to shows its right to be. This was effectually excluded all possibility of inquiries as to the relative perfection or justification for the existence of, *de facto* social and political institutions.

The political and administrative ideas have been discussed in the Dharam Sutras. Although none of the existing Dharamasutras is probably older than 600 B.C. They are no doubt based on earlier works of this class and have preserved strata of earlier thought.

The Dharma-Sutras do not contain any systematic exposition of legal principles and political doctrines such as we find in the Dharamsastras and Arthsastras of the later age. Nor does their conception of law and politics conform to our present ideas on the subject. As we shall see later, they cover for more than law and do not cover the whole of law. As regards politics they view the state of society as an organic whole, in which the different elements, such as the king and the people play their part according to Dharma or Law, imposed or at least sanctioned by the Divine will. Life is also regarded as whole without any sharp distinction between public and private, or individual and collective. As a matter of fact the collective organisation of society dominates over the idea of individual person. Each individual has his duty and responsibility, rather than rights and privileges, fixed by law and custom. Each man has a recognized function, which he inherits as a member of a group rather than selects of himself. To perform this function successfully is his highest object in life, a duty not merely political, social and moral, but also religious in character. For this depends not only his well-being in this life but also his salvation in the next world. Like the modern collectivist theories (such as Fascism) this view raises society above individual but there is an important difference. For the allegiance here is not to any party or political principle, but to Dharma conceived as an eternal and immutable Law or Order, which is divine in character and does not emanate from human will.

Administrative Organisation

The king was the head of administration and his jurisdiction extended to all walks of life. To quote V.D. Mahajan, "According to the Dharma Sutras, the sovereign was not the source of law but merely the upholder of law. " To quote Gautama, "The administration of justice shall be regulated by the Veda, the Darma Sastras, the Vedangas, the Puranas and the Upvedas. Again, "The king must protect the castes and different stages of life. Authoritative in the realm shall be all laws of castes and clans as well as the laws of religions not opposed to Vedic tradition, while for their respective orders, ploughmen, traders, herdsmen, moneylenders and artisans may make their own laws" ' According to Vasistha, "The king's duty is to pay attention to the special laws of regions, castes and clans and keep the four orders to their prescribed duty. " The various guilds were allowed to frame their own laws.

To quote V.M. Apte, "His supreme duty, as noted above, was the protection of the people and maintenance of the rules of caste and order "As a corollary to this he must punish the thieves and other criminals as well as those who stray from the path of duty laid down in the Sastras. His authority and jurisdiction thus extended practically over the entire activities of his subjects. One of his most important duties was to decide legal disputes. He was to protect the interest of a minor until he attained majority. He was also to support learned priests, the widow of his soldiers, those who are exempted from taxes (to be specified later) and Brahmacharins. He must preserve fruit-bearing trees. He must make an equal division of the booty secured in battle and distribute it equitably among those who shared the risks of war with him. He must prevent the use of false weights and measures.

Under the king there were regular hierarchy of officers. The village was the basic administrative unit. According to Apastamba the king shall appoint men of the first three castes who are pure and truthful, over villages and towns for the protection of people. These officials were to appoint subordinates possessing the same qualities. They were to protect the towns and villages from thieves and must be made to repay what is stolen within their jurisdiction. These passages, though brief, hold out the picture of a regular administrative machinery which was set up for the security of life and property.

Special branches of administration were for collection of taxes and military matters. According to Gautama, the king was entitled to take as tax one-tenth, one-eight or one-sixth of the produce and one day's work per month from artisans. He could also charge one-twentieth on merchandise, one-fifteenth on cattle and gold and sixtieth flowers, herbs, honey, meat, grains, fruits etc. The right of inheritance was given to the Sapindas. Widow were not given the right to inherit. A daughter could inherit only if there was no son, pupil or teacher of the deceased. Women were not allowed to offer sacrifices. They were considered as property.

A special mention may be made of the administration of justice. The administration of justice was not only restricted to public but covered all facets of life. Under the criminal law, theft and adultery are the main general topic discussed in the Dharma-sutras. To quote V.P. Apte, "That the king himself personally administered civil and criminal justice appears from certain indications in the Sutras (Gau. Dh. S. XII. 43). The administration of justice was to be regulated by the Vedas, the Dharmasastras, the Angas, and Puranas (Gau. Dh. S. XI. 19), due regard being paid to local and family usage of (in other words) to the laws of districts, castes, and families which the king must learn from those who in each case have authority to speak (Gau. Dh. S. XI. 20-22). It seems to have been permissible for the king to delegate his judicial authority or at least the supervision of punishments to a royal officer or a Rajanya who could act as an adhyaksha (overseer). Difficult cases were referred to the Parishad whose composition has been mentioned above. When it failed to arrive at any satisfactory solution in doubtful cases, the king referred the matter to a Srotriya or Brahamana of high learning (Gau. Dh.S. XXVIII. 50). The theory of the rod punishment as the symbol of penal powers vested in the king had now fully developed.

Reference is made to three kinds of important crimes and those were assault, adultery and theft. The punishments awarded to persons belonging to the various castes varied. If a Kshatriya abused a Brahman, he was fined 100 coins. If a Vaishya abused a Brahman, he was fined 150 coins. If Brahman abused a Kshatriya he was fined 50 coins. If he abused a Vaishya, he was fined 25 coins. If he abused a Shudra, he was not fined at all. Interest at the rate of 15 percent was allowed.

Dharma-Sutras also paid attention to village, sanitation and buildings of towns. To quote V.D. Mahajan, "The Dharma Sutras preferred the life of villages and condemned the life of cities. According to Baudhayana. It is impossible for one to attain salvation who lives in a town covered with dust". No wonder, good people were asked to avoid going into the towns. The Mantras were not be recited in the towns at any time. However, there are some references to the building of towns by certain kings and the establishment of their palaces, assembly halls, etc. The people were not allowed to go to foreign countries. A taboo was put on sea voyage.

Kautilya and Arthashastra

R.S. Tripathi in his book "History of Ancient India" mentions that Magasthenes and Kautilya are two most important authors, whose writings throw a flood of light on the people, government and institutions of India under Chandragupta Maurya. The 'Indika' of Megasthenes is now lost but happily it is still preserved in the form of quotations by later writer. Kautilya or Chanakya, is reputed to have been the minister of Chandragupta. His production the 'Arthashastra' is a compendium on polity and statecraft, and it would perhaps be no overestimate of its value to say that despite its theoretical character, it is a unique work in early Indian Literature. According to V.D. Mahajan "The most important source for writing the history of the Mauryas is Kautilya's Arthashastra. The book is divided into 15 Adhikarnas or sections and 180 Prakaranas or sub-division. It has about 6,000 slokas. This was discovered in 1909 and has been ably translated by Shamasastri. The book is more a manual for the administrator than a theoretical work on polity discussing the philosophy and fundamental principles of administration or of political science. It is mainly concerned with the political problems of the government and describes its machinery and functions, both in peace and war.

Book one deals with the duties of a king and the appointment of ministers and other high officers. Book Two gives a picture of State activities. Book Three discusses a code of law. Book Four deals with the suppression of crime. Book Five deals with salaries of state servants and other matter. Book six is an introduction to the State's relations with its neighbouring States. Book seven deals with the various aspects of foreign policy. Book Eight deals with calamities or weaknesses. Book Nine is concerned with preparation for war. Book Ten deals with fighting. Book Eleven, Twelve, and Thirteen deal with the problems related to war and conquest.

The machinery of the Government was highly organized and can be divided into four elements, the King, the Ministers, the Council and the Bureaucracy.

The King : The King was the head of all branches of the Government. Kings were mostly hereditary, though there were examples of elected kings.

According to Kautilya, the calamity of a king is more serious than that of a minister (Amatyas). The king alone appoints the minister, the domestic priest and servants. He employees superintendents. He applies remedies against troubles. As is the conduct of the king, so is the conduct of the people. A king is the head of the state. He is the government itself (Raja Rajyamiti). Government is ultimately resolvable into one ultimate and that is the king. The king absorbs all the rest of the elements. The kings were given training. There day and night schedule was divided into Eight parts which are given below as given by R.C. Majumdar.

Day

1. Receiving reports about the accounts and the defensive measures of the kingdom.
2. Considering the prayers and petitions of the subjects.
3. Bath, meal and study.
4. Attending to revenue and department heads.
5. Attending to the business of the council and confidential reports from spies.
6. Recreation or deliberation on State affairs.
7. Inspection of royal forces.
8. Consultation with the commander-in-chief about military affairs.

Night

1. Receiving the spies.
2. Bath, meal and study.

3. Sleep.
4. Reflection on sacred literature and his own duties.
5. Consultation with the ministers and sending out spies.
6. Attending to domestic duties, religious rites, ceremonies etc.

The paramount duty of the king was to protect the people and seek their welfare, Kautilya sums up the position very beautifully in the following verse:. "In the happiness of his subjects lies his happiness; in their welfare his welfare; whatever pleases himself he shall not consider as good, but whatever pleases his subject he shall consider as good".

The Ministers : Next in importance to the king were the ministers. Kautilya says:

"Sovereignty is possible only with assistance of Ministers: A single wheel can never move. Hence the king shall employ minister and hear their opinion."

Kautilya discusses that selection of ministers must be done on merit and should mainly depend on qualification and not on the considerations of family of backs fair influence. The ministers used to advise the kings on all important matters.

The following remarks of Kautilya indicate the nature of ministerial power and responsibility. A single minister proceeds with fully and without restraints. In deliberating with two ministers, the king may be overpowered by their combined action, or imperilled by their mutual dissension. But with three or four ministers he will not come to any serious grief, but will arrive at satisfactory results. In accordance with the requirements of place, time and nature of the work in view, he may, as he deems it proper, deliberate with one or two ministers or by himself. The king may ask his ministers for their opinion, either individually or collectively, and ascertain their ability by judging over the reason they assign for their opinions".

The Council : The Council assists the king in the administrative work. This body occupied a great importance. It used to concentrate on all important issues.

The Bureaucracy : As stated by R.C. Majumdar that while the policy was formulated by the council and the ministers, the detailed work of administration was carried on by a bureaucracy. At the head of the bureaucracy were a few high officials whose numbers and status must have varied in different ages and different status. The following list includes the more important ones:

1. The High Priest.
2. The Commander-in-chief
3. The Chief Judge
4. The Door keeper (Pratihan)
5. The High Treasures (Sannidhata)
6. The Collector-General (Samahartta)

The general nature of their is indicated by their names. There were also ceremonial officers, such as "The bearer of the Sunshade of the State," and "the State Sword-bearers". There were other officers like Viceroys and Viceroys and Ambassadors, whose sphere of work lay in distant parts of the country. All these formed the member of the highest branch of administration. Next come the lower branch, consisting mainly of the Superintendents of the various departments into which the administration was divided, and their staff. The number of these Superintendents must have varied in different kingdom. In Kautilya's Arthashastra we read of the Superintendents of the following:

1. Ocean-mines, 2. Treasury, 3. Mines, 4. Metals, 5. Mint, 6. Accounts, 7. Gold, 8. Storehouse, 9. Commerce, 10. Forest produce, 11. Passport, 12. Weights and Measures, 13. Lineal measures, 14. Tolls, 15. Weaving, 16. Agriculture, 17. Liquor, 18. Slaughterhouse, 19. Prostitutes, 20. Ships, 21. Cows, 22. Horses, 23. Elephants, 24. Chariots, 25. Infantry, 26. Armour, 27 Pasture, 28. Harem.

Besides, there were officials dealing with local administration at the district and lower levels.

Financial Administration : The most important contribution Kautilya was in the field of the financial administration. The

Department of Revenue was one of the important department of the Government, as finance was the motive power and the basis of all the activity, Kautilya paid great attention towards this department.

Kautilya mentions two high officials *Samabarta* and *Sannidhatea* who practically were vested with the immediate control of the whole administration. In their financial capacity, the functions of the samahartas relate to the whole range of state income and expenditure. The task was assisted by the *Sthanikas* and under them were the *Gopas* each of whom was in charge of the five or ten villages. The work undertaken by the Samaharta guidance and direction prepare various registers and census list of the villages. This has to be checked by spies during emergency. Samaharta had to raise taxation. Agents of local government were gopas in local areas. Their work was to collect and maintain registers in income and expenditure. Basically they maintained reports about the following:

1. Varieties of land product and their produce.
2. Areas under cultivations.
3. Irrigation laws.
4. Privileges and immunities enjoyed by individuals, local traditions etc.,
5. Transfer and sale of land.
6. Occupation of the people.

The duties of Samaharta comprised the following:

1. Division of the kingdom into four parts apparently corresponding to jurisdiction of the four sthanikas.
2. The arrangement of the villages were done according to the grade like best, middle and lowest.
3. Preparation of the revenue free land that is 'Nibandha'.
4. By means of inspection of village boundaries he was to ascertain the total area of villages within bi-circle.

Maintaining the :

1. Register of boundaries and villages fields.
2. Register of uncultivated lands.
3. Register of transfers.
4. Register of the amount of loan advanced and revenue remission.

He mentioned that all administrators must take care of finance as money is like honey and there are chance of its sticking.

Administration in Muslim India

Next stage in public administration in India came with the coming of the Muslims in India. They were autocrats and they did not cherish the idea of establishing a sound public administrative set-up. They had of course their ministers but were more interested in keeping the sovereign in good mood rather than looking after the welfare of the subjects. Ain-i-Akbari is one such treaty of this period which gives detailed information about administrative set-up under Akbar, the Great. It will be more or less a futile attempt to prove that public administration under the Muslim rulers in any way was run and managed in accordance with any of the sound principles of public administration which are commonly accepted and honoured these days. But the king had servants to run administration.

Administration under East India Company

In 1600, East India Company was established by a charter of Queen Elizabeth of England by which some of the traders were allowed to trade with India. The traders, were for a century, busy in their own affairs and they had neither time nor resources nor energy for organising or establishing a sound system of public administration. The situation however, changed after 1773. By this time the powerful Mughal empire had completely given way under its inefficient, luxury loving and incompetent sovereigns. This had provided the company to have a strong hold over many parts of India. The traders were now becoming rulers of the Country.

After obtaining Diwani rights the situation altogether changed. One of the serious problems faced by the Company was how to collect Diwani of Bengal, Bihar and Orissa. Equally important problem was how to check corruption which had become a way of life of public servants of the Company. No less important problem was the extent of the Parliament's control over the traders, because the 'New Nawabs' as the moneyed servants of the Company were called were creating a serious problem in England. They were finding a way to parliament by purchasing rotten boroughs. It was, therefore, imperative that on the one hand some sort of public administrative system should be evolved by which the process of tax collection could be made easy. On the other hand, an administrative system was needed which could check the leakage of revenue so that the servants of the Company did not become wealthy at the cost of Company.

The Regulating Act, 1773 : Regulating Act of 1773 can easily be called as a first land mark in the history of public administration in India. It was with the enforcement of this Act that skeleton of the present administrative set-up in India was laid. The act divided the administration of the country into Supreme and Central Government and the Provincial Governments. For the management of Company's possessions in India, the Act provided for a Governor General at Fort William in Bengal. The Governor General was to be assisted by a Council of four members. The Council was to manage all territorial and revenue affairs of the Company. The Council was also empowered to superintendent and manage the affairs of presidencies of Madras and Bombay in certain matters. The affairs of the Council were to be decided by majority of votes. It also provided for the creation of a Supreme Court of adjudication at Fort William which consisted of a Chief Justice and three other judges. No distinction was maintained between executive and legislative functions and both continued to be discharged by the Council of the Governor General.

From 1773-1833 : The Regulating Act of 1773 initiated the system of parliamentary control over the affairs of the Company. During the period under review the Pitt's India Act 1784. The Charter Acts of 1793, 1813 and 1833 were passed. The significant feature of these Acts was that these provided for more effective control of British parliament over the affairs of the Company. Another feature was visible tendency towards centralisation of authority. Gradually and step by step the provincial governments began to be stripped of their powers and authority and instead the grip of Supreme Government became tighter and stiffer over provincial governments.

A very significant change in administrration was introduced with the passing of Charter Act of 1833. It was with the passing of this Act that a distinction was made in the executive and legislative functions of the Governor General. Separate Executive and Legislative Councils were created. A law member was added to the Council of Governor General who participated in the deliberations of the Council when it sat to transact legislative work.

Charter Act of 1853 : The Charter Act of 1853 was the last granted to the East India Company by the British Parliament. The Act of 1853 provided for a legislative council with a strength of 12 members. It provided for setting up a Law Commission. Some of the thinkers are of the view that it was with the passing of this Act and setting up a separate law Commission that the seeds of parliamentary government in India were sown.

Administration since Independence

This environment and situation changed suddenly with the coming of independence. The most important new factor was the emergence of the Indian politician as an effective ruler. The civil servants at the top of the administrative apparatus no longer acted as representatives of the English Crown, but had to act as servants of Indian Ministers. This could have meant a very large change in the situation of civil servants and in the functioning of the administrative system. However, in effect, this change was insignificant. Partly it was due to the fact that the Indian Statesmen, even Jawahar Lal Nehru, were not anxious to affect adversely the prestige and the commanding position of the administrative system and particularly of the top operators. Nehru did not evidently want to change the position of members of the Indian Civil Service in any way and they were guaranteed, like princes, a number of privileges. Even so, the exercise of political power by Ministers and later on by legislators eroded gradually the privileged position of the top civil servants, and they had to learn more and more the art of the management of their political masters. The change in relations between the highest civil service cadres and other elements of administration was thus gradual.

The other extremely important aspect of the changed situation was that the civil servant could no longer look upon himself as an outsider or representative of an outside authority. He began by slow degrees to function more and more as part of the Indian Society. The distinction of ruler and ruled did not become completely blurred but the involvement of the civil servant in public affairs, in particular groups, or interests, his affiliation with regions and castes came more obviously to the surface. However, even today the transition period has not been completed and in a large part vestiges of the older bureaucracy linger on.

Today, the 'generalist' i.e. the Indian Civil Servant and his successor, the I.A.S., still completely dominate the scene. There is an enormous concentration of power on top; in this ladder new elements of specialist or managers of business still rank low in prestige and authority. The I.C.S. and the I.A.S. still function with an exclusive status in the administration. The attitudes of the public towards officials and of the officials towards the public are still coloured largely by the older psychology of antagonism and this has had adverse effect in the context of the plans of development.

The British concepts of the single British District Officer or Collector, co-ordinating all authority in all departments over an entire area in his hands still continues to be an important feature of the local administrative structure and colours the whole of its operation.

The civil service enjoys very effective power even today. However an extremely important aspect is that the older combination of power and responsibility are no longer to be found. In the older regime when power vested largely in their hands the senior group of members of the civil service also accepted accompanying responsibility. They were responsible ultimately to the Crown for proper management of Indian affairs and always behaved with a full sense of responsibility. Today the civil servant no longer feels responsible in this manner because power is supposed to reside in any directly wielded by the political Minister. The curious situation that exists at present is, therefore, that while the actual day-to-day exercise of the power rests in the hands of the civil servant, the civil servant no longer feels any overall responsibility. This he feels rests with the Ministers who exercise it fitfully largely on the advice of the civil servant themselves. However, as this exercise, especially in relation to personal or party matter may be on considerations other than those accepted by the civil servant or put forward by him, the advice is likely to be disregarded in some contexts and occasions. This change seems to have relieved the civil servant of any feeling of carrying the overall burden of administration. The informal operation of a group of top civil servants as generally looking after the total situation has, therefore, vanished and the Cabinet or an inner group of Ministers have not taken over this function in any perfect effective manner.

As against this, one has to consider the relevance and appropriateness of the present state of administrative arrangement in India to the specific requirements of the effort at planned economic development. Apart from the result of transition to self rule after independence, it is planned economic development that has added enormously to the dimensions of Government effort. The activities of Government have increased tremendously both in width of coverage and in depth and intensity. The direct responsibilities that Government now undertakes cover large fields of social and economic life. Government takes upon itself the responsibility of erecting the structure of public services and utilities required for development of a modern industrial society and continuously maintaining that structure. It undertakes in addition a large variety of welfare activities and conducts a large number of industrial production businesses which are basic to the industrial structure. Government occupies large sections of trading and it tries to regulate many other aspects of social and economic life. The number of administrator at various levels required in Government service has increased enormously and the qualifications needed by them have become extremely enormously and the qualifications needed by them have become extremely varied. The contrast with the situation in 1939 is extremely glaring.

Not only has the sphere of direct Government activity and of official regulation of socio-economic activity immensely widened but also the conduct of operations has become extremely detailed. The task undertaken by government, of the transformation and activization of rural economic society, is in itself immense. This in effect operating on the millions of small dispersed units of fanning and other rural activities. Development of agriculture and its improvement are essentially specialised tasks which must be performed in relation to every locality. In British times, in some States the collection of revenue was related to maintenance of detailed village records and village officials. However, in the landlord provinces the rural administrative structure was very rudimentary. Looking at the area of the landlord provinces and of the Indian States, it may be said that for the large part of the country an administrative structure for regulating the activities of individual local communities was not available at the time of independence. This had to be constructed, widened and strengthened.

Apart from undertaking multifold activities and activizing or regulating economic life all over the country, planning requires continuous maintenance of a long-term and co-ordinated direction to socio-economic development. This is both a highly important and difficult function which has become all the more important and complicated because of the large size, the diversity and the federal political structure of the country. Administration has to be geared to all these ends.

It will thus be seen that very large ground has yet to be covered as between the highly limited Government activity of British times for which the particular structure was fashioned and the requirements of the administrative system of the planned development today.

It must, in the first instance, be recognized that Indian administrative system has grown rapidly, adapted itself partially to the changed situation and tried to meet the large manifold new requirements. Inefficiency and corruption has not mitigated but on the whole there has been no breakdown of the system. However, huge problems remain unsolved and need urgent attention.

Nature of Administration

It is no gain saying that perforce of circumstances, the traders become administrators. They were neither highly educated, nor they had any training dealing with administrative problems, nor they had any bent up of mind of an administrator. They were primarily interested in earning money. They had no concept of public relationship.

But when the traders became administrators, the question of providing them better pay scales, eradication of corruption, devotion to duty, efficient administrative set up and hierarchy, which had hitherto been neglected assumed priority problems requiring immediate solution. During 1773-1853, thus, the Directors of the Company under pressure from the government tried to have, an efficient administrative set-up. It was, therefore, in the year 1800 that a College at Fort William was set-up with a view to training civil servants for running the administration of the Company. In 1853 certain rules were adopted for entry into civil service of the Company. It inter-alia provided that a candidate should be in the age group of 19-23 years and be a university graduate.

A very important salient feature of the administration was that the Indians had no hand in running their own administration with the result that public administration in India was alien for the public of India and both had no relationship with each other.

We can thus observe that during this period the Company was more concerned about setting its own house in order rather than establishing any healthy relations and contacts with the people of India.

3

Structure of Administration

India, as an ex-colonial country, has a variety of traditional structures, habits and behavioural patterns. It also has modern political and economic structures. Her administrative system is therefore a blend of the administrative system of the former colonial administration and concepts and directions of the new system established by the Government of free India after independence.

The basic framework of administration is based on the theory of decentralization of structures and functions, under which autonomy and initiative are vested in the States and local units of Government. But it also accepts central planning and direction, articulated both through the governmental machinery and the ruling political party. Leadership both political and administrative, being committed to the welfare of the state, and other goals of egalitarianism and social service, keep the administration engaged in the achievement of the vital objective of integrating ,the people politically and emotionally into a nation. This involves communication of administrators with the most isolated sectors of the society and the development of a channel of identification, by administrators and citizens, to the broad goals of the total society. The administrative system, emphasises on the development of a public hierarchy motivated to share effectively the responsibilities of development.

Here below we are discussing the administrative structure:

Central Secretariat

Indian system of government and administration is largely a legacy of British colonial rule. Our Constitution has borrowed abundantly from the various constitutions of the world, particularly, it has modelled itself on the lines of British Constitution. Indian constitution establishes neither a purely federal polity nor exactly a unitary system.

However, the opening article of the Indian constitution says that (I) India, that is Bharat shall be union of states, (2) the states and the territories there of shall be as specified in the first schedule, (3) the territories of India thereof shall comprise the territories of the states, the union territories as specified in the first schedule and such other territories as may be acquired, article says that parliament may by law admit into the union, or establish new states on such terms and conditions as it thinks fit. Thus India is a 'UNION OF STATES' with some centrally administered territories and having flexibility in regard to change in the political map or the territories.

As regards the system of governments, Indian constitution has adopted the Westminster model of government with separate constitutional and real heads. The executive power of the union government is vested in the President and his council of ministers, headed by a Prime Minister. Although in theory, the President does not possess vast legislative, emergency, executive and judicial powers, in practice he is a mere figurehead and the power in reality is exercised by the Prime Minister and his cabinet. For all their administrative and legislative actions, they in turn are responsible to the Parliament. The council of ministers is a body referred to include all the ministers i.e., cabinet ministers, ministers of state and deputy ministers. It is the cabinet which actually meets and supervise the whole of the administrative machinery. Each cabinet minister is not only the co-ordinator of all executive policies and actions, but is also the leader of the cabinet, and in reality a leader of the nation. The number of ministers changes from time to time and generally around twenty.

The work of various ministers is coordinated by the cabinet secretariat headed by a cabinet secretary. Some coordination work is also done by the Prime Minister's Secretariat,. These two offices serve as the staff agencies of the entire administration. At the apex of the hierarchy of administrative organisation, there is central secretariat which occupies key position regarding the policy making, programming and their implementation. Apart from this we have certain independent bodies which are not directly controlled by the ministries. The most important of these are : The Planning Commission, the Union Public Service Commission, the Election Commission, the Finance Commission, the office of the Controller and Auditor General of India. Besides these agencies, there has been a growth of a large number of public enterprises Departmental Undertakings, Public Corporation and Government and Joint Stock Companies. As regards personnel management, there is a provision of three kinds of services in the constitution. The All-India Services, The Central Services and The State Services.

The Central legislature of Parliament consists of the President and two Houses- the Rajya Sabha (Council of States) and the Lok Sabha (House of the people). The Lok Sabha consists of the people 'selected representatives' whereas the Rajya Sabha consists of members mostly elected by the state legislative and a few nominated members by the President. The President, summons each House from time to time to meet. The Parliament has been conferred powers by the constitution to make laws. However, these laws are subject to judicial review, i.e., the High Courts and the Supreme Court have the power to declare an act of the parliament unconstitutional and void on the ground that it violates the provisions of the constitution.

Broadly speaking, the pattern of the government in states is the same as that for the union, namely the parliamentary system. The executive head being a constitutional ruler who is to act according to the advice of the ministers is responsible to the popular house of the state legislature. As the head of the executive powers of the state, the Governor just as the President stands as the head of the executive power of the state. The Governor of a state is not elected but is appointed by the President. Actually it is the Prime Minister who recommends a person to be appointed as Governor. The Governor is bound to act on the advice of his council of ministers. The council of ministers in the state is organised on the same pattern and practically in the same manner as is done at the centre. Leader of the majority party in the state legislature is invited by the governor to be appointed as Chief Minister. There is a Cabinet as the head of the state executive, the functions and powers of which are similar to that of union Cabinet. Each minister (including the chief minister) is in charge of a department. Each of the Department's as control led by a permanent official called the Secretary.

State administration is further subdivided into Districts, which is the smallest unit of administration in the country. The district chief is known as Commissioner, Deputy Commissioner, or Collector depending upon the status of the district and pattern in a particular state. Every district has some field officers of the central or state governments.

At the local level, we have a system of local self-government or democratic decentralisation. There are two separate sets of local government in urban and rural areas. In urban areas, depending upon the size, population and level of development there may be municipal corporation, municipal committee, notified area committee or town area committee. In the areas occupied by the Defence Ministry or Military these are cantonment boards as the local government. Most important of all these are the first two. All these lack bodies function independently and have no organic link with each other. In the rural areas we have a system of Panchayati Raj started in the fifties. On the recommendations of Committee recommended a three tier structure, i.e., Grant Panchayat at the village level, Panchayat Samiti at the block level, (comprising of about 80-1000 villages with a population of around one lac) and Zila Parishad at the district level. However, variations in pattern exist in different states in terms of nomenclature, organisational structure, constitutional frame work, system of elections, provisions of finances, delegation of powers and so on. But in most of cases there is a support for effective decentralization of powers. In fact the most important difference among various models of Panchayati Raj is regarding the assignment of the pivotal powers to one tier out of Zila Parishad and Panchayat Samiti. Most of the local bodies-both rural and urban, have elected members as well as permanent officials and look after some of the local services, civic as well as developmental. Although the institutions of local government have presented a lot of problems in respect of co-ordination of work multiplicity of authority and the life. But in general they have found to be very useful in the political and administrative set up of both developed and developing countries. It is an admitted fact that system of local government is essential not only to educated people and to train them in the act of self-government but also to check the centralising tendencies.

Composition of Central Secretariat : The secretariat consists of the council of ministers, the secretaries and the staff. It functions as the nerve centre of government. It is here that all policies and programmes get formulated and executive orders originate.

It also provides overall supervision, guidance and leadership. It sets the pattern of efficiency for every branch of administration. The efficiency of the central administration as a whole depends largely on its working.

Functions of Secretariat

The Secretariat plays a key role in assisting and advising the Council of Ministers in the shaping of government policies and programmes. It has to collect necessary materials for the formulation of government policies, analyses and present them to the different aspects of problems so as to enable the council of minister to take appropriate decisions. The secretariat provides guidelines to the executive agencies for the speedy and efficient implementation of government programmes and assists them in all possible manner, including removal of difficulties. The secretariat also keeps a watch over the implementation and presents a correct appraisal of progress made in it to government from time to time. At the state level the state secretariat has been set in each state.

1. Assisting the minister in policy making and in modifying policies from time to time, as and when necessary.

2. Framing legislation and rules and regulations.

3. Sectoral planning and programme formulation.

4. (a) Budgeting and control of expenditure in respect of activities of the ministry and

   (b) Accounting or securing administrative and financial, approval to operational programmes and plans and their subsequent modifications of policies and programmes by the executive departments or semi-autonomous field agencies and evaluation of the results.

5. Coordination and interpretation of policies assisting other branches of government and maintaining contact with state governments.

6. Initiating measures to develop greater personnel and organisational competence both in the ministry and its executive agencies.

7. Assisting the minister in the discharge of his parliamentary responsibilities.

The Administrative Reforms Commission considered the secretariat to be an essential ingredient in our system of government. The secretariat system of work has lent balance, consistency and continuity to the administration, and served as a nucleus for the total machinery of a ministry. It has facilitated inter-ministry coordination and accountability to parliament at the ministerial level. As an institutionalised system it is indispensable for the proper functioning of government. Not withstanding its indispensability, the secretariat is an overgrown, ponderous and slow-moving organisation. The secretariat at the centre is thus today encumbered with non-essential work and has for a large part become a widely and overstaffed organisation. This leads to occasional blurring of responsibilities, and choking of the administrative machinery, which thus finds excuse for dilatoriness and delay. Further, the overgrowth of personnel has resulted in deterioration in quality. Thus has inevitably meant increased burden for officers at the higher levels.

This has happened because it has also taken up work which falls within the states jurisdiction under our constitution or which legitimately belongs to the domain of its attached offices. It is necessary in the interest of economic development itself to rearrange the centre-state relationship in a manner that will enable the centre to manage more efficiently in the tasks which clearly fall within its jurisdiction and encourage the states to take over from it progressively the responsibilities in areas which undoubtedly belong to them. The central ministries have the following legitimate relation to the subject failing within the sphere of the states:

1. Providing initiative and leadership to the states, and a particular serving as a clearing house of the information, intimating details and data about good programmes and methods adopted in our part of the country to the rest of the country.
2. Undertaking the responsibility for drawing up the national plan for the development sector in questions in close collaboration with the states, and developing for this purpose well-manned planning and statistical units.
3. Undertaking research at a national level confining attention to matters which are beyond the research resources of states.
4. Undertaking training programmes of foundational nature, e.g., training of planners and administrators and training of trainers.
5. Taking the initiative in evaluation of programmes with the object of checking progress, locating bottlenecks, taking remedial measures, making adjustment etc.

6. Providing a forum and meeting ground for state representatives for the exchange of ideas on different subjects and for the evaluation of guidelines.
7. Attending to functions of the nature of coordination which can only be handled at the centre.
8. Maintaining relations with foreign and international organisations.

At present while the secretariat bears the responsibility for formulating policies their execution as a norm, rests with separate organisations called attached and subordinate offices. The arrangement reflects a commitment to policy administration dichotomy.

The present style of decision-making in the secretariat seeks indiscriminate participation of too many levels in the hierarchy and, what is more, the business methods in vogue leave initiative in the hands of the clerical personnel. These two features conspire to render the secretariat as a bewilderingly slow-moving machine. There are, at present, as many as six levels of proceeding on the decision-making, namely, the dealing hand, section officer, under secretary, deputy secretary, join secretary/secretary and minister. Broadly speaking, at least four or five levels are generally involved in the disposal of any substantive case.

A serious defect which has developed in the system during the last four decades concerns the rise in the level of financial decision-making. There has been a marked tendency to send up cases for decision to higher levels even though these can be decided at a lower one. As a result, the senior officers have often too heavy a burden to bear in the area of decision-making. It is being felt that the present system under which each paper has to travel down to dealing assistant and then travel back through a number of levels till the final decision is taken is highly unsatisfactory. It leads to excessive nothing causes delay and diffuses responsibility. Above all, it undermines initiative and sense of responsibility at senior levels. Every paper has to be first noted upon by the office. This excessive dependence on the office promotes a 'file-dealing approach'. As a result, many of the senior officers do not perceive it as their role to initiate action or reflect upon the complex problems on their own. The commission was emphatic in its view that as a rule, there should be only two levels of consideration and decision below the minister. At the lower level of consideration a case may be handled by an under secretary or a deputy secretary and at the higher level by the joint or additional secretary or the secretary.

Cabinet Secretariat

The union cabinet being the chief political and executive body in India, formulates all major national policies, makes all major appointments, coordinates the various activities of government and handles various other tasks of executive. To handle the burdensome and multifarious tasks the cabinet requires adequate staff and secretarial assistance. The cabinet secretariat fills this role. It serves ministers collectively in the conduct of cabinet business. Cabinet secretariat in India has played an important role to bring about efficiency and co-ordination in the working of the cabinet. Such an office is therefore indispensable for the chief executive. In England, there is cabinet office for this purpose, which comprises the cabinet secretariat to central statistical office, the historical section and the central policy review staff. The Cabinet-office is headed by the cabinet secretary and work under the overall direction of the Prime Minister. In addition, there is also a separate office of the Prime Minister known as Prime Minister's Secretariat.

The cabinet secretariat has an important coordinating role in the process of decision-making at the highest level and operates under the direction of the Prime Minister. It submits the cases to the cabinet and its committees, prepares the records of decision taken and follow up action on their supplementation.

The political headship of the cabinet secretariat rests with the Prime Minister, and the administrative head of the secretariat is the cabinet secretary, who is very senior civil servant and plays the role as the pivot of the cabinet system. The cabinet secretariat is organized into departments wings and units. There is permanent department, i.e. Department of Cabinet Affairs. Besides this department from time to time a few other department have also been working under the cabinet secretariat, these are Department of Statistics and Department of Personnel and Administrative Reforms.

As on 1-01-2001, the following was the overall set up of the cabinet secretariat:

(a) Main Secretariat

(b) Advisory Board of Energy

(c) Office of Scientific Advisor to Prime Minister

(d) Adviser to Prime Minister on Heritage on Cultural Resources

(e) Adviser to National Security

(f) Commission on Economic Efficiency, Productivity and Exports

(g) Department of dis-investment

Main Secretariat

The main secretariat is headed by the cabinet secretary, below him there are three secretaries including one secretary (Co-ordination). One Additional Secretary, on Joint Secretary and one Secretary (TPIC) and Ex-office Joint Secretary and six deputy secretaries.

The main secretariat also accommodates the officer of the Security Advisor to Prime Minister and the office of Scientific Commission which is headed by a Chairman.

The work of the main secretariat is divided into different wings. The civil wing is responsible for secretariat work connected with the meetings of the cabinet and its committees standing as well as ad hoc committees and also the committees of secretaries which meet periodically under the chairmanship of the cabinet secretary to consider and advice on problems requiring inter-ministerial consolation and co-ordination. The civil wing is also concerned with the formulation of the Rules of Business of the union government and the allocation of the business of the government to the ministers and departments under the direction of the Prime Minister and with the approval of the President. The civil wing is divided into four sections, namely, (i) co-ordination section, (ii) cabinet section, (iii) general section, (iv) administrative section. The military wing is responsible for all National Defence Council, Military Affairs Committee and other committees concerned with defence matters. The economic wing is responsible for the secretarial matter connected with the Joint Intelligence Committee of the cabinet.

Role of Cabinet Secretariat : The cabinet secretariat plays an important role in securing the co-ordination among different ministries ad in the working of the cabinet. It provides full secretarial assistance to the cabinet and its committee and keep all the records concerning their meetings. The main area of activities of the cabinet secretariat becomes clear from the list of subjects with which the cabinet has to deal:

(a) Cases involving legislation including the issues of ordinances.

(b) Cases concerning negotiations with foreign countries on treaties and government.

(c) Addresses and messages of the President to Parliament.

(d) Proposals to summon or prorogue Parliament.

(e) Appointment of public enquiry committees and consideration of reports of such committees.

(f) Cases of disagreement between ministries of the issues which an individual minister may like to discuss in cabinet meetings.

(g) Recognition of any previous decision taken by the cabinet.

(h) Appointment of delegations of withdrawal of prosecution instituted by the government.

The cabinet secretariat helps the cabinet in all ways to perform these activities. However, there are many other functions which are not obvious but which a cabinet secretariat has to perform during varied situations. The role of the cabinet secretariat towards the success of cabinet is quite significant which can be discussed under the following headings:

As the Secretariat of the Cabinet : The obvious role of the cabinet secretariat, in the first instance is to provide full secretariat assistance to cabinet and its committees. A number of files and papers are to the presented to the cabinet or its committees during their meetings and there are a number of other papers which are circulated to the President, the vice president, the members of the cabinet/cabinet committees/council of ministers for information. A list of such papers is given in the fourth schedule to the Transaction of Business Rules, 1961. The papers which are at present circulated by the cabinet secretariat are an economic review, fortnightly political reports from state governments and centrally administered territorial administration, monthly summaries from the minister/s departments giving a brief account of their activities and decision, monthly notes from missions abroad, quarterly reports on the economic situation, reports on prices of food articles, review of the five year plans, reports on agricultural production, reports on production in public sector undertaking, reports on administrative reforms, reports on the union public service commission, reports on the working of industrial and commercial undertakings of the central government, brief notes on important matters from ministries, trade agreements/arrangements in pursuance of the general directions/decisions of the cabinet, white papers on various topics, and any other paper which the Prime Minister may wish to circulate to the ministers.

As an Originating Office : Whenever a new government is formed it becomes a smooth affair to complete all the formalities only due to the handling by the cabinet secretariat. The first item of work relates to the appointment of ministers, minister of state, deputy minister and parliamentary secretaries and the allotment of portfolios to the ministers. Once the recommendation of the Prime Minister on the appointment of a minister is accepted by the President, matters like the swearing-in ceremony, assumption of office, and so on is handled by it. Likewise, work relating to resignation, relinquishment of the charge, in portfolios, and so on, of ministers falls in the charge of cabinet secretariat.

There are certain rules of business which the president makes under the article 77 (3) and allocates the business among the ministries. Work relating to the drafting of such rules is handled in the cabinet office. The President, on the advice of the Prime Minister allots ministries/departments to the charge of ministers from time to time. Ministries are merged or reorganised and the subject dealt with by them are reallocated or readjusted or transferred from the one ministry to another according to administrative needs from time to time. This is more or less continuing process, and the proposals which arise or are received in this connection are processed by the cabinet secretariat.

The third original items of work relates to certain aspects of co-ordination and expenditure in the implementation of the policies of government. In this matter the cabinet secretariat does not supersede other ministries nor does it relive them of their responsibilities. It is the duty of the cabinet secretariat.

(i) to assist in resolving difficulties or delays which may arise in any field of activity between the ministers and departments.

(ii) to watch the progress of important administrative measures of the government of India which affect more than one ministry.

(iii) to assist in co-ordinating the major administrative activities and policies of the government of India, and

(iv) to watch the implementation of decisions in which the cabinet as a whole or Prime Minister is interested.

In performing the duties mentioned above, the cabinet secretariat issue circular and instructions for the guidance of ministers. It also conveys the directives of the cabinet of the Prime Minister on administrative and allied matters, to various functionaries and agencies.

Role in Co-ordination : A highly significant role is played by the cabinet secretariat by achieving interdepartmental co-ordination which is basic requirement towards the success of any administrative system and which becomes more important when it is closely linked with the task of policy formulation and implementation. Over the years, various type of mechanism have been evolved for the purpose of having quick and efficient inter-departmental consultations and of securing co-ordination of activities of different ministers and departmental consultation and of the executive council of the viceroy was established to perform the following duties.

(a) To assist in co-ordinating the major administrative decisions and policies of government.

(b) To assist in resolving difficulties or delays which arises in the administrative field whether between ministries of the government of India/ and provincial governments.

(c) To watch the progress of important administrative measure of the government of India which affected more than one ministry.

(d) To submit to the co-ordination committee of the council such matters as required its decisions and instructions.

The ministries or administrative agencies of the government were never superseded by the co-ordination committee's secretary or the secretariat nor they were relieved of their duties by the latter. The secretary served all ministers and was at the disposal of ministers for consultation on any matter in which his assistance was required.

The work of co-ordination previously done by the co-ordination committee is now undertaken by the cabinet and its committees. At the official level a number of standing committees of secretaries with the cabinet secretary as chairman have been set up. Specific functions have been assigned to these committees. Some of them viz., the Committee of Economic Secretaries, the Secretaries's Committee on Foreign Affairs and Scientific Advisory

Committee to the Cabinet assist and advice the Cabinet/on matters which fall within the scope of their functions. In cases where there is a difference of opinion among various ministries, the cabinet secretary assists in resolving such differences and in arriving at agreed or acceptable decisions. As head of the cabinet secretariat, he is entrusted with the positive functions of securing co-ordination as well as timely and effective action by all ministeries/department of the government of India in all matters in which the cabinet as a whole or the Prime Minister is interested. For this purpose apart from the meetings of regular Committees of Secretaries he convenes meeting of secretaries and senior officials, whenever necessary. Rule 4 of the transaction of business rules lays down that when the subject of a case concerns more than one departments, no order shall be issued until such departments have concurred, or failing such concurrence, a decision there on has been taken by the authority of the cabinet. In accordance with this rule for consideration of complicated questions concerning more than one department, interdepartmental consultations are held or meetings of the representatives of ministries are convened. This results in faster disposal of disputed matters and eliminates elaborates correspondence.

Role in Implementation : The Cabinet decisions are communicated to all the concerned ministeries or other agencies by the cabinet secretariat which also keeps a watch on the progress of the implementation of the same. In accordance with the instructions issued by the cabinet secretariat, a monthly statement showing the progress on the cases relating to each ministry is sent to the cabinet secretariat. These statements are scrutinised in the context of the decision taken. If in any case it is noticed that the ministries are not making substantial progress in the implementation of the decision, the matter is taken up with them at a higher level to expediting implementation action. Records of such cases are kept by the cabinet secretariat.

Role as a Staff Agency : The role played by the cabinet secretariat is truly of staff agency. It is a walking stick for the cabinet. As a staff agency, it ensures that the cabinet, which is the chief executive in India is adequately and correctly informed. It assists and even advises the cabinet in for seeing problems and planning future programmes. For this purpose there are experienced administrators and expert advisers working in the cabinet secretariat. Besides this, the cabinet, secretariat ensures that matters for cabinet's decision reaches to it promptly so that no decisions are taken in haste and without proper information or judgement. At the same time, the precious time of the cabinet is saved.

The Administrative Reforms Commission (1966) suggested reorganisation of the cabinet secretariat so as to have cells specialising in broad areas of governmental functioning. The main functions of such cells of the cabinet secretariat would be:

(a) to keep the Prime Minister posted with happening in ministers;

(b) To receive memorandum of major decision from ministers and put them up to the Prime Minister;

(c) To serve cabinet committees, if any, relating to the group of ministers assigned to them.

(d) To act as the aides of the Prime Minister the cabinet and the cabinet committees in giving shape to new policies in supra-ministry fields; and

(e) To keep in touch with follow-up of the Prime Minister's suggestions or the decisions of the Cabinet and its Committees.

It was also suggested by the ARC that the Cabinet Secretary should act as the principal staff advisor of the Prime Minister, the cabinet and the cabinet committees on important policy matters.

As has been noted earlier, the cabinet secretariat is performing the functions as suggested by the ARC. In fact the role of the cabinet secretariat (as well as that of PM's Secretariat) depends a great deal on the personal style of the Prime Minister and the political strength of the party in power and the balance of forces in party system. On the other hand, the administrative output or the efficiency of the cabinet secretariat depends much on the leadership of the cabinet secretary.

4

Protection of Civil Servants

We shall discuss with you procedural safeguards to civil servants which have been given in the Constitution of India. As you known that in any welfare state civil servants play a crucial role in executing the policies and laws for the benefit of the people without a team of dedicated civil servant. It was due to this reason that in India there is a tremendous expansion of the civil service. According to an estimate in 1949, there were 14 lakhs civil servants. In 1978 this number just doubled. This is apart from the large number of employees of the public sector undertakings. By March, 2001, the number of civil Servants has gone upto 32 lakhs.

A civil servant is expected to be devoted, dynamic, honest, impartial and fearless in the face of external pressures so that they may exercise their functions honestly and impartially. Constitution has given them a security of service by providing certain procedural safeguards. In this lesson we shall examine these procedural safeguards in detail as interpreted by the courts in India.

Constitutional Provision

In part XIV of the Constitution Articles 309, 310 and deal with the service matters of government servants in India. Article 309 empowers the appropriate legislatures to make laws relating to the recruitment, conditions of service and disciplinary matters not only of persons serving the Union or the State but with respect to person appointed to public services and posts in connection with the affairs of the Union or the State.

However, this power of passing Law or making rules there under by the competent authority is subject to the other provisions of the Constitution. Therefore, such laws/rules are subject to judicial interrelations.

Process with far-off roots it is not merely an adjudicatory body but it is also a consultative body. In 1979 it considered 147 draft laws which were placed before the Parliament in 1980 and also considered 489 decrees.

The early common criticism of the Droit Administration in France has been that it cannot protect the private citizen from the excesses of the administration. However, later researches have shown that no single institution has done so much for the protection of private citizens against the excesses of the administration as has been done by the Council d'Etat.

From the above discussion of the growth of administrative law in India and France it becomes clear that in France the sense in which administrative law differs from the sense in which we understand administrative law in India. In France administrative law is a law which is developed by special, administrative courts on case-to-case basis whereas in India the administrative law is partly statutory and partly developed by the ordinary courts on case-to-case basis. Furthermore, in France the administrative law basically regulates the relationships of a private individual with the State and its officers, whereas in India the administrative law deals with the administration as a whole and also deals with the legislature and judiciary. In France there is a dual judicial system (1) which regulates the relationship of individuals interest and the other (2) which regulates the relationships of the individual with the State. This later part of the judicial system is known as the administrative law in France. However, in India there is only single judicial system that deals with the relationship of the individuals interest and their relationship with the State. It also becomes clear that the peculiar administrative law in France is a by-product of a very special historical context whereas in India the administrative law is a natural development of the judicial process. Article 310 (1) which lays down pleasure doctrine. Article 311 which given protection against arbitrary dismissal, removal etc., and part III dealing with fundamental rights. Consequently if any law/rule is made which violates any of the above provisions, it would be unconstitutional and hence, void. In exercise of this, power the Union and the State Legislatures have passed various laws governing the recruitment, conditions of service and discipline of government servants. These laws are supplemented by various rules framed by the executive in exercise of rule making power delegated to them under various Acts.

Article 310 contains what is popularly known as 'pleasure doctrine'. It provides that every government servant shall hold his post during the pleasure of the President or the Governor of a State as the case may be. However, this pleasure doctrine though not subject to the law made by the Parliament or the State legislature yet is subject to the provisions expressly provided in the Constitution. Thus, 'pleasure doctrine' is subject to the provisions of Article 311 which provides safeguards against dismissal, removal or reduction in rank of a government servant. The result that no government servant can be dismissed or removed or reduced in rank at the pleasure of the government, in violation of the provisions of Article 311.

Article 311 provides Constitutional Protections to civil servants against their dismissal or removal or reduction in rank. These protections have been provided in the public interest for, public good in as much as they give a feeling a security of service to a civil servant. Article 311 as amended upto date provides:

"Dismissal, removal or reduction in rank of person employed in civil capacities under the Union or a State."

1. No person who is a member of civil service of the Union or an All-India-Services or a Civil Service of a State or holds a civil post under the Union or a State

shall be dismissed or removed by an authority subordinate to that by which he was appointed.

2. No such person as aforesaid shall be dismissed or removed or reduced in rank except after an inquiry in which he has been informed of the changes against him and given a reasonable opportunity of being heard in respect of those charges.

Provided that where it is proposed after such inquiry, to impose upon him any such penalty, may be imposed on the basis of the evidence adduced during-such inquiry and it shall not be necessary to give such person any opportunity of making representation on the penalty proposed.

Provided further that this clause shall not apply:

(a) where a person is dismissed or removed or reduced in rank on the ground of conduct which has led to his conviction on a criminal charge; or

(b) Where authority empowered to dismiss or remove a person or to reduce him in rank is satisfied that for some reason, to be recorded by that authority in writing, it is not reasonably practicable to hold such inquiry; or

(c) where the President or the Governor, as the case may be, is satisfied that in the interest of the security of the State it is not expedient to hold such inquiry.

If, in respect of any such person as aforesaid a question arises whether it is reasonably practicable to hold such inquiry as is referred to in clause (2) the decision there on of the authority empowered to dismiss or remove such person or to reduce him in rank shall be final.

Safeguards provided under Article 311 are available only to those who are members of Civil Service of the Union or of an all-India service or of a civil service of a State or to persons who hold a civil post under the Union or a State. Therefore, these safeguards are not available to a person serving in any public undertaking or a government company. These safeguards are also not available to a person in defence services and they are governed by the Arm of the Act.

Who is a civil servant in a complex question? A person cannot be said to be a civil servant merely because his salary is paid out of State funds or the State exercises certain control over him. There must exist a relationship of master and servant between the persons and the State. This relationship is indicated by the State's right to select and appoint, its right to control and payment of salary. Hence, whether a person is a civil servant or not is a question of fact to be determined in conjunction with these various factors.

It is important to note that the protection of Article 311 is available both to the permanent and temporary servants. Courts have gone even to the extent that even the service of a probationer cannot be terminated at will if it is done by ways of punishment.

Protection of Article 311 is not available if a person is retired after he reaches the age of superannuation which has been reasonably fixed. Protection is also not available if a person is compulsorily retired according to the service rules. However, if power is exercised in an arbitrary manner to punish the person the courts have granted relief.

Article 311, therefore, provides two important safeguard to the government servants. Under class (1) no civil servant can be dismissed or removed or reduced in rank from service by an authority subordinate to that by which he was appointed. Under Clause (2) no civil servant can be dismissed or removed or reduced in rank without any inquiry in which he has been informed of the charges against him and given reasonable opportunity of being heard in respect of such charges. Reasonable opportunity means that the inquiry be conducted according to the principles of natural justice. Should the report of the Inquiry Officer be shown to the employee before final action is taken? This question has raised controversy. However, Central Administrative Service Tribunal has recently held that if the report is not shown, it shall violate the norm or reasonable opportunity in Article 311.

This matter is still subject to the consideration by the Supreme Court of India. Before 1976 there was one more protection available to a civil servant which provided for a second opportunity for making a representation against the penalty proposed to be imposed upon him. This protection was taken away by the Constitution (Forty-Second Amendment) Act, 1976.

However, the safeguard provided under Clause 2 (opportunity of being heard) is not available in three situations provided in clauses (a), (b), (c) of Article 311 (2). Therefore, a civil servant can be dismissed, or removed or reduced in rank without an opportunity.

(a) Where such person has been convicted on a criminal charge by a court; or

(b) Where the authority is satisfied, for the reasons to be recorded in writing, that it is not reasonable principle to hold inquiry, or

(c) Where the president or the Governor as the case may be is satisfied in the interest of security of the state it is not expedient to hold an inquiry.

It is, therefore, evident that the rule of the natural justice available to Civil Servants under Article 311(2) has been expressly excluded in these situations.

The language of these three clauses of Article 311 (2) is plain and unambiguous. Further the words in Article 311 (2) "this clause shall not apply' make these three clauses mandatory. There is thus no scope for allowing opportunity for hearing in these three situations by any implication or inference. Constituent Assembly debates indicates that these clauses were deliberately introduced in Article 311 (2) as a matter of public good. Consequently Rule 19 if the Central Civil Services (Classification, Control an Appeal) Rule 1965, rule 14 of the Railway Servants (Discipline and Appeal) Rules 1960, Rule 3 7 of the Central Industrial Security Forces Rules 1969 provide substantially for the same exceptions to the rule of notice and hearing as are provided in clauses a, b and c of Article 311 (2) because anything contrary to his would be unconstitutional and hence void.

Judicial Interpretation

Article 311 which gives protection to the government servants against dismissal, or reduction in rank has been subjected to judicial scrutiny on numerous occasions. However, the three clauses of the second provision to Article 311 (2) which allow disciplinary action against a government servant without notice and hearing have come under detailed scrutiny lately. In order to understand and appreciate judicial interpretation of these 3 clauses, one may start with Challapan and end with Tulsi Ram Patel.

Challapan Case (1976) : Divisional Personnel Officer, Southern Railway V.T.R. Challapan provided the first opportunity to the Highest Bench to interpret Article 31-1 (2) (a) conjunction with Rule 14 of the Railway Servants (Discipline and Appeal) Rules 1968. This case disposed off three appeals against a common judgement of the High Court of Kerala allowing writ petitions filed by three railway servants. Challapan, the respondent in one of three appeals, was a railway post man. He was arrested at Olabakhot Railway Station platform for disorderly drunken and indecent behaviour and was prosecuted and convicted under Kerala Police Act. So far as other two railway employees were concerned, one was convicted under Section 3 of the Railway Property (Unlawful Possession) Act, 1966 for possessing stolen properties and the other under Section 420 of the Indian Penal Code for the offence of cheating. However, instead of sentencing them, magistrate released them on Probation Offenders Act, 1958. Thereafter they were removed from the service by the Department without holding any inquiry on the basis of conviction in Criminal cases.

It is pertinent to not that Rule I (i) of the Railway servants (Discipline and Appeal) Rules 1968 provides for the same exception to the rule of notice and hearing as is provided in Article 311 (2) (a). It lays down that where any penalty is imposed on a railway servant on the ground of conduct which has led to his conviction on a criminal charge, the disciplinary authority may consider the circumstances of the case and may make such orders there on as it deems fit. Kerala High Court allowed the writ petition solely on the ground that the orders of the Magistrate releasing the concerned railway employee on probation does not amount to imposition of 'penalty' as contemplated by Rule 14 of Railway Servants (Discipline and Appeal) Rules, 1968. However, the Supreme Court did not agree with this view and held that the word 'penalty' does not refer to a sentence awarded to the accused on his conviction but it merely indicates the nature of penalty impossible by the disciplinary authority if the delinquent employee has been found guilty of conduct which has led to his conviction on a criminal charge. Nevertheless the order of Kerala High Court was upheld by the Supreme Court on the ground the words "the disciplinary authority may consider the circumstances of the case and make such order there on as it deems fit". The Rule 14 incorporates the rule of fair hearing before a person can be dismissed on the ground of the conviction by a Court.

Supreme Court held that the use of the word 'consider' implies consideration of all aspects of the matter after hearing the aggrieved person. However, the court was quick to add that inquiry in such cases may be summary and the conviction of the delinquent employee would be taken to be sufficient proof of misconduct and the inquiry will be taken to be sufficient proof of misconduct and the inquiry will be only as to the nature and the extent of the penalty to be imposed. The Highest Bench did not express any opinion on the argument of the appellant that in cases where proviso (a) of Article 311 (2) applies departmental inquiry is completely dispensed with and the disciplinary authority can on the basis of doctrine of pleasure terminate the services of the delinquent employee. It was not necessary also because the court interpreted role by itself and not in conjunction with clause (a) of Article 311 (2) of the Constitution. Therefore, Challapan's case is an authority only for the proposition that under Rule 14 of Railway Servants Discipline and Appeal Rules 1968 the delinquent employee is entitled to summary hearing at on the quantum of punishment being imposed upon him in pursuance of his conviction by a court on a criminal charge. The rationale behind this proposition is that it is just possible that the employee may have been convicted on a minor or technical criminal charge.

However, the correctness of the law laid down in Challapan's case was doubled from the very beginning. Judgement in this case was delivered in September 15, 1976 and was reported in 1976. Immediately thereafter in the next group of appeals in which the same question was raised the matter was referred to a larger Bench by an order made on November 18, 1975 in view of the earlier decision of another three-judges Bench M. Gopala Krishna Naidu v. State of M.P

Tulsi Ram Patel's Case : After Challappan case the Union of India v. Tulsi Ram Patel (1983) decided by Five-Judges Constitution Bench which evoked nation wide controversy. In order to understand the true importance of law laid down by the Highest Bench in this case it is necessary to understand the factual matrix of the case.

All government servants involved in this case had either been dismissed or removed from without holding any inquiry. The penalty of dismissal or removal had been imposed upon them under one or the other of the three clauses of the second proviso to Article 311 (2) or under similar provisions of the rules under the proviso to Article 309, such as, Rule 19 of the Central Civil Services (Classification, Control and Appeal) Rules, 1965, Rule 14 of the Railway Servant (Discipline and Appeal) Rules, 1958 and Rule 37 of the Central Security Force Rules, 1969.

This case is unique because the court had the opportunity of deciding on the scope and ambit of all the three clauses of proviso (2) of Article 311 (2). The case of Tulsi Ram Patel falls under clauses, (a) and rest all other cases fall under clause (b) (c) of Article 311 (2). A brief statement of the factual situation in each category is essential in order to appreciate the law as laid down by the Supreme Court in correct perspective.

The respondent, Tulsi Ram Patel, was a permanent auditor in the Regional Audit Office, M.E.S. Jabalpur. It appears that orders were issued by Headquarters, C.D.A. Meerut stopping the increment of the respondent for one year. One Raj Kumar Jairath was at the relevant time the Regional Audit Officer, M.E.S. Jabalpur. On July 27, 1976, the respondent went to Mr. Raj Kumar's Office and demanded an explanation from him as to why he had stopped his increment whereupon Mr. Raj Kumar replied that he was no body to stop his increment. Tulsi Ram thereafter struck him on the head with an iron rod. Raj Kumar fell down with his head profusely bleeding. Tulsi Ram was tried and convicted by the Magistrate who instead of sending him to jail released him on probation. His appeal against his conviction was dismissed by the Session Judge. Thereafter, because he had been convicted on a criminal charge by a court, the penalty of compulsory retirement was imposed upon him under clause (i) of Rule 19 of Civil Service Rules which contains law substantially similar to Article 311 (2) (a) of the Constitution. It may be noted that compulsory retirement in this case was by way of penalty, hence amounts to removal from services and thus the provisions of Article 311 (2) (a) are attracted.

The respondents in the second category are dismissed members of the Central Industrial Security force a (CISF) posted at Bokaro Steel Plant in Bihar and at Security Paper Mill at Hoshangabad in Madhya Pradesh. The members of the CISF Unit at Bokaro had formed an all India association in March, 1979. Thereafter, a country wide agitation was carried on for the recognition of the association. In 1979 some members of the association were invited to meet the Home Minister at Delhi. While they were staging a demonstration, some demonstrators were arrested, but later released on bail. At Bokaro Steel Plant, the agitation which was going on assumed aggravated violent proportions. Out of 1, 19000 persons of the CISF, about 1,000 participated in violent demonstration and indulged in collective violence and intimidation. These violent activities reached to such a proportion that Army had to be called in June, 1979. On seeing the army the agitators started making preparations for armed resistance by putting sand bags floodlights and barricades. The agitators who were in the control of armoury also exchanged fire with the army which continued for three hours. It resulted in the death of one Army Major and two other army personnel on the spot. Nineteen person of CISF also died in this pitched battle. About 800 persons of the Unit were arrested and a substantial number either fled away or went underground with large quantity of arms and ammunition with them. Situation continued to be tense and CRPF was devolved from security duties. This situation continued for a long time. Under these circumstances authority came to the conclusion that any inquiry is impracticable and therefore, the penalty of dismissal was imposed on the general secretary of the association without any hearing under Rule 37 of CISF Rules, 1969 read with Article 311 (2) (b) of the Constitution.

To the same category belonged the cases of those railway employees who participated in All-India strike of 1974 in order to press for their demands. In this All-India strike large number of railway workers had struck work, the railway service paralysed, loyal workers and superior officers were assaulted and intimidated, the country held to ransom, economy of the country prejudicially affected and properly damaged and destroyed. Under these circumstances action was taken against key figures and penalty of dismissal was imposed without any notice and hearing on the ground that in such a situation any hearing is impracticable and hence the penalty of dismissal was imposed under clause (ii) of Rule 14 of the Railway Servants (Discipline and Appeal) Rules, 1968 read with second proviso to Article 311 (2) of the Constitution.

In the third category those members of the Madhya Pradesh District Police Force of Madhya Pradesh Special Armed Force are included who were dismissed by an order of the Governor by applying Clause (c) of the second proviso to Article 311 (2) which provides that where that President or the Governor, as the case may be, is satisfied that in the interest of the security of the State it is not expedient to hold inquiry. The case arose out of an incident at the annual Mela at Gwalior in 1981 in which one person was burnt alive. Two persons belonging to two forces were arrested and this led to a large scale rioting and violence at the Mela. Constables attacked police station and ransacked it. Situation become so worse that there was no alternative out to release the arrested persons. As the disciplinary proceeding started, members of the force started secret meetings, distributing leaflets and inciting constabulary to rise against the government.

The court by single judgement dismissed all appeals, writs and transferred cases and firmly held that if a case is covered under clause a, b and c of Article 311 (2) of the Constitution no hearing is necessary for dismissal or removal or reduction in rank of any government servant and thus fixed as final seal of disapproval on the law laid down in Challapan's case. Supreme Court held that the three judges Bench of the Supreme Court in Challappan's case erred in interpreting Rule of the 14 of the Railway Servants (Discipline and Appeal) Rules, 1968 by itself and not in conjunction with Article 311 (2), the court said, the interpretation of the word 'consider' would not have been different from that to be placed upon the second proviso to Article 311 (2). The court thus observed that the view taken in Challappan's case that a "Consideration of the Circumstances "under Rule 14 must therefore be exparte by the disciplinary authority himself without affording to the concerned Civil Servant in opportunity of being heard. The disciplinary authority in such case however, shall take into consideration the facts and circumstances of the case, judgement of the criminal court, entire conduct of the Civil Servant, gravity of the offence committed, importance of the administration, whether office is of technical or trivial nature and the extenuating circumstances; if any. But, this has to be done by the authority himself without hearing the concerned employee. It may be noted that in case falling under clause (a) of Article 311 (2) hearing is not impracticable as in clause (b) and (c), therefore, heavens would not fall, if the person convicted by a criminal court was allowed hearing at least at the final stage of imposing the penalty. Fairness runs like golden thread through all the pages of the Constitution and is not excluded by it.

Regarding Clauses (b) and (c) of Article 311 (2) it is clear beyond doubt that in such cases hearing is excluded because it is not just practicable to afford hearing to the delinquent government servant. Therefore, if it is shown that hearing was practicable, then order of the discipilinary authority as final, nevertheless, final to is not so 'final' that the courts cannot do anything. Within the parameters of the law relating to the privilege of the government to withhold documents, court can decide the question of expediency and practicability of not holding the inquiry. In this case, it is pertinent to note that government did not claim privilege and placed all documents at the disposal of the court.

Replying to the argument of the respondents courts further held that no matter Article 14 is Constitutional guardian of the principles of natural justice yet when it is expressly excluded by

Article 311 (2) Clauses a, b and c its requirement cannot be read in Article 14 simply because it is not just possible to afford an inquiry under the circumstances. Same law was reiterated in Satyavir Singh v. Union of India (1985).

In this case all the appellants who were employees of the Research and Analysis Wing (RAW) resented the introduction of identity card system introduced by the Counter-Intelligence Section (CIS), a branch of RAW, for going from one floor to the other as a security measure. This resentment later on took an ugly turn. There were violent demonstrations and the officers were made hostages. Situation became so tense that police had to be called in to release the hostage. Demonstrations were held on the precinct of the Office. Under these circumstances witnesses were non-available and services of the notice was not practicable. Therefore, delinquent employees were dismissed without hearing under Rule 19 of the Central Rules Services read with clause (b) of second proviso to Article 311 (2) of the Constitution.

A bare reading of the facts of each case mentioned above will show that one thing is common in all these fact situations and that is 'violence'. The opinion on courts ruling in this case is sharply divided. Those who believe that even in a democratic society violence is justified hence they support the judgement. This brings us to a question of legitimacy of violence'. It is argued that the police personnel who had taken part in 1979 police movement, locomen who had participated in 1974 movement and members of the CISF who had participated in 1979 uprising were doing it for acceptance for their long standing legitimate demands for higher pay, better conditions of service and better facilities, which from all angles had sunk very low, therefore, violence is justified because without this it is not possible to energise and activate the indolent pachyadermic administration which has become emboldened by the anesthesised public conscience.

It is a fallacious logic, the fact remains that there cannot be anything like Justified violence in a democratic society. Violence is the negation of any civilized existence in a society. No matter, however, the laudable the purpose may be, violence cannot be justified. Anything contrary to this would be glorifying violence and thus reverting the humane existence of an animal existence. Right to protection is a fundamental right in a democratic society. There is always a constitutional and legal way of the settling disputes and grievances even if it is against the government itself, because the government can also be changed through the prescribed constitutional procedure. The people of India have demonstrated beyond doubt that this is not a myth but reality when the government in power was ousted by the ballot.

The decision of the court in Tulsi Ram's case is highly contextual and it is confined only to case of mass violence where hearing is not practicable. Subsequently, the apprehension that the decision adversely affects the right to strike and leaves the government servant's high and dry is imaginary and pollustic.

To sum up, one can say that the real message of Tulsi Ram Patel's case is that in our democratic process, one must not be guilty of violence and wrongful deeds for getting any of his demands accepted by the government on matter, howsoever, legitimate these may be. One is reminded of Martin Luther King who said, "We must conduct our struggle at a high plane of dignity and discipline. We must not allow our creative violence to degenerate into physical violence." Protest minus violence, the precious right of any person in a democratic society is still untouched. At the most, Tulsi Ram Patel sounds like the bell of a fire brigade which wakes up people at midnight and thus causes annoyance but it also saves them from burning alive. Fact remains that without discipline no nation can progress.

Comptroller and Auditor General

An important office in the Government of India is that of Comptroller and Auditor-General who controls the entire financial system of the country (Article 148). The President appoints the Comptroller and Auditor-General to perform all duties and exercise powers in connection with the accounts of the Union and the States. The independence of the Comptroller and Auditor General has been ensured by the Constitution.

Terms and Service Conditions

1. Though appointed by the President, Comptroller and Auditor-General may be removed only on an address from both Houses of Parliament on the grounds of 'proved misbehaviour' or 'incapacity'. He is thus exempted from the general rule that all civil servants of the Union hold their office at the pleasure of the President.

2. His salary and conditions of service are statutory (i.e., as laid down by the Parliament by law) and are not subject to variation to his disadvantages during his term of office.

The term of office is six year. His age of retirement is 65 years. He may resign his office at any time by writing a letter to the President. He may be removed by impeachment.

On retirement he is eligible to an annual pension. In other matters his conditions of service are determined by the Rules applicable to a member of I.A.S, holding the rank of a Secretary to the Government of India. He is not eligible for further office either under the Government of India or under any State. Government after he ceases to hold his office.

The Functions : His duties include : (a) to audit and report on all expenditure from the Consolidated Fund of India and of each State and each Union Territory having a Legislative Assembly as to whether such expenditure has been in accordance with the law, (b) to audit and report on all expenditure from the contingency fund and public accounts of the union and of the states, (c) to audit and report on all trading, manufacturing, profit and loss accounts, etc., kept by any department of the Union or a State and (d) to audit and report on the accounts of government Companies and other Corporations when required by law.

His reports relating to the accounts of the Union and of the States are submitted to the President and the Government concerned. These reports are placed before Parliament and Legislatures.

The accounts compiled by the Comptroller and Auditor-General and the audit reports laid before the Parliament, are in two parts : (i) Finance accounts giving a picture of the entire receipts and expenditure of the Government, and (ii) Appropriate accounts in which are given details of the amount sanctioned in the appropriation act or acts and the amount actually, spent under each grant. Thus he keeps vigilance on the finance of the country.

Election Commission

The control of elections in the Union of India and the States has been vested in the Election Commission. The Chief Election Commissioner and other Election Commissioners are appointed by the President, and are important and independent person under the Constitution. The Chief Election Commissioner cannot be removed from office except in the manner as the Judge of Supreme Court can be removed. The Commission as an election body has very wide powers and functions. It is responsible for elections to the Parliament, State Legislatures, and to the offices of the President and the Vice-President. It has judicial powers to decide disputes between the political parties. Election Commission appoints the returning officers for every constituency. The President can seek its advice on prescribing laws and disqualifications of the members. The Election Commission can suggest reforms in electoral system. This part has not been divided into chapter. Articles 324 to 329 deal with elections, and the Election Commission.

Important Provision : The superintendence, direction and control of the preparation of the electoral rolls for, and the conduct of, all elections to the Parliament and to the Legislature of every State and of elections to the offices of the President and the Vice President held under this Constitution, shall be vested in a Commission (referred to in this Constitution as the Election Commission).

The Election Commission shall consist of the Chief Election Commissioner and such number of other Election Commissioners, if any, as the President may from time to time fix and the appointment of the Chief Election Commissioner and other Election Commissioners shall, subject to the provisions of any law made on that behalf by the Parliament, be made by the President.

When any other Election Commissioner is so appointed, the Chief Election Commissioner shall act as the Chairman of the Election Commission. Before each general election to the House of the People and to the Legislative Assembly of each state, and before the first general election and thereafter before each biennial election to the Legislative Council of each State having such Council, the President may also appoint after consultation with the Election Commission such Regional Commissioners as he may consider necessary to assist the Election Commission in the performance of the functions conferred on the Commission by clause (1) subject to the provisions of any law made by the Parliament. The conditions of service and tenure of the office of the Election Commissioner and the Regional Commissioners shall be such as the President may by rule determine:

Provided that the Chief Election Commissioner shall not be removed from the office except in like manner and on the like ground as a Judge of the Supreme Court and the conditions of service of the Chief Election Commissioner shall not be varied to his disadvantage after his appointment.

Provided further, that any other Election Commissioner or a Regional Commissioner shall not be removed from office except on the recommendation of the Chief Election Commissioner.

The President, or the Governor of a State, shall, when so requested by the Election Commission, make available to the Election Commissioner or to a Regional Commissioner such staff as may be necessary for the discharge of the functions conferred on the Election commission by clause (1).

Since 1991, Election Commission of India has been made a three member body. (A Chairman and two members).

There shall be one general electoral roll for every territorial constituency for election to either House of the Parliament or either House of the Legislature of a State and no person shall be ineligible for inclusion in any such roll or claim to be included in any special electoral roll for any such constituency on grounds only of religion, race, caste, sex or any of them.

The elections to the House of the People and to the Legislative Assembly of every State shall be on the basis of adult suffrage; that is to say, every person who is a citizen of India and who is not less than 18 years of age (61 Amendment 1989) and such date be fixed on that behalf by or under any law made by the appropriate Legislature and is not otherwise disqualified under this Constitution of any law made by the appropriate Legislature on the ground of non-residence, unsoundness of mind, crime or corrupt or illegal practice, shall be entitled to be registered as a voter at any such election.

Notwithstanding anything in this Constitution:

1. The validity of any law relating to the delimitation of constituencies or the allotment of seats to such constituencies, made or purporting to be made under Article 327 or Article 328 shall not be called in question in any court;

2. No election to either House of the Parliament or to either House of the Legislature of a State shall be called in question except by an election petition presented to such authority and in such manner as may be proved for by or under any law made by the appropriate legislature.

Other Noteworthy Provisions : Power of the Parliament to make provision with respect to elections to the Legislature : Subject to the provisions of this Constitution, the Parliament may from time to time by law make provision with respect to all matters relating to, or in connection with, elections to either House of Legislature of a State including the preparation of electoral rolls, the delimitation of constituencies and all other matters necessary for securing the due constitution of such House or Houses.

Power of the Legislature of a State to make provision with respect to elections to such Legislature : Subject to the provision of this Constitution and in so far as provision on that behalf is not made by the Parliament, the Legislature of a State may from time to time by law make provision with respect to all matters relating to the House or either House of the Legislature of the State including the preparation of electoral rolls and all other matter necessary for securing the due consideration of such House or Houses.

Lok Adalat (People's Court) : For the last few years, Lok Adalats have very much come to limelight. Lok Adalats have opened a new vista for providing speedy justice to the people. A Committee under the Chairmanship of Justice Bhagwati had been appointed to suggest, among other things, the means and ways to provide legal aid to those who are not in a position to engage lawyers. The various recommendations of the Committee included a suggestion to institute Lok Adalats.

Meaning : As is evident from the very title the Lok Adalat means "People's Court". This court endeavours to settle disputes between the litigants through mutual agreements or understanding. From time to time these courts have been held in Gujarat, Delhi and various other States. People engaged in public welfare, social workers and young students of law have contributed in a big way to the institution of Lok Adalats. These people were helped by judges who showed them the files of cases which were pending in their courts. On the basis of this information they met the parties involved in litigation and persuaded them to withdraw their cases from the courts of law and move the Lok Adalats for redress.

The Working of Lok Adalats : The judges of Lok Adalats do not act as judges but as counsellors. The judges as well as the students and public workers inform the litigants about their rights and duties. They make an endeavour to bring compromise or agreement between the parties. On October 6, 1985 for the first time the Lok Adalats were held in Delhi. Justice P.N. Bhagwati inaugurated the Adalats. On the first day five Lok Adalats, organised by the Legal Aid and Advisory Board of Delhi, held their sessions. On this day 116 persons received compensation to the tune of Rs. 35 lakhs. These people had been contesting their motor accident claims since 1978-79. Delhi Transport Corporation immediately made payment to the victims of accidents. On 22nd January, 1989 Ninth Lok Adalat held its session in Delhi. On that day about 850 motor accident claims and 150 claims against the

Railways were settled by the Lok Adalats. While inaugurating the Ninth Lok Adalat the Lt. Governor of Delhi observed, "the jurisdiction of Lok Adalat should be expanded so that cases related to dowry and family affairs also get speedier settlement."

Evaluation of Lok Adalats : The work done by the Lok Adalats in Delhi, Gujarat and other places has been highly appreciated. Primarily three arguments are presented in support of Lok Adalats

(i) The Lok Adalats work in the spirit of compromise.

(ii) Lok Adalats deliver speedy and inexpensive justice.

(iii) The Lok Adalats shall reduce the work load of other courts and would consequently reduce delay in justice.

It is the need of the hour that Lok Adalats are organised more frequently and their jurisdiction is expanded. The voluntary organisations can organise such Adalats in their areas of operation. These courts can play important role in settling the family feuds, disputes between the neighbours and minor cases of assault and injury. There are more than fifty places where Lok Adalats are working. The lawyers and the jurists are of the opinion that the poor people cannot fight the long and expensive legal battle. So their cases should be settled on the basis of priority.

Speedy and Inexpensive Justice : How long a case in a court of law in India would take to reach the final settlement through the long drawn legal procedure is beyond one's imagination. There were 1,65,106 cases pending before the Supreme Court in December, 1990. The High Courts had more than ten lakh cases in abeyance. If we add up the cases pending in the lower courts as well, it would show how lax and lengthy is the legal procedure in India.

5

Parliamentary Democracy

The constitution of India has adopted a parliamentary form of government on the British model but its republican character necessitated the creation of the office of the President who acts as the constitutional head of the state. The real executive power of the union of central government is vested in the Council of Ministers headed by the Prime Minister. The responsibility of the executive to the legislature has been called the essence of parliamentary democracy, accordingly the Council of Ministers is collectively responsible to the union Parliament (Sansad), particularly its lower house, called House of the People of the Lok Sabha which consists of members, elected directly by the people on the basis of universal adult franchise. The union government thus consists of three main organs the President, the Council of Ministers and the Parliament.

In the Parliamentary form of government there are two executives, one real and the other nominal. In India, while the President is the nominal executive, the Council of Ministers headed by the Prime Minister is the real executive . It means that formally all executive power of the Union are vested in the President of India under Article 53 but in reality he does not exercise these powers, himself. Rather he exercises them on the advice of the Cabinet or more precisely the cabinet exercises them on his behalf and in his name.

Article 74 (1) of the constitution provides that there shall be a council of ministers, headed by the Prime Minister to aid and advise the president in the exercise of his powers and performance of his function. In 1976 the Forty-second Amendment Act made it binding on the President to accept the advice of the Cabinet. After this amendment, the President could not even ask the Cabinet to reconsider its advice to him. Thus, he became totally a rubber stamp in the hands of the Cabinet. However, when Janata Party came to power this position was changed by the Forty-fourth Amendment Act (1978). The amendment allows the President to refer back a matter to the Cabinet and ask it to reconsider its advice, but if the Cabinet again sends its advice to president, he will have to accept it. Thus in ultimate analysis the President is only a nominal executive and the real executive is the Union Cabinet. The second important feature of the parliamentary government as it obtains in India is that theoretically the Council of Ministers holds office during the pleasure of the President but in reality, it is responsible to the union Parliament.

Under the constitution a bicameral legislature, called Parliament, has been established at the Union level. It has two houses, the Rajya Sabha and the Lok Sabha. As the Constitution establishes a federal system of government, there was almost unanimity among the framers for achieving a balance between the direct representation of people and the representation of units as such, by setting up two Houses, one representing the people as a whole and the other, the federal Units. The two houses of Parliament are the Council of States (the Rajya Sabha) and the House of people (Lok Sabha) which fairly reflect the nature of their composition. The Lok Sabha is composed of directly elected representatives on the basis of adult franchise. The Rajya Sabha is composed mainly of representatives of the States, elected by the Legislative Assemblies of the States.

According to Article 79 of the Constitution: Parliament consists of the President and the two houses viz the Rajya Sabha and Lok Sabha. Making the President an integral part of Parliament is in conformity with the principles and traditions of a parliamentary system of government. (In Great Britain, Parliament consists of the Queen, the House of Lords and the House of Commons).

Although the President himself is not a member of the legislature, his participation in the legislative process is ensured by making him a part of Parliament. The fact that he is the chief executive authority and that the executive power is co-extensive with the legislative power also makes it necessary that he should become an integral part of legislature.

However in practice, the Parliament has not been as effective as it is supposed to be because of the increasing influence of the Council of Ministers.

The Planning

Planning substitutes order for chaos and introduces rationality into decision-making process. It reduces random and haphazard activity. Planning makes personnel conscious of the objectives of the enterprise and thus encourages their involvement and participation. Planning promotes internal co-ordination and thus helps in making possible the integrated and co-ordinated effort. It facilitates control as the top executives can compare the performance with the standards of targets laid down by the process of planning. Planning generate economy and efficiency. Terry has rightly stated that "planning is the foundation of most successful action of an enterprise."

In 1934, Sri V. Visvesvaraya, published his book "Planning Economy in India" in which he formulated a 10 year Plans for the economic development of the country. In 1938, after the popular rule in a number of provinces, a National Planning Committee was set up in 1938 under the Chairmanship of Pt. Jawahar Lal Nehru with Prof. K.T. Shah as its General Secretary. In 1941 eight leading industrialists of India prepared a plan of economic development of India. An interim Govt. appointed in August 24, 1946 appointed an Advisory Planning Board with Mr. K.C. Neogy as its Chairman.

Just after the attainment of Independence the government set up the Planning Commission in 1950 to assess the country's need of material capital and human resources so as to formulate a plan of their more balanced and effective utilisation. The First Five Year Plan commenced in 1950-51 and it was followed by a series of Five Year Plan.

The Directive Principles of our Constitution laid down: "The State shall in particular, direct its policy towards securing- (a) that citizens, men and women equally have the right to adequate means of livelihood; (b) that the ownership and control of the resources of the community are so distributed as best to sub-serve the common good; (c) that the operation of the economic system does not result in the concentration of wealth and means of production to the common detriment."

Four long term objectives were set out by the planners in India. They were:

1. to increase production to the maximum possible extent so as to achieve higher level of national and per capita income;
2. to achieve full employment;
3. to reduce inequalities of income and wealth;
4. to set up a socialist society based on equality and justice and absence of exploitation.

The First-Five-Year Plan expressed clearly that the long-term objectives goals of economic planning in India as follows: "Maximum production and full employment, the attainment of economic equality or social justice which constitute the accepted objectives of planning under present day condition are not really so many different ideas but a series of related aims which the country must work for. None of these objectives can be pursued to the exclusion of a plan of development must place balanced emphasis on these" B.S. Minhas states: "Securing rapid economic growth and expansion of employment, eradication of disparities in income and wealth, prevention of concentration of economic power, and creation of the values and attitudes of a free and equal society have been among the objectives of all our plan."

Various Aspects

Planning machinery at the national and state level consists of a network of agencies and institutions which are concerned with the various aspects of the planning process—plan formulation; plan implementations, plan appraisal and evaluation, plan financing, etc. Thus viewed, planning machinery at the national and state levels include the following:

(i) The Planning Commission and the State Planning Boards.

(ii) The Central Ministries and the State Governments.

(iii) The National Development Council, and

(iv) The Commission's associated bodies and its 'Liaison Agencies'.

Let us now discuss in brief the role of Planning Commission in the formulation of plan in India:

India has perhaps the largest tradition of planning in any non-socialist country. The nearest parallel to it in Western Europe is the French System of Planning. The main difference, however, is that India has a federal structure of government and the achievement of socialistic pattern of society is her a vowed objective. The Planning Commission was established in March, 1950. The Commission was required:

(a) To make an assessment of material, capital and human resources as well as to formulate development plans for the most effective utilisation of these resources for improvement of social, human and economic conditions in the country.

(b) To indicate the obstacles in the way of planned economic and social development in the Country and suggest ways and means to the government to deal with them.

(c) To suggest any changes or additions to the administration system for effective implementation of development plans proposed by it and approved by the government.

(d) To carry out appraisals, from time to time of the progress achieved in implementation of the development plans by the administrative agencies or departments concerned and to suggest ways and means for improving the scale and quality of this implementation.

The Commission comprises a number of members at its head as well as a body of experts, administrators and house keeping personnel which constitute its secretariat. So far as the members are concerned some of them are whole time while a few are part time. There is, however, no fixed strength and thus the exact number of members may vary from time to time, depending upon several factors.

The Secretariat of the Commission includes three wings—(i) General Divisions, (ii) Subject Divisions and (iii) House-Keeping Divisions.

There are at present fourteen General Divisions which concern themselves with the studies relating to the Plan as a whole. The branches are : (i) Perspective Planning, (ii) Statistics and Surveys; (iii) Economic Research, (iv) Socio-Economic Research, (v) Plan Co-ordination (vi) Programme Administration, (vii) Multi Level Planning, (viii) Project Appraisal; (ix) Employment and Man-Power, Health and Family Welfare, (x) Housing and Urban Development, (xi) Industry and Minerals; (xii) Village and Small scale Industries; (xiii) Social Planning and (xiv) Social Welfare.

These divisions maintain intimate relations with their counterparts in the Central Ministries and State Government Departments. They collect, process and analyse relevant information and data as well as sponsor research for use by the commission in the formulation of sector plans and programmes.

The House-keeping Divisions deal with records, accounting and routine administration.

The subject division carry out most of the planning exercises. Each division utilises working of expert groups on which the concerned ministry is represented.

State Planning Boards have been set up in many parts of India. These Boards are to prepare the drafts for state plans by bringing about consultations among the experts, ministers and other decision makers as well as by seeking the views and demands of the district administration and other organisations. Except in a few states, the state planning boards have, however, yet to establish their role in a meaningful manner. They lack adequate expertise and creativity. Their position as the thinking tank' of the government on social and economic problems has yet to be demonstrated and proved. 'The Tribune' has rightly stated that:

"In most states, the Planning Boards, like several 'autonomous' corporations have been made sanctuaries for disgruntled, defeated or troublesome politicians who tend to treat plan funds as discretionary grants. Sinecures were deemed necessary to ensure the political support of such politicians in the struggle for ministerial survival amidst recurring toppling drives. Inevitably, such political accommodation has led to the minimum involvement of economic experts who alone would comprise State Planning Boards".

It is the time that the pollution of planning through politics was ended.

The programme advisers are responsible for co-ordination and co-operation between the Union Ministries, the Planning Boards at the State level, the Planning Bureaus of the State Departments especially as regards the allocation of resources and the determination of priorities during five year-plan. The various groups concerned have strong preferences and influences. The programme adviser have to reconcile these conflicting interests without much friction. Planning Commission submits the plans to National Development Council. This Council comprises of Prime

Minister as the Chairman and the Chief Minister of Planning Commission are its ex-officio members. Several Ministers of the Central Government are also invited by the Chairman to attend the meetings as non-members in order to put forward their view point on matters within their respective ministerial jurisdiction. The Council may set up a committee for various subject or field of planning. The main function of the Council may be summarised as :

(i) To formulate and prescribe guidelines for the preparation of the National Plans as well as to suggest ways and means for mobilisation of resources for the Plan.

(ii) To discuss and scrutinise the Draft National Plan as prepared by the Planning Commission.

(iii) To examine policy questions arising with regards to the Plan.

(iv) To review relevant questions relating to the implementation of the Plan.

The decisions of the National Development Council along with the Draft National Plan are sent to the cabinets and legislatures of all the government in the country for discussion. These high powered organs of the government have thus the final voice in regard to the nature and scope of plans as well as the strategy and resources for its implementation.

6

Constitution of India

The very fact that the constitution of Indian Republic is the product not of a political revolution but of the research and deliberations of a body of eminent representatives of the public who sought to improve upon the existing system of administration, makes a retrospect of the constitutional development indispensable for a proper understanding of this constitution.

Practically the only respect in which the constitution of 1949 differs from the constitutional document of the preceding two centuries is that while the latter had been imposed by an imperial power, the Republican constitution is made by the people themselves, though representatives assembled in a Sovereign constituent Assembly. That explains the majesty and ethical value of the new instrument and also the significance of those of its provisions which have been engraved upon the pre-existing system.

The British Crown assumed sovereignty over India from the East statue for the governance of India under the direct rule of the British Government, under the Government of India Act, 1858. This act serves as the starting point because it was dominated by the principle of absolute imperial control without any popular participation in the administration of the country, while the subsequent history upto the making of the constitution is one of gradual relaxation of imperial control and the evolution of responsible government. By this Act the powers of the Crown were to be exercised by the Secretary of State for India, assisted by a Council of fifteen members (known as the Council of India.) The Council was composed exclusively of people from England, some of whom were nominees of Crown while others were the representatives of Directors of the East India Company, the Secretary of State, who was responsible to the British Parliament, governed India through the Governor-General assisted by an Executive Council, which consisted of high officials of the Government.

Indian Councils Act (1861)

The Indian Council Act, 1861 introduced a gain of popular elements in so far as it provided that the Governor-General's Executive Councils which was so long composed exclusively of officials, should include certain additional non-official members, while transacting legislative business as a legislative council. The Legislative Council was neither representative nor deliberative in the sense. The members were nominated and their functions were confined exclusively to a consideration of the legislative proposal placed before it by the Governor-General.

Indian Councils Act (1892)

Two improvements upon the preceding state of affairs as regards the Indian and Provincial Legislative Councils were introduced by the Indian Council Act, 1892, namely.

(a) though a majority of the officials members were retained, the non-official members of the Indian Legislative Council were hence forth to be nominated by the Bengal Chamber of Commerce and the Provincial Legislative Councils, while the non-official members of the Provincial Councils were to be nominated by certain local bodies such as universities, district board, municipalities.

(b) The Council were to have the power of discussing the annual statement of revenue and expenditure i.e., the Budget and of addressing to the Executive.

The first attempt at introducing a representative and popular element was made by the Morley-Minto Reforms, known by the names of then Secretary of State for India (Lord Morley) and the Viceroy (Lord Minto), which were implemented by the Indian Councils Act, 1909.

Subsequent to this, Government of India Act, 1915 was passed merely to consolidate the provisions of all the preceding Government of India Acts so that the existing governmental provisions relating to the Government of India in its executive, legislative and judicial branches could be had from one enactment.

Montague-Chelmsford Report (The Government of India Act, 1919)

The next land mark in the constitutional development of India is the Montague-Chelmsford Report which led the enactment of the Government of India Act, 1919. It was in fact, an amending Act, but the amendments introduced substantial changes into the existing system.

Simon Commission

The Commission headed by Sir John Simon reported in 1930. The Report was considered by a Round Table Conference consisting of delegates of the British Government and of British India as well as rules of Indian States (in as much as the scheme was to unite the Indian States with rest of India under a federal scheme). A White Paper prepared on the results of this conference was examined by a Joint Select Committee of the British Parliament and the Government of India Bill was drafted in accordance with the recommendations of that select committee, and passed with certain Amendments; as the Governments of India Act, 1935.

The Act of 1935, provided a separate representation not only for the Muslims, but also for the Sikhs, the Europeans, Indians,

Christians and Anglo-Indian and thus created a serious hurdle in the way of building national unity which the makers of the future constitution found it almost insurmountable to overcome even after the Muslims had partitioned for a separate state.

Philosophy of the Constitution

The changes introduced by the Indian Independence Act, 1947 into the structure of the government pending the drawing up of a constitution for independent.

The Constitution of India, unlike the preceding Government of India Acts, is not a gift of British Parliament it is ordained by the people of India through their respective representatives assembled in a sovereign Constituent Assembly which was competent to determine the political future of the country in any manner it liked. It declares, therefore, in univocal terms that the source of all authority under the constitution is the people of India and there is no subordination to any external authority.

As a form of government, the democracy which is envisaged is, of course a respective representative democracy and there are in our constitution no agencies of direct control by the people, such as "referendum "or "initiative". The people of India are to exercise their sovereignty through a Parliament at the Centre and a Legislature in each state, which is to be elected on adult franchise. Thus, Indian Administration operates within the framework of the constitution which has been in operation since 1950.

The main features of the constitution which condition its functioning are:

1. Parliamentary type of democracy, both at the centre and in the states, in which the Executive is held responsible to the elected legislature.
2. Federal nature of the constitution in which functions have been constitutionally divided between the Union Government and the States. The former playing a more important role and in time of emergency, its authority

extending even to taking over of administration of individual states in its own hands.

3. The constitution of India grants a number of fundamental rights to the citizens of India. The presence of these rights in the constitution guarantees the liberties of the people against any governmental excessiveness. Even the slightest encroachment by the Government on the citizen's right can be remedied through independent courts.

4. By the 42nd amendment of the constitution adopted in 1976, fundamental duties of the citizens have been enumerated. These enjoin upon citizens, among other things, to abide by the constitution.

5. One of the most novel features of the Constitution of India is the provision of Directive Principles of Stale Policy. The main object of this part is to provide guidelines to the state Government while framing their policies.

6. To help the backward classes and communities, provision was made to help them for bringing them at the level of advanced classes. It was done by reservation of seats for 10 years but this period has been extended from time to time.

7. The minorities communities have been provided equal rights with the majority community in religious, cultural, economic and political spheres.

In this part, attempt has been made to study the some of important features of the constitution of India which condition its functioning .

Indian Federation

The establishment of an integrated unitary state in British India was one of the outstanding achievements in British rule in the country. The earlier tendency was towards increasing centralisation which reached its high watermark during the regime of Lord Curzon. But it was evident that this policy of concentrating all powers in the Central Government (C.G.) had been carried too far. Measures were therefore, adopted to bring about administrative decentralisation and financial devolution culminating in the introduction of Provincial Autonomy under the Government of India Act, 1935.

The idea of constituting India into a federation was definitely mooted in the Simon Commission Report, and later embodied in Government of India Act, 1935. But as we know that the All India Federation proposed under this Act did not see the light of the day because it was rejected by almost all sections of organized public opinion in India. That is why the federal system proposed for the Central Government in the Act of 1935, never came into force.

It was, however, generally agreed that, in view of India's vast size and the diversity of races, cultures and languages found in her, a federal form of government was better suited to our country than the existing unitary system.

Naturally, therefore, the framers of free India's constitution accepted federalism as the basis of the country's new constitutional set up. The constitution does not use the word federation. Instead it calls India a 'Union of States'. A federation is characterised by the following features which are enshrined in the Indian Constitution, thus entitling India to call itself a federally governed state.

Federal Features of Constitution

It possesses the following distinctive features of a federation:

1. There must be two levels of government, the Central Government and the State Government. Both being autonomous in its own sphere of functioning.

2. The powers and functions of the Central Government and the State Government must be defined in a written

Constitution. Hence, there is the constitutional distribution of functions between the two levels of government. The Central Government has jurisdiction over 97 subjects : Strictly, speaking there are 96 subjects, the last one being any other matter not enumerated in list II and III including any tax not mentioned in either of these lists. This is really the residuary power. The state list includes 66 subjects, which are within the exclusive legislative jurisdiction of the State legislature. Also, there is a concurrent list consisting of 47 items over which both the governments have concurrent jurisdiction subject, of course, to the superiority of Central Government.

3. The disputes regarding the power and functions of the Central Government and the State Government are to decided by the Supreme Court which is an independent body under the constitution.

4. The strength of the centre can be immensely increased in times of war and other national emergencies when the constitution can be converted into a unitary one without the need of constitutional amendments. By issuing a Proclamation of Emergency, the President of India can assume extra ordinary powers which may amount to the suspension of autonomy of states. While a Proclamation of Emergency is in operation the executive power of the Union shall extend to the states in all matter and Parliament shall be empowered to frame laws even on those subjects which are included in the state list. Similar effects will follow if the Governor of a state declares that the government of a state cannot be carried in accordance with the provisions of the Constitution and the President, by Proclamation, assumes to himself all or any of the functions of the government of the state. Administration of the state shall be exercisable by order and the authority of Parliament. The President can also modify the provisions of

the constitution relating to the distribution of powers between the Union and the State. This is an unparalleled features of the Indian Constitution which is at once unitary and federal according to the circumstances. Normally, it is meant to be federal but in an emergency it can assume a unitary character.

5. In the fifth place, the territories of the units of the Indian Union are not treated as inviolable. The Union Parliament can (a) form a new state by separation of territory from any state or uniting two or more states, (b) increase or diminish the area of any state, and (c) alter the boundaries or name of any state. Article 3 of the constitution provide that these changes can be made by passing a Bill introduced in Parliament on the recommendation of the President provided that the views of the legislature of the state or states concerned have been ascertained by the President.

Problems of Parliamentary Democracy

The Constitution establishes the parliamentary form of Government in India. This applies to the states as well as the Union. The President of the Indian Union and the Governors of the States are constitutional rulers with nominal powers. Real executive authority is exercised by the Council of Ministers which is responsible to the Parliament and holds the reins of power only so long as it enjoys the confidence of the latter.

The Parliamentary democracy which is enshrined in the Indian Constitution has numerous implications but the following have direct relevance to the public administration of the country.

1. The supremacy of Parliament over the executive and the right of Parliament to review the working of administrative machinery.
2. The collective responsibility of council of Ministers to Parliament and the determination of major policies by the cabinet.

3. The individual responsibility (as a part of the collective responsibility) of each minister holding a portfolio for formulating policies to oversee their implementation and to ensure efficient working of the administrative machinery under his charge.

4. The obligation of ministers as well as of civil servants to uphold the constitution and the rule of law.

5. The obligation of every civil servant implement faithfully all policies and decisions of the ministers, even if these be contrary to the advice tendered by him.

6. The freedom of civil servants to express themselves, frankly in tendering advice to their superiors, including ministers, and

7. The observance by civil servants of the principles of political neutrality, impartially and anonymity.

Let us now examine some of the problems of parliamentary democracy.

One of the major problems of parliamentary democracy at present is the decay of political institution which has arouse during the past few years. Political parties are losing their organisation's strength and the gap between the electorate and the elected representative is increasing. Defections are conducive to undisciplined in parties which leads to decay all the more.

In the second place, the constitution creates a very strong centre. In the three fold distribution of powers, the most important subjects are placed in the Union List which is the longest of the three lists. Besides, there is concurrent list over which the Central Government can exercise legislative and administrative jurisdiction if it deems necessary.

The other problem of parliamentary democracy can be said to be of Centre-State relationship. Because of centralization of power at the Union level, there is always a conflict between the Centre and States primarily relating to autonomy and the financial aspect. As each state has its own set of peculiar problems and wants solutions to them seeing to the local needs. On the other hand, the Centralised approach of Union Government poses a problem of implementation in uniformity. Hence, the State Government insists on more autonomy. The other problem relating to finances is of acute nature. As the C.G. always has upper hand at the time of allocation of funds.

Further, because of the gulf between the electorate and elected representatives, there arises the need of accountability. It is not possible for the common citizen to have first hand information relating to actions taken by the government.

In the end, there have been growing inequalities of income and wealth in India. As the big industrialist finance the part of election campaign, they get rewards from the government when it comes into power. Hence, the economic concentration is in the hands of big business houses, thereby, depriving the larger section of the society.

Structure of Indian Constitution

India achieved freedom from British colonialism in August 1947 when it was partitioned into two dominions of India and Pakistan respectively. The Dominion of Pakistan formally came into being on 14 August while the Dominion of India viz. the erstwhile British India, minus Pakistan, was born a day later i.e., on 15th August 1947.

To prepare the new constitution of free India, a Constituent Assembly was brought into existence under the Cabinet Mission Plan in 1946. It consisted of 389 members, including 93 members for the native states. The seats were allocated to different provinces and the princely states roughly in the ratio of one member to a million of the population. Whereas the modalities for the representation of native states in the Constituent Assembly were left to be determined by negotiations with their rulers. Elections to the assembly from the provinces were held in July, 1945.

The Constituent Assembly held its inaugural meeting on 9 December 1946. Dr. Rajendra Prasad was elected its permanent Chairman two days later. Dr. Sachindanand Sinha was the first President of the assembly for two days. On 13 December Jawahar Lal Nehru moved the Objective Resolution in which the assembly declared 'its firm and solemn resolve to proclaim India as an independent, sovereign republic and to draw up for future government a Constitution befitting here national aspirations. The resolution was passed by the Constituent Assembly on 22 January 1947. To quote the resolution:

Constitution Assembly declares its firm and solemn resolution to proclaim, India as an independent Sovereign Republic has to draw up for her further governance a constitution:

(i) WHEREIN the territories that now comprise British India, the territories that now form the Indian States, and such other parts of India as are outside British India and the States as well as such other territories as are willing to be constituted into the independent Sovereign India, shall be a Union of them all; and

(ii) WHEREIN the said territories whether with their present boundaries or with such others as may be determined by the Constituent Assembly and thereafter according to the law of the Constitution, shall possess and retain the status of autonomous units, together with residuary powers, and exercise all powers and functions of Government and administration, save and expect such powers and functions as are vested in or assigned to the Union or as are inherent or implied in the union or resulting there from; and

(iii) WHEREIN all powers and authority of the Sovereign Independent India, its constituent parts and organs of Governments are derived from the people; and

(iv) WHEREIN shall be guaranteed and secured to all the people of India, Justice-social, economic and political;

equality of status, of opportunity and before the law, freedom of thought, expression, belief, faith, worship, vocation, association and action, subject to law and public morality; and

(v) WHEREIN adequate safeguards shall be provided for minorities, backward and tribal areas and depressed and other backward classes;

(vi) WHEREIN shall be maintained the integrity of the territory of the Republic and its sovereign rights on land, sea and air according to justice and the law of civilised nations; and

(vii) The ancient land attain its rightful and honoured place in the world and makes its full and willing contribution to the promotion of world peace and the welfare of mankind.

Seventy-three of its members, elected from the provinces on Muslim League tickets, boycotted the proceedings of the assembly from its very inception. They subsequently formed a separate Constituent Assembly for Pakistan which was formally inaugurated by Lord Mountbatten at Karachi on 14 August 1947. After the dawn of independence, the Constituent Assembly became a sovereign body, and it took about three years to frame the new constitution of free India; it came into force on 26 January 1950. The new constitution which declares India, that is Bharat to be a sovereign, democratic republic, is a very bulky document.

The basic framework and ideology of the Constitution is reflected in the Preamble which reads as:

WE, THE PEOPLE OF INDIA, having solemnly resolved to constitute India, into a SOVEREIGN SOCIALIST SECULAR DEMOCRATIC REPUBLIC and to secure to all its citizens : JUSTICE, social economic and political.

EQUALITY of status and of opportunity, and to promote among them all FRATERNITY assuring the dignity of the individual and the unity and integrity of the nation.

IN OUR CONSTITUENT ASSEMBLY this twenty-sixth day of November, 1949, do HEREBY ADOPT, ENACT AND GIVE TO OURSELVES THIS CONSTITUTION.

Though the Preamble is not a part of the constitution yet it serves as a key to the constitution. To quote Pandit Bhargave "it is most precious part of the Constitution. It is the soul of the Constitution. It is key to Constitution........It is jewel set in the Constitution. It is a superb prose poem, may be it is perfection in itself." Chief Justice Hidayathullah has said "Preamble resembles the Declaration of Independence of the United States of America but is more than a declaration. It is the soul of our constitution which lays down the pattern of our political society.........It contains a solemn resolve which nothing but a revolution can alter."

An analysis of the preamble shows that it intends India to be a Sovereign, Socialist, Secular and Democratic Republic. Let us describe them briefly.

The basic principles and ideology, on which the Indian Constitution is based, are discussed below:

Sovereignty : The Indian Constitution is based on the principles of sovereignty meaning, thereby, that India is an independent and autonomous and not dependent upon any foreign government for its administration.

Republic : The concept of Republic implies that Head of State would be, directly or indirectly, elected by the people themselves, and he would not be appointed on the basis of heredity. Consequently, the Indian Constitution provides for the election of the President not his nomination.

Democracy : As a form of Government, the democracy which is envisaged is, representative democracy and there are in our constitution no agencies of direct control by the people, such as 'referendum' or 'initiative'.

Socialism : The world 'Socialism' has been added in the Preamble of the Indian Constitution by 42nd amendment (1976). The socialist orientation of the Indian Constitution is evident, particularly, from Article 39 which provides: (a) that all citizens have the right to adequate means of livelihood, (b) that the ownership and control of the material resources of the community have to be so distributed as to sub-serve the common goods; (c) that the operations of the economic-system should be so organised as not to result in the concentration of wealth and the means of production to the common determent and so on.

Secularism : The word 'secular' to the existing description of the country as a sovereign democratic republic was added in the Preamble by the 42nd amendment (1976) further strengthens the non-religious approach of the Constitution. A secular state implies that there is no state religion and in the formulations of its policies, the state would remain neutral in religious matter- neither supporting nor discriminating against any religion of the country.

Federation : The Constitution is a Federation Constitution in as much as it establishes what may be called a Dual Polity (which) consists of the Union at the Centre and the States at the periphery each endowed with sovereign powers to be exercised in the field assigned to them respectively by the Constitution. Yet the Constitution avoids the tight mould of federalism, and could be both unitary as well as federal according to the requirements of time and circumstances.

Constitution of India 1950, declares India a "Union of State". The world 'Federalism' has not been used anywhere in the constitution. But certain features like the distribution of powers between the States and Union, presence of a Supreme Court to review the laws passed by the government etc. seem to give us the impression of a federal constitution. The Federal nature of the Indian Constitution as has been said earlier, has always been a matter of controversy. The reason behind this is nothing but the presence of unitary as well as federal characteristics in the same constitution

Division of Power

Division of powers is generally considered to be the most important part of a federation. In the present world of cooperative federalism, the federal government has virtually taken away many of the powers of the units and the traditional definitions of identifying federalism with the constitutional autonomy of the States or strict compartmentalisation no longer hold water. Similarly many other characteristics of the federation which were considered to be the very bases of federal constitution, have lost their importance in the highly dynamic nature of the present world society. This has made the centralisation in every walk of life inevitable. However, the division of power is still considered to be the very essence of federalism and any constitution which forbids this division of powers between the Union and the units, can not claim to be federal, however, flexible the criterion of federation may be.

A brief account of these three divisions is given below:

Legislative Relations

The Indian Constitution divides the legislative powers into three lists which have been given in the Seventh schedule that is, Union List, State List, and the Concurrent List.

The Union List: It includes the subjects which are considered to be of the national importance, such as Defence, Foreign Affairs, War and Peace, Citizenship, Railways, Currency, Posts and Telegraphs, Banking etc.

The 42nd Amendment to the Constitution inserted a new entry, 3A after entry 2 in the Union list. This new entry deals with the employment of any armed forces of Union or any other force subject to the control of the Union or any contingent of unit thereof in any State in aid of the civil power.

The State List: This includes the items which were left to the States. Initially, the list included many items such as Public Order, Public Administration, Justice, Prisons, Public Health, Education, Agriculture and Forests etc. But the 42nd Amendment Act which was a comprehensive attempt to change the federal division of powers, shifted some of these subjects to the concurrent list. This led to the transfer of administration of justice, constitution and organization of all courts, education, weights and measures, forests and protection of wild animals and birds, etc. from List II to List III.

The Concurrent List : This list includes the items on which both the union and states governments can legislate. This includes such items as criminal law and procedures, civil procedures, contracts, torts, trusts, welfare of labour etc. As we have seen in preceding lines, many more subjects have been removed from the State list and added to the Concurrent List.

Residuary Powers: Residuary Powers in the Constitution have been left with the Union. This is contrary to the provisions in the U.S. Constitution which leaves the residuary power with the States.

Apart from these three lists, the Union-State legislative relations are also governed by some articles which give to the parliament power to overrule State legislation in certain cases.

Administrative Relations : The administrative relations have been designed in such a way as to ensure the smooth working of the Union and the State Governments avoid any such incidence which runs contrary to the spirit of harmonious working. Articles 256, 257, 258, 262 and 263 broadly deal with these provisions. Article 256 provides that the executive has to ensure compliance with the laws made by Parliament.

Article 257 provides that the States will exercise their executive power in such a way as not to impede or prejudice the exercise of the executive power of the Union and Government of India might give to a State such directions as might appear to it necessary for that purpose.

Article 258 provides that the President can constitute the State as the agents of the Union with their consent and can entrust conditionally or unconditionally to them or to their officers, functions in relation to any matter to which the executive power of the Union extends.

Article 262 empowers the President to provide by law for the adjudication of any dispute among States with respect to the use, distribution and control of river waters or valleys.

Articles 263 deals with the establishment of an inner-State Council.

Financial Relations : The financial relations of the Centre and the States can briefly be summarised as below:

Tax Jurisdiction of the Union : The Union has tax jurisdiction over the subjects which have been included in the Union list. These include corporation tax, taxes on income other than from agricultural land, custom duties of exercise on tobacco, estate duty in respect of property other than agricultural land terminal taxes on goods or passengers carried by railways, sea or air taxes on the sale or purchase of newspaper and any other tax which has not been mentioned in the other two lists.

Tax Jurisdiction of the States : These taxes include mainly the following taxes: Estate duties in respect of agricultural land, taxes on lands, buildings, taxes on consumption and sale of electricity, taxes on the entry of goods into local area for consumption, use or sale them taxes on sale and purchase of goods other than newspapers, duties in respect of succession to agricultural land, duties or excise on certain goods purchased or manufactured in the State, land revenue, taxes on vehicles, taxes on entertainments etc.

Taxes levied by the Union but collected and wholly appropriated by the States : This includes stamp duties and excise duties on medicine and toilet preparations.

Taxes levied and collected by the Union but assigned to the States : It includes taxes on railway freights, taxes on the sale and purchase of newspaper and advertisements, published therein, terminal taxes, taxes on goods and passengers carried by railway, sea or air, estate duty in respect of property other than agricultural land, duties in respect of succession to property other than agricultural land etc.

Taxes levied and collected by the Union but necessarily shared between the Centre and States : It includes taxes on income other than agricultural income.

Taxes which are levied and collected by the Union but may be shared between the Union and the States : It includes excise duties other than those on medical and toilet preparations mentioned in the Union list and collected by the Government India.

Analysis : The analysis of the provisions in the constitution indicate that India is federal in form and unitary in spirit. Sardar K.M. Panikkar justified a strong centre thus: "The purpose which the Founding Fathers had in view was not only to hold in or check the fissiparous tendencies which led to the disruption of former empire and to maintain the unity which has been achieved after so much struggle, but to endow the Central government with all powers necessary in the political and economic field to enable India to undertake a policy of planned development which would raise her to the position of a modern nation, unhampered by the statutory rights to state government.

Prof. Wheare states "The new Constitution establishes a unitary State with subsidiary federal features rather than federal State with subsidiary unitary features." P.B. Gajendragadkar, a former Chief Justice of India also says, "The Indian Constitution could be both unitary as well as federal according to the requirements of the time and circumstances. The Constitution-makers were fully impressed by the need to emphasize the unity of the country when they set up, though it partakes some of the characteristics of a federal structure can not be said to be federal in the true sense of the term".

7

The Executive (Union)

President of India

The President is elected by the members of an electoral college consisting of the elected members of Houses of Parliament and of the legislative assemblies of States in accordance with the system of proportional representation by means of single transferable vote. To secure uniformity among the States *inter se well* as parity between the States as a whole and the Union, suitable weightage is given to each vote. The President must be a citizen of India, not less than 35 years of age, and qualified for election as a member of the Lok Sabha. His term of office is five years and he is eligible for re-election. His removal from office is to be in accordance with the procedure prescribed in Article 61 of the Constitution. He may, by writing under his hand addressed to the Vice-President, resign his office.

The executive power of the Union is vested in the President and is exercised by him either directly or through Officers subordinate to him in accordance with the Constitution. The supreme command of the defence forces of the Union also vests in him. The President summons, prorogues, addresses, sends messages to Parliament and dissolves the Lok Sabha; promulgates ordinances at any time, except when both Houses of Parliament are in session; makes recommendations for introducing financial and money bills and gives assent to bills; grants pardons, reprieves, respites or remissions of punishment or suspends, remits or commutes sentences in certain cases. When there is a failure of constitutional machinery in a state, he can assume to himself all or any of the functions of the government of the state. The President can proclaim emergency in the country if he is satisfied that a grave emergency exists whereby the security of India or of any part of its territory is threatened whether by war or external aggression or armed rebellion.

In India the President is the Head of the State but not of the Executive. He represents the nation, but does not rule the nation. His place in the administration is that of a ceremonial head. His position is that of constitutional President. The Ministers are responsible to the Legislature and tender advice to the President who is bound to act according to that advice.

As India was proclaimed a Republic, the Head of the State had to be an elected one. The Head of the Indian Union was called the President. According to the Constitution, the Executive power of the Indian Union is vested in the President and is exercisable by him either direct or through Officers subordinate to him in accordance with the provisions of the Constitution (Article 53).

The Head of the State in the Union and the States is also called the President but the position of India's President is entirely different from that of the American President. The latter is a real executive and exercise the powers vested in him by the Constitution; not necessarily on the advice of his (Ministers) secretaries but in his own discretion.

When the question of the form of government for India came before the Constituent Assembly, a small minority recommended the adoption of the Presidential system of government as prevalent in the United States. One member pleaded for the Swiss form of Collegiate Executive which combines the merits of both the

Presidential and the Parliamentary systems-stability and responsibility. However, an overwhelming majority was in favour of the Cabinet system of government, as in England.

The features of the Indian Constitution are in favour of the Cabinet System for several reasons. K.M. Munshi stated the reasons in his speech in the Constituent Assembly.

(i) The Cabinet system means the rule of the majority in the legislature. As such, the legislature is only supporting its leaders who are in the cabinet. Relationship is more harmonious.

(ii) During the British period Indian public life had largely drawn upon the traditions of British Constitutional law which is parliamentary in character.

(iii) During previous thirty to forty years (after 1919 reforms) some kind of responsible government was introduced by stages in the government of country. Thus our constitutional traditions had become parliamentary to a great extent.

(iv) The Dominion Government of India, as set up in 1947, also functioned as a full-fledged parliamentary government.

Qualifications : A candidate for the office of the President should possess the following qualifications:

(a) He must be a citizen of India.

(b) He must not be less than 35 years of age.

(c) He should be qualified for election to the House of People.

(d) He should not hold any office of profit under the Government of India or any State Government or Local Authority. (Certain positions in the Government are excluded from the scope of this provision, the President, the Vice-President, Governors and Ministers of the Central and State Governments.)

(e) The President cannot be a member of Parliament or of a State Legislature. If any member of the Union or State Legislature is elected President, his seat in the Legislature shall be deemed to have been vacated from the date on which he assumes office of the President.

Terms and Emoluments : The President hold office for five years unless he resigns or is removed by impeachment before the expiry of his term. The President is eligible for re-election. The President receives a salary of Rs.50,000 per month besides other allowances. He is entitled to a rent-free official residence named Rashtrapati Bhawan.

Removal : The President can be removed by impeachment "violation of the Constitution". Impeachment is a kind of trial. Charges may be framed by either House of Parliament in the form of a resolution passed by a two-third majority.

The other House will investigate the charges and if it declares in a resolution passed by a two-third majority that the charges have been proved, the President shall vacate the office.

Elections Procedure : The President of India is indirectly elected by an electoral college consisting of the elected members of both Houses of Parliament and the elected members of the Legislative Assemblies of the States in accordance with the system of proportional representation by means of a single transferable vote. In this election the number of votes to be exercised by each member of the electoral college is determined in such a way that the voting strength of the two Houses of Parliament is equal to that of the Legislative Assemblies of the States taken together. Uniformity of representation of the different States at the election is also ensured by seeing that the votes have a value in proportion to the population that the votes represent. To achieve this aim, a special method has been devised:

The total population of each state is divided first by the total number of elected members in the Assembly. The quotient is then divided by 1000. For example, the actual number of votes enjoyed by each member of Uttar Pradesh Legislative Assembly in the Presidential Election of 1957 was calculated as below:

(i) Total Population of Uttar Pradesh 63.215.742

(ii) Total number of elected members in the Uttar Pradesh Legislative Assembly 430

(iii) The Number of votes enjoyed by each member

$$\frac{63{,}215.742}{430 \times 1000} = 147$$

The number of votes each elected member of Parliament is entitled to, in the election is arrived at by dividing the total number of votes given to all the elected members of the State assemblies by the total number of elected members of both the Houses of Parliament.

Direct election of the President by the people would have been more democratic. The President would have been the direct choice of the nation. But such a directly elected President would not have been content with the position of a mere constitutional ruler. He would have tried to assume real power and there would have been a deadlock. A nation wide direct election would have also prevented practical difficulties. If the President were to be elected, it would have robbed him of all appearances of independence, impartiality and dignity. Election by the members of the Central Parliament and members of the State legislatures, with equal parity, makes him a national figure. The electoral college is quite large and broad based.

The Presidential election system appears to be quite a complicated process but in practice it is a simple one. It has all-India significance but passes off in a quiet, business like manner. It is in consonance with the federal principle and does not create any complication.

In Case of Vacancy **:**A vacancy occurs in three ways : death, resignation or impeachment. The vacancy is filled by the Vice President until the new President is elected and before six months elapse from the date the vacancy occurred.

Powers of the President

The Constitution confers extensive powers on the President of the Indian Republic. These may be conveniently classified under the following heads :

Executive Powers **:** As the President is the Head of the Union Executive, his executive powers embrace the entire field of activities of the Union:

(a) He is the Commander-in-Chief of the Defence forces and has the power of declaring war and concluding peace.

(b) He has vast powers of appointment. He appoints the Ministers. He appoints Governors of the States, Ambassadors and other diplomatic representatives, the Chief Justice and Justices of the Courts and those of the High Courts, the members of the Union Public Service Commission, the Attorney General, the Election Commissioner, the Comptroller and Auditor-General of India, Commissioner of the Scheduled Castes, Tribes, Backward Classes and Minorities etc.

Legislative Powers **:** The Union Legislature consists of the President and the two Houses of Parliament.

(a) The President summons, adjourns and prorogues both the Houses and dissolves the House of the People.

(b) He may summon a joint session of both the Houses, especially if the two disagree on a bill.

(c) He nominates 12 members for the Council of State Rajya Sabha and two Anglo-Indians to the House of the People.

(d) He opens the first session of the Parliament with a speech outlining the national and foreign policy of his government along with the legislative programme. He may give assent or withhold his assent or return it to Parliament for reconsideration.

(e) Every bill passed by Parliament must be presented to the President for his assent. He may give assent or withhold his assent or return it to Parliament for reconsideration.

(f) Under Article 123 the President is empowered to promulgate Ordinances, except, when the two Houses are in session. A Presidential ordinance has the same force as an Act of Parliament. However, every such ordinance should be laid before both the Houses within six weeks from the reassembling of Parliament. Failure to comply with this condition makes the ordinance invalid.

(g) During an emergency arising from the failure of the constitutional machinery in a State, the President may make laws for such a State when authorised by the Parliament.

Judicial Powers : Under Article 72 the President has the power to grant pardon or any other appropriate mercy, as reprieve, respite, remission, suspension or communication of the sentence.

Financial Powers

(a) Before the beginning of a financial year the President causes to be laid before the Parliament the annual budget and supplementary budget, if any.

(b) No money bill can be introduced in the Parliament without his prior recommendation.

(c) He distributes the shares of the income tax receipts between the Centre and the States.

(d) He is empowered to create a Contingency Fund out of which he can make advances to meet unforeseen expenditure subject to the subsequent sanction by the Parliament.

(e) He is empowered to appoint Finance Commissions from time to time for allocation of the shares of the States in regard to receipts from other taxes. Union-State financial relations are determined on the basis of these recommendations.

Emergency Powers : The President is empowered to declare three different types of emergencies :

National Emergency : Emergencies caused by war or external aggression or internal disturbances (Article 352)

(i) The President can issue such a proclamation even before a war or external aggression or civil commotion takes place, if he is satisfied that there is imminent danger.

(ii) The President's decision to issue a proclamation of Emergency cannot be challenged in a court of law and the President is the sole judge to decide whether an emergency exists.

(iii) Parliament shall have full powers to frame laws for the entire country or any part on subject of the State List.

(iv) The Union Executive and Legislature shall have the power to control and supervise the work of the State Executive and Legislature.

(v) The President will have the power to modify the normal distribution of the sources of revenue between the Union and the Sates.

(vi) The autonomy of the States is suspended and the federal structure is converted into a unitary one.

(vii) The authority of the President is subject to the control of the Parliament. The proclamation is to be laid before both the Houses and ceases to operate at the end of one month unless it has been approved by the two Houses in the meanwhile. This is a democratic safeguard.

Constitutional Emergency : Emergency arising out of the failure of the constitutional machinery in the States (Article 356). Under Article 356 the President is armed with special powers to discharge this duty.

(i) On receipt of a report from the Governor of a State or otherwise that the Government of a State cannot be carried on according to that provisions of the Constitution, he may issue a proclamation to that effect and suspend the Constitution in that State.

(ii) Under such an emergency the President may assume to himself any or all functions of the government of the State except the judicial functions. The autonomy of the State is suspended and is brought completely under the authority of the Union in all legislative and executive matters.

(iii) The proclamation ceases to be effective after two months unless, in the meantime it has been approved by the two Houses. At one time it cannot be issued for more than six months but it can be extended every six months upto a maximum of three years, each extension being subject to the approval of the President.

Financial Emergency : Emergency arising out of threat to financial stability or credit of India (Article 360).

Such emergency can be declared for the country as a whole or apart thereof.:

(i) In such cases the President can issue instructions to any State, he may deem fit and ask it to observe certain canons of financial propriety.

(ii) He may order reduction in the salaries and allowances to all or any classes of persons serving in connection with the affairs of a State or the Union including the Judges of the Supreme Court and the High Courts.

(iii) He may require a State to submit to him a money bill for his assent before it is passed by the legislature.

The President : A Despot or a Constitutional Ruler? —Certain authorities on Indian Polity feel that the President of India can become despot if he so likes. It is only a legalistic and judicial view.

Gladhill, in his book, "The Republic of India" has drawn a highly exaggerated picture of the President of India when he becomes determined to become a dictator. Suppose the evil designs of the President become known one-fourth of the members of a House can give notice of a resolution to impeach the President. Fourteen day's notice is needed to move such a resolution. Before the expiry of 14 days, the President can dissolve the Lok Sabha. A new House is to be elected but it need not meet for six months after such an election. He may dismiss his Ministers because they hold office at his pleasure. He may appoint his own men as Ministers who too may not be Members for the next six Months. He may issue ordinances. He may suspend the autonomy of the States. As Supreme Commander of the forces he may utilise them to suppress his political opponents and civil liberties. Thus he can become a Dictator. This is how the Weimar Constitution was destroyed in Germany by Hitler. But no one President will like to be so ambitious. A President who disregards the Cabinet's advice would precipitate a constitutional crisis. Article 53 (1) of course lays down that the executive powers of the Union are vested in the President and shall be exercised by him directly or through Officers subordinate to him. But the clarification is made in Article 74 (1) : "There is a Council of Ministers to aid and advise the President in the exercise of his functions". But as Dr. Banerjee asks the question, "Is the President legally bound under Article 74(1)?" Evidently, not during the Constituent Assembly session Dr. Rajendra Prasad suggested that a specific provision be made requiring the President to abide by the advice of the Ministers in all matters.

The fathers of the Constitution had adopted the Cabinet system and it is the essence of the cabinet system that real executive power should be exercised by a Cabinet or a Council of Ministers responsible to the legislature. According to S.N. Mukherjee, they preferred to leave this to conventions as in the case of United Kingdom. Dr. Ambedkar was very clear: "He will be generally bound by the advice of Ministers. He can do nothing contrary to their advice, nor can he do anything without their advice."

Thus the President is only a constitutional ruler, possessing glory but no real power. He cannot afford to act against the advice of the Ministers. If he does so, the Ministers can resign and create a constitutional deadlock and the President can be impeached. In a Parliamentary system of government, the Executive is responsible to the legislature. The Council of Ministers do not hold office as a grace of the President during his pleasure but because they have the confidence of the Parliament.

The Supreme Court, too, in the case of Ram Jawaya Vs. the State of Punjab in 1955 viewed that the President has been made a formal or constitutional head and the real executive powers are vested in the Ministers or the Cabinet.

In 1974 the verdict given by five judges was "wherever the Constitution requires the satisfaction of the President or the Governor for the exercise by the President or the Governor of any power or function, the satisfaction required by the Constitution is not the personal satisfaction of the President or Governor but the satisfaction of the President or Governor in the constitutional sense in the Cabinet System of Government, that is, satisfaction of his Council on whose aid and advice generally he exercises all his powers and functions.

Influence of the President

That the Indian President is just a constitutional ruler also does not mean that he is just a rubber stamp or a dumb statue. He is the first citizen of India and his office carries great dignity and prestige. A man of dynamic personality will always succeed in influencing the decisions of the Cabinet. His advice cannot just be brushed aside. Like the British King, he has a right to be informed, to encourage and to warn his Ministers. In fact, if the President, after his election, forgets his old political affiliation and acts in a dignified and impartial manner, he is bound to be listened to be the Prime Minister. During his tenure as the President, Dr. Rajendra Prasad tried to exercise more power than was given by the Constitution. In September 1951 when the Hindu Code Bill was introduced in the Parliament he sent a note to Nehru, expressing his desire to act solely on his own judgement, independently of the Council of Ministers, when giving assent to the bills, when sending messages to Parliament and when returning bills to Parliament for reconsideration. He advised the Prime Minister against the desirability of hasty legislation. Pt. Nehru asked Sir Alladi Krishnaswami Aiyar and M.C. Setalwad to examine the position of the President under the Constitution. The Government had to postpone its consideration of the Hindu Code Bill. Dr. Prasad also objected to the Government's proposals for imposing ceiling on land holdings, introducing cooperative farming and resorting to State trading in food grains. In 1960 in a speech to the Indian Law Institute, he said "There is no provision in the Constitution which in so many words lay down that the president shall be bound to act in accordance with the advice of his Ministers ".

Dr. Radhakrishnan is said to have strong views on the question of removal of Krishna Menon from the Cabinet after Chinese invasion on India in 1962. On a few occasions he was very critical of Government's inefficiency. In his Republic Day Broadcast in 1964, he cautioned the country against complacency about corruption. Regarding V.V.Giri, though the general belief has been that he was a more "rubber stamp" it has been asserted that it was a mere political nonsense. In a preface to a book on " The President of India" he claims to have differed from the Government on several occasions, e.g. the general strike of the Railways, dissolution of Gujarat Assembly and Telengana-Andhra tangle. However, he admits that the President does not function in competition with his Council of Ministers. When he expresses his views, "he does not do so to embarrass the Government but to strengthen their hands?

Fakhruddin Ali Ahmed is also said to have differed from Indira Gandhi on several questions, such as the proclamation of emergency. However, if the Prime Minister is strong and dynamic and has received a mandate from the people, the President cannot do otherwise than sign of the dotted line. He can never seek to defy the constitutional constraints on his authority.

Only on two occasions the President can exercise his discretion-appointment of the Prime Minister if there are several candidates and a breakdown of constitutional machinery. Because of the mushroom growth of political parties and spate of political defections, a stage does come when the President has to exercise his discretionary powers for the furtherance of parliamentary democracy. Morarji Desai was of the opinion that in times of crisis the President can form a national government. Sanjiva Reddy definitely played a very decisive role in the midst of uncertainty in 1979.

Criticism of Emergency Provision : During discussions in the Constituent Assembly, several members considered the Emergency provisions as "too sweeping and autocratic". They were regarded as totally "inconsistent with the democratic provisions embodied elsewhere. Professor K.T. Shah felt that liberty or democracy will remain under the Constitution only in name H.V. Kamath opined "we are seeking to lay the foundation of a totalitarian state, a police state, a state completely opposed to all the ideals and principles that we have held a lot during the last few decades..."

Although the entire chapter on emergency provisions was under fire during discussions, provisions made for suspension of freedom guaranteed and suspension of the provisions for moving the courts for enforcement of Fundamental Rights (under articles 358 and 359) were very strongly criticised. A member described the position as the "grand final and crowing glory of the most reactionary chapter of the Constitution . Emergency has been called a fraud on the Constitution, an instrument to keep the citizens' Fundamental Rights under 'eclipse'. K. Subba Rao, Ex-Chief Justice of India, was also of the same view. The judgement of the Supreme Court that all or any of the Fundamental Rights can be suspended further strengthened the Emergency Powers of the President.

Justification for the Emergency Provisions : The justification for the Emergency Provisions lies mainly in the past history of India. Whenever there has been a weak centre, it has brought about ruin in the country. The founding fathers of the Constitution did not want history to be repeated.

The conditions prevailing at the time of framing the Constitution had an important bearing on the inclusion of these provisions:

(i) The country was facing separatist tendencies. The problem before the fathers was not only to give a democratic constitution but also to provide safeguards against anti-national and anti -democratic forces. The whole atmosphere was explosive. The partition of India let loose communal conflict, with tales of arson, murder and loot.

(ii) The federal constitutions have certain inherent weaknesses especially in times of crisis. There was the problem of Kashmir, Junagarh decided to accede to Pakistan and Hyderabad declared itself independent. Military action was essential as a matter of geographical compulsion.

(iii) The leaders of the nations did not have enough experience of working democratic government.

(iv) The divisive forces of linguism, regionalism, casteism and communalism were disturbing the peace of the country. The number of opposition parties at national and state levels were increasing fast. The communists were becoming a potential threat to peace.

(v) There was also a marked deterioration in the economic situation of the country. The foreign exchange reserves had fallen considerably.

It was necessary to remain in a state of preparedness to meet sudden crises and avert hostility and calamities. Fear of foreign aggression due to Pakistan's hostility and internal dissensions because of separatist tendencies created abnormal circumstances.

Hence the emergency provisions were made to preserve the integrity of the Constitution and the state against foreign aggression, imperialistic designs of big powers, economic rivalries, dangers from outside and disruptive tendencies within the country. The emergency provisions are equally meant to strengthen the working of the federal structure. A state contravening the principle of the federal system has to be put back to its old position. Economic crises were also to be averted by emergency action, as may become necessary during times of economic depression.

National Emergencies

The first proclamation of National Emergency was made in October 1962 on the occasion of the Chinese aggression. It continued to be in operation from October 26, 1962 to January 10, 1968.

The second proclamation was made on December 4, 1971 on Pakistan's declaration of a full scale war.

National emergency was again declared in June 26, 1975 when the country was threatened i with chaos and anarchy and extra-constitutional methods were adopted by some opposition parties to give a wider base to the concept of so called 'total revolution'.

Failure of Constitutional Machinery in States

So far the President has acted only on a report from the State Governor; he can act "otherwise", if he is satisfied that an emergency has arisen. Action may be necessary for one of the following reasons; mass violence and unrest with the sympathy of the party in power; the State's economic plans may be contrary to the economic programmes of the Centre; Centre's imposition of its economic linguistic or prohibition policy on a recalcitrant State; gross mal-administration, simple non-compliance with some federal law; failure to find a party in clear majority in form a government; or a coalition failing to function and causing a political deadlock. In such cases, the Centre steps in to bring order out of chaos. According to Lylee, it is a protective device for responsive government in politically unstable states. At the termination of emergency a stable ministry has generally emerged. There is no doubt that during emergency the Central executive becomes usually powerful but the Parliament continues to be vigilant.

Up till 1972 article 356 had been promulgated in States twenty times. In most of the cases trouble arose because of mutual bickering of rival groups within the ruling party, constant defections of legislators, failure of coalition ministries due to internal dissensions and consequent law lessens the political instability. Kerala came under the President's rule five times. Critics of the emergency provisions allege that the centre has never been tolerant of opposition parties forming governments in the States, specially in Kerala and West Bengal, where the Communists have succeeded from time to time in forming governments. It is also alleged that the ruling party in power at the Centre encourages the "see-saw game of defection and counter defections and at times the "Defectionist-in-Chief' becomes the next Chief Minister.

Precautions against Misuse of Emergency Powers : Authorities of Indian Constitution have suggested that healthy and sound conventions should be established for careful and cautious use of this emergency power by the President. Constitutional or political deadlock should not automatically lead to emergency action.

Certain proposals have been made to prevent the misuse of this power:

(i) Delimiting the exercise of this power by imposition of certain restrictions.

(ii) Making the exercise of this power justiciable by Supreme Court of by making it compulsory for the President to obtain an advisory opinion of the Supreme Court before imposing Article 356 in a State.

(iii) Making the office of the Governor elective, as is the case in the United States, making him not an agent of the Centre but an impartial judge in times of crises.

Any one of such proposals will obviate the fears of the State and also check political use of the Article. But the Centre's control will definitely become weak.

It is true the emergency powers vested with the President are "unparalleled in the history of democratic world. It is true that during emergency the federal character is destroyed and the Union becomes all powerful. It is also true that the powers of the state-both the Union and the federating units-become concentrated in the hands of the Central Executive. The financial power of the State is also nullified. Above all, the Fundamental Rights are totally suspended.

But the authority of the state as a whole is of far greater importance than the individual liberty of a few citizens. It is the state which is to safeguard the liberties of the citizens and if the state is destroyed the liberties of the citizens too will come to an end.

Vice-President

The Vice-President is elected by the members of an electoral collage consisting of the members of both Houses of Parliament in accordance with the system of proportional representation by means of the single transferable vote. He must be citizen of India, not less than 35 years of age, and eligible for elections as a member of the Rajya Sabha (Council of States). His term of office is five years and he is eligible for reelection. His removal from office is to be in accordance with the procedure prescribed in Article 67(b).

The Vice-President is the ex officio Chairman of the Rajya Sabha and acts as the President when the latter is unable to discharge his functions due to absence, illness or any other cause, or till the election of a new President (to be held within six months) when a vacancy is caused by death, resignation or removal, or otherwise of the President. While so acting he ceased to perform the function of the Chairman of the Rajya Sabha.

Prime Minister

"The Prime Minister is really the keystone of the Cabinet and unless and until we create that office and endow that office with statutory authority to nominate and dismiss ministers, there can be no collective responsibility." Dr B R Ambedkar

"I am also something, after all I am the Prime Minister of India and the Prime Minister is the Prime Minister. He can lay down the Policy of Government and the Constitution, the Prime Minister is the linchpin of Government. To say that the Prime Minister cannot make a statement is a monstrous statement in itself. Jawaharlal Nehru

Prime Minister's Position and Power

The Indian Prime Minister occupies a unique position. He enjoys vast powers. Indira Gandhi in her time enjoyed much more powers than ever enjoyed by the British Prime Ministers. She was even accused of 'authoritarianism'.

Jawaharlal Nehru enjoyed no less power. No Minister could ever afford to displease him. If any one differed, he had to resign. The Prime Minister's will prevaile.

Rajiv Gandhi also enjoys unfettered power. He has reshuffled his Cabinet quite a few times to push out his Ministers who may differ with him on any basic issue.

Quite a few eminent persons had to resign due to differences with Nehru. Dr. S.P. Mukherjee and K.C. Neogi resigned on the question of Nehru-Liaqat Pact, Dr Ambedkar resigned on the Hindu Code Bill. C.D. Deshmukh on the question of Bombay and Maharashtra, V.V. Giri on matters of labour policy. As explained above, Nehru was not merely first among equals. He was essential to the very life and death of the whole Council of Ministers. He was the keystone of the Cabinet Arch.

The following powers enjoyed by the Prime Minister give an idea of the magnitude of his authority;

(a) The President appoints Ministers on the advice of the Prime Minister. He distributes portfolios according to his choice. Although to some extent he/she is bound by certain other factors, both Nehru and Indira Gandhi have allocated portfolios as they have liked. What Ambedkar said in the Constituent Assembly is very correct today, "No person shall be retained as a member of the Cabinet, if the Prime Minister says that he shall be dismissed." Dismissal is, of course, a very harsh word but reconstituting the Cabinet and excluding an undesirable Minister or elevating him to governorship or ambassadorship was never a problem for Nehru. Indira Gandhi has been much more powerful. During emergency, top leaders, like Yell. Chavan, Jagjiwan Ram, T.A. Rai and others, could not dare differ with her. This had been possible because of her charismatic personality and the fact that the Indian masses were with her *en masse* and her policies were thought to bring up the most vulnerable and downtrodden people.

(b) As Chairman of the Cabinet, the Prime Minister presides over the meeting and determines the agenda. He/She rejects or accepts proposals for cabinet discussions.

(c) As the Prime Minister, he coordinates the activities of all Ministers who are heads of different departments. Government activities have multiplied a lot as the Government is wedded to the objective of socialism and a Welfare State. It is the job of the Prime Minister to see that all activities are carried on harmoniously.

(d) As the leader of the House of the people, the Prime Minister makes all important policy announcements on internal policy matters, on matters of world peace, and foreign policy. He initiates and leads the parliamentary debates on all important matters.

(e) The Prime Minister is the link between the President and the Cabinet. He communicates to the President all decisions taken by the Cabinet relating to administration of the affairs of the Union and all proposals for legislation. He furnishes such information to the President, as and when the latter asks for.

(f) The Prime Minister is the spokesman of Indian's policy abroad. He very often visits foreign countries. He represents India in various International conferences and Commonwealth conferences. Indira Gandhi visited a large number of countries on diplomatic and goodwill missions and invited the heads of many countries to India. Wherever she went she created a good impression and was able to sell our country's policies. Foreign journalists have described her as a sweet dove symbolising peace with sharp claws. In 1971 before Indo-Pak war, she visited a number of European countries and built public opinion in favour of India. Later also her visits to Arab countries and African countries and her speeches on foreign policy or Indian Ocean politics won for her wide acclaim.

(g) The Prime Minister is not only the leader of the majority party in the House of the People, he is also the acknowledged leader of the nation. As long as Nehru lived, he was the synonym for the Congress party and India. Mrs. Indira Gandhi has been often hailed as 'Indira is India. She won the mandate from the electorate in 1971 and again in 1980.

Council of Ministers

Article 53 of the Indian Constitution lays down that the executive power of the Union shall be exercised by the President of India, either directly or through officers subordinate to him. These officers, subordinate to him, are the Ministers.

According to Article 74, there is to be a Council of Ministers with the Prime Minister, to aid and advise the President, in the exercise of his functions.

Article 75 explains the process of formation of the Council of Ministers. According to this article, the Prime Minister is to be appointed by the President, and the Ministers are appointed on the advice of the Prime Minister. The Council of Ministers much be collectively responsible to the House of the People. This establishes the Parliamentary form of Government in India.

According to Article 75 (2) the Ministers hold office during the pleasure of the President. Collective responsibility to Parliament and holding office during President's pleasure are two contradictory things in practice.

Can the President exercise his discretion in calling any one for appointment as the Prime Minister? Can he legally dismiss a Ministry even if it enjoys the confidence of the House of People? The answer is 'No'.

The fact is that the Parliamentary Government is based on certain conventions which do not lend themselves to formal statements in the provisions of the Constitution. The pattern of British Parliamentary Government has been followed in India.

The President, as such, has no other choice but to invite the leader of the party or group commanding a majority in the House of the People. If no single party commands a majority two or more parties may form a coalition and select a common leader.

It is not necessary that the Prime Minister must belong to the House of the People. Jawaharlal Nehru and Lal Bahadur Shastri were the members of the House of the People. Indira Gandhi, at the time of her first appointment, was a member of the Council of States. However, no outsider has so far been appointed as Prime Minister, though in the States, 'outsiders' have been the Chief Ministers.

In case the Prime Minister or any of the Ministers is not a member of either House, he ceases to hold his office on the expiration of six months from the date of appointment.

After constituting the Council of Ministers, the Prime Minister distributes the portfolios among the Ministers. creation of a homogeneous ministry with satisfaction of all regarding the portfolio he/ she gets is not an easy task. The hands of the Prime Minister are quite tight. He has to think of the capabilities of different persons; he has to think of representation of different regions and communities in the Ministry; he also cannot afford to annoy his senior colleagues in regard to choice of a portfolio.

The Cabinet

A distinction between the Council of Ministers and a Cabinet is to be understood. The Constitution provides only for a Council of Ministers. The Cabinet is an informal body of senior ministers who form the inner core of administration.

The Council of Ministers consists of three categories of Ministers:

(i) Cabinet Ministers

(ii) Ministers of State

(iii) Deputy Ministers

There is not a word in the Constitution regarding the Cabinet. It is the best example of the convention so far established under the Constitution. The Cabinet has gradually become a distinct entity. The Cabinet meets as a body and takes policy decisions. It is an extra legal growth but it is the steering wheel of the ship of the State. It is the key-stone of the constitutional arch. It is the hyphen that joins the buckle that fastens the executive and the legislature. The Cabinet is supposed to present to the Parliament and to the world a unified policy of action. The individual Ministers just carry out the decisions of the Cabinet faithfully.

Besides the Cabinet there is also a Super-Cabinet. Nehru and Patel formed the Super-Cabinet. After Patel, Nehru, Azad, Ayyangar and Kidwai fanned the inner cabinet. Nehru's last inner cabinet included Shastri and Menon. The members of the inner-cabinet of Indira Gandhi had been changing frequently.

The Council of Ministers as a whole does not meet frequently. The Cabinet, presided over by the Prime Minister, meets once a week. The agenda is determined by the Prime Minister. Besides the Cabinet Ministers, the Ministers of State may be asked to attend, if matters connected with their Departments are being discussed. Deputy Ministers and Planning Commission Members are also at times asked to attend the Cabinet meetings. A matter is discussed till the consensus is reached.

Before assuming office the Prime Minister and all other Ministers take oath of their respective offices as provided under the third schedule of the Constitution. They affirm or swear in the name of God that they shall uphold the sovereignty and integrity of India and defend the Constitution of India as established by law. They also affirm that they shall perform the duties of their offices faithfully and maintain secrecy of the deliberations of the Council of Ministers.

The Cabinet in India works on the lines of the Cabinet in England.

The President of India does not attend and preside over the meetings of the Cabinet. Although all executive actions are taken in his name, yet he is not held responsible for the wrongs done by the Ministers. In England the King can do no wrong; so in India the President does no wrong. He is not responsible for the acts of omission and commission of his Ministers.

All the members of the Cabinet are the members of either House of the Parliament. The Ministers have a double role to play. They hold different portfolios and carry on the administration of the country. They also attend the legislature's meetings and take an active share in discussions. This brings about very close and harmonious relationship. The Cabinet guides the legislature and it has earned the fame of the Cabinet Dictatorship. The Legislature, on the other hand, controls the Cabinet by asking questions, moving motions for adjournment, making cut motions in the budget grants or making motion of no confidence.

Ministerial Responsibility : Although the Cabinet, as the inner group of the majority party in the legislature, assumes dictatorship, constitutionally it is responsible to the House of the People and through it to the electorate. It remains in office as long as it enjoys the confidence of the majority of the members of the House. The moment it loses the confidence of the majority, it has to resign.

Collective and Individual Responsibility

The Constitution lays down that the Council of Ministers is collectively responsible to the House of the People. The entire body sinks and swims together. The Ministry works as a team and should resign in a body when necessary. There is individual responsibility also. If a single Minister is at fault, he may resign and the rest of the Ministry may continue. In case of disagreement with the Prime Minister, an individual Minister may resign or the Prime Minister may ask him to quit.

It is expected that all Ministers have the same political views. The Ministry has to act as a team, and face the legislature as one team. The Ministers are not supposed to express dissenting opinion, as they did during the days of Janta Party rule when they indulged in factionalism.

Jawaharlal Nehru did include eminent personalities in his earlier Cabinets, such as Shanmukham Chetty, Dr. John Mathai, Dr. B.R. Ambedkar, Dr. S.P. Mukherjee, Sardar Baldev Singh etc., but it was only a temporary phase. The experiment did not prove very successful. After 1952 the Cabinets became more and more homogeneous. Indira Gandhi took care to choose as Ministers only such persons as were loyal to her. Thus political homogeneity was maintained without much effort. The Ministry was purely a single party Minister.

The leadership of the Prime Minister is an acknowledged fact. He is the chief architect of the Council of Ministers. He is not merely primus inter pares i.e. first among equals; he is much more. Nehru was described as 'Moon among lesser Stars' by Harcourt and as 'Sun around which Ministers revolve like planets' by Dr. Jennings. Lal Bahadur Shastri, who succeeded Nehru, could not have attained a position so high. He adopted the policy of 'collective leadership'. When Indira Gandhi took over, other senior Congress leaders thought of the 'Syndicate' rule but gradually she emerged more powerful. She shuffled her Ministers and reallocated portfolio as she pleased. She deprived Morarji Desai of Finance portfolio before the split of the Congress in 1969. After taking over in 1980 she unceremoniously removed two of her senior ministers, Kamlapati Tripathi, and V.C. Shukla, because they tended to act against her wishes and caused indiscipline in the party.

The Constitution does not fix the size of the Council of Ministers. It is for the Prime Minister to determine the size according to the requirements of the occasion. After the first General Elections when the Council of Ministers was reconstituted, a change in the classification of Ministers was made, the Ministers of States being elevated to the Minister of Cabinet rank. But the abolition of the designation of Ministers of State and their re-designation as Ministers of Cabinet rank created confusion as to relative functions and responsibilities of the ministers concerned. The result was that when the second government was formed in 1957 after the General Election, the old practice was reverted to the appointments were made in the three ranks of Cabinet Minister, Minister of State and Deputy Minister. But shortly thereafter, Ministers of State were re-designated as before. After the third General Elections the old practice of making appointments in the three ranks has been followed.

The Deputy Ministers do not hold charge of independent portfolios. They assist the senior Ministers and perform such functions as are entrusted to them by the Ministers. There are no rigid rules defining the relations between the Minister can be made use of depends largely on the personal equation between a Minister and his Deputy and measure of confidence which the former is prepared to give to the latter. Some enthusiastic Ministers are also not inclined to share authority and power with their deputies. It is necessary to make the Deputy Minister fulfil a useful role that there must be established a relationship of understanding and confidence between the Minister and his deputy. The Deputy Minister should be entrusted with definite functions.

Regarding the composition of the Council of Ministers may also be remarked that there was a time when political offices were distributed as a reward to the prominent political workers who participated in the struggle for independence. But the time has now come, after fifty years of independence, when political considerations should not be made to weigh much and appointments should be made on non-political consideration.

8

The Executive (State)

In the identical fashion to the centre, the states are provided with separate constitutional and real political executive, i.e. Governor and the Council of Minister respectively. The office of the governor is a constitutional one, very much resembling that of the President of India. Article 154 of the constitution grants all the executive powers of the state to the Governor. Similarly, article 164 makes the Governor an integral part of the legislature of a state like the president who is a part of the Parliament. Similarly, article 202 of the constitution has made it the duty of the Governor to lay before the house or houses of the state legislature an annual financial statement (budget) of receipts and expenditure of the state for the year.

No money bill or other financial bill can be introduced in the legislative assembly except on the recommendations of the Governor. The contingency funds of the states is placed at the disposal of the Governor. Similarly article 161 vests the Governor with important judicial powers. But whatever the case may be the normal role of the Governor is that of a constitutional head ordinarily, he has to act according to the wishes of the council of ministers. However, there are three major areas in which the Governor is in a position to exercise his discretion (i) the appointment of the Chief Minister, (ii) the dismissal of council of ministers;

and (iii) the dismissal of the legislative assembly. Again in the periods of governmental instability in the states. The Governor can exercise his discretion. Thus, it is quite clear that unlike President, the Governor is neither a rubber stamp nor a nominal head. He is such an important functionary who can play a vital role in running the life and administration of the state.

Governor being a constitutional heads, it is the council of ministers which is the real executive in a state corresponding to that of the union council of ministers. To be more specific, it is the Chief Minister of a state who stands at the top of power mechanism at the state level. He enjoys supreme command over the executive as well as legislative branch of the government. Being a top most political executive he occupies a unique position in the political system of a state similar to the Prime Minister at the union level, and thus reminds the expressions as the key stone of the cabinet arch coined for the office of Prime Minister. He leads and guides his ministers, achieves co-operation and co-ordination between the ministers and patches up disputes or differences arising among the ministers. Apart from this he provides important link between the Governor and the cabinet, Legislature and the cabinet and between the people and government. He in this way, is the top leader in the State and leader of the people. However, there are some weak points of his position. The position of the Chief Minister of a single majority party, different from the party in power at the centre is not so strong. He enjoys sole power as political chief executive in the state but always faces opposition from the centre. Moreover, he faces an opponent in the office of governor, who is an appointee of the centre. However, the position of the Chief Minister, who is the leader of the coalition government; is virtually of a prisoner of the circumstances. He does not enjoy much powers and may even be ineffective. The weak position of such a Chief Minister is obvious as he holds his office at the pleasure of parties which join together to constitute majority for making the government.

Similarly, at the local level urban and rural local bodies have been set up. At the rural level Panchayati Raj institutions have been set up. In India we have a three tiered structure of Panchayati

Raj. The political executive at the Panchayat level is Sarpanch (Pradhan) and the political executive of other two levels of Panchayti Raj such as Panchayat Samiti and Zila Parishad are known as Presidents and Chairman respectively mostly elected through indirect election. Similarly, urban local bodies such as Municipal Corporations and Municipal Committees too have representative bodies. The political executive of these bodies are known as Mayors and Presidents respectively.

In fact, the political executive is, by and large, unsettled issue of local government in all over the world. In India, attempts have been made to institute a local executive. The result has been the dispersal of executive authority among different agencies, in case of co-operations, the council and its committee but there is a demand for reforming local executive. The Calcutta Municipal Corporation Act-1980 has adopted a Mayor-in-Council of government for the city government. It is a step towards a structural reform.

Powers of the Governor

Executive Powers

The power to appoint his Council of Ministers.

Appointment of High Officers of the State.

Rules for the convenient transaction of the business of the Government.

Asking information from the Chief Minister.

Legislative Powers

Sessions of the State Legislature.

Nomination to the State Legislature.

Right to address and send Messages.

Assent to Bills.

Power to promulgate ordinances.

Financial Powers

- No Money Bill can be introduced except on the recommendation of the Governor.
- In every financial year the Governor shall cause laid before the State Legislative the annual financial statement (Budget) showing the estimated receipts and expenditure for the year.
- The State Legislature may by law establish a Contingency Fund of the State. The said Fund is placed at the disposal of the Governor for meeting unforeseen expenditure.

Judicial Powers

- The Governor has the power to grant pardons, remissions of punishment or commute the sentence of any person convicted of any offence relating to a matter to which the executive power of the Steve extends.
- The appointment, posting and promotion of district judges, are made by the Governor in consultation with the High Court. This does not mean that the Governor must accept whatever advice is given by the High Court its views on the merits of the persons who have to be appointed or promoted as District Judges.

The institution of Mayor or the Deputy Mayor in India have not been listed authorities in any of Acts as they do not appear to have been vested with executive powers are treated as a part of the council or the standing committee. Even U.P. Act which vest on mayor the power of making certain appointments to the higher posts and thus having statutory control over such officers does not have an authority of the corporation of mayor and deputy mayor are to be given specific powers as representatives of the elected wing. They will have to be listed one of the authorities.

From the preceding it is quite clear that a heavy responsibility is thus cast on the political executive for providing a meaningful and purposive sense of direction to the community. It is ultimately true to say that every Nation gets the Government it deserves. And yet the leadership in a community has to accept responsibility for all that the Nation has to face.

There need, therefore, be no doubt or question about the location of responsibility for failures on any front of the social, economic or political life of the Nation. This is, however, more so in respect of the particular factor which may be designated as "the general atmosphere prevailing in a Nation" or, for want of a better expression of the Time Spirit, the creation of which is in their hands and for which they must be held fully responsible. To be more specific we can say that the King is responsible for the creation of the Time Spirit. In a democracy, where people are sovereign this responsibility must be necessarily accepted by the political executive as they are representing the people.

It is the Time Spirit which ultimately decides whether the nation as a whole, is one the upgrade or is consciously or unconsciously slipping downwards. In particular, the Time Spirit is the regulator of the National Conscience which determines whether the great majority, which are always on the fence, cast their weight on the right side of all that is good in national life thus enriching it and making it grow from strength to strength or, on the other hand, get corrupted and act as a weighty drag pulling the nation fast one the slippery path of National Decay.

As the political executive is at the top to the national life it is but natural that people should look up to it for setting and maintaining the highest standards. Integrity, austerity and hard-work are expected from each individuals but the standard of expectation and performance expected of him must be directly proportional to his position in life. The task of enforcement of appropriate standards at all levels would be much easier if these are strictly applied at the highest level. It is a mere truism to state that one who is not himself adhering to the principles he preaches, cannot with any conviction or moral courage, ask others to follow them. If he does so, he would not be taken seriously.

Discretionary Powers of the Governor : The Governor has to act on the advice of the Council of Ministers except when he may be called upon to exercise his power in discretion. The occasions which will give such an opportunity to the Governor seem to be the following :

- Circumstances can arise when no party commands an absolute majority in the House. In such a case the Governor will have to exercise his personal judgement in selecting the Chief Minister.
- If the Ministry has lost the confidence of the Legislative Assembly, it must resign. But a situation may arise that the Ministry insists on remaining in office and asks for the dissolution of the House on the plea that the House has lost the confidence of the people. In such circumstances the Governor will be within his right not to accept the advice of the Chief Minister to dissolve the Assembly.
- The Governor may report to the President that a situation has arisen under which Government of the State may not be carried on in accordance with the provisions of the Constitution. It will result in the imposition of the President's rule in the State.
- The Governor may refuse to give assent to a Bill or he may send it back for reconsideration. He may also reserve a Bill for the assent of the President.
- There are some provisions as to the administration of Tribal Areas in the States of Assam, Meghalaya, Tripura and Mizoram. The Governor of each of these States exercise these functions in his discretion.

Thus we can say that it is for the political executive of the country to create the new climate in which with the help of non-official leadership and the administrative apparatus, it will be possible to instill a sense of dedication all round, to reward merit and hard work, to punish idleness, sloth and indifference, to root out corruption and so set the tone that the best in the national life is thrown up in the process.

Political Executive and Civil Servants

In assessing this responsibility of the political executives we would like to make it clear that it is not intention to foist the whole blame on the political leaders for the present shortcomings of the administration. On the contrary, the services must accept in a full measure their share of the blame too. Can there be any excuse for the failure on the part of a civil servants to offer frank advice on the ground that it may not be liked or appreciated? If he is not able to muster even this much courage in a free India, there must be said to be something positively wrong with his makeup and character. It is to secure independent and well considered advice from them that they are so well paid and constitutional guarantees are provided to protect them from any action springing from prejudice. It should be realised that such an excuse only recoils on the one who made it.

It is being felt by the scholars that there has been a basic failure on the part of the administrative leadership which has contributed to the present situation in the administration and not all of it can be attributed to the impact of democratic institutions. There has been a recognisable fall in service standards for which full responsibility must be accepted by the heads of the administration. There is no valid explanation for failure to exercise supervision, for the various instances of administrative slackness and for the tacit acceptance of the present state of the administrative machinery by a fraternity who had seen it in a better form in the past. It does not seem to have liked to any heart-searching amongst them and to any effective move on their part to improve conditions.

While the leadership of the Minister in the entire sphere of administration is undoubted, both in law and in fact the complexities of modern government, the time he has to devote to parliamentary activity, the necessity of keeping in close touch with the people and the increasingly technical nature of the various decisions that have to be made, necessarily limit his sphere of direct participation in all the intricate and detailed aspects of administration even on the part of most dynamic and competent of personalities. All that one can succeed in doing is to see that one's policies, attitudes and directions are well-understood and that implementation is according to them.

The minister's only instrument is his Secretary on whom he relies for constant advice and guidance. He can, of course, take any additional assistance he needs, but never in such a manner that he generates a feeling of lack of confidence in his sole instrument. He has to secure that complete confidence and understanding prevails between him and his Secretary. He must be able to draw the best out of the permanent staff and make them willing partners in all he intends to do.

All this puts a great responsibility on the Secretary. He must be open enough to understand his political chief and see that his undoubted capacities which have brought him to the top of the administrative ladder are so used as to encourage the political chief to open out his mind to him. His capacities must act as the manure and water with which the seed to knowledge of what his political chief wants and desires can grow to its full height in the departmental soil of the administration. He must be eager to ascertain how his political chief likes things to be done and act accordingly. It is the lack of this openness, the harbouring of the feeling that everything that is being done is all right, that anything new is unnecessary interference and must be scotched out, that leads to the criticism often heard from the leaders of the nation of their being unable to achieve anything because of the iron frame of the administration.

Once this understanding is secured, the political chief should leave the actual implementation to his executive head. He can always ask questions on any matter to satisfy himself that things are going on all right. But before he interferes, he must not only be very sure of his ground but he must also proceed in a way that his Secretary continues to feel the same confidence in his attitudes judgement as when they started. Any feeling that the political executive is acting out of political weakness or to secure an unfair advantage or any other consideration which an honest and a sincere person would scorn to harbour, starts a deteriorating process which may ultimately lead to a situation where each utilises the other for his own ends and the whole administration suffers. So, intimate is this relationship that the present practice is to give the minister the choice of his secretary out of a panel of three prepared by the Appointments Committee of the cabinet. While this gives a certain choice to the minister, it also opens up a possibility of approaches to him on the part of .service. We are providing for the contingency of their being unable to get on, by the recommendation that it should be open to either of them to ask for a change. In view of this, the balance of the consideration appears to be in favour of a single nomination to the post, recommended by the Central Personnel Agency so as to eliminate all personal elements in the appointment.

No hard and fast rules can be laid down to describe this delicate relationship between the political executive and his secretary. The dividing line between their respective functions is generally indicated by the statement that while the laying down of policies is the privilege of the political executive, their execution should be left to the administrative and execution beings. Besides these difficulties of basic principles, there are personality factors and degrees to mutual adjustment, which go to determine the actual role of the two partners. Initially there were certain built-in obstructions to the development of harmonious relationship between them. The services were used to the ways of the old administration. Its essential feature was that it was leisurely, not achievement-oriented and not responsible. The heads were drawn from the same service and therefore there was an understanding which tampered the demand of answerability.

The situation at the dawn of independence was different. The new executive was anxious to do their bit for the country, which was hungry for development. They were answerable to Parliament and Assemblies. They were in a hurry and had no patience with the leisurely functioning of the past. Most of them during the course of the National struggle had crossed swords with the very service whom they had come to rule. Another complicating factor was that except for the top leadership, many had not only no previous experience of the administration, but in intellectual capacity and comprehension, were not always as highly gifted as the services. These circumstances were not conducive to the development of mutual respect.

In spite of these handicaps, it must be said to the credit of the services and the political leadership that, though none of them had any previous experience of running a democratic state, their initial impact was not as inharmonious as their differing backgrounds would have indicated. By and large, the services adjusted themselves to the demands of the new situation and did their best to co-operate with their new masters. It is because of this that the government at the centre and the states were able to withstand the critical situation created by the partition, the refugee problem and three wars with China and Pakistan. The fact that India has been able to maintain and run a democratic system for decades in a world climate which does not appear to be particularly favourable to democratic institution must also be set down as due to this factor once again. Significant changes are taking place. Democratic institutions are strengthening. However, over a period of time, certain defects in the working of this relationship have become apparent. On their part, the services have failed to exercise supervision and control over the administrative apparatus to see that it becomes achievement oriented to secure, that good work is rewarded and bad work punished, and in maintaining the general efficiency of the administrative machine. They however, feel that to the extent, this result has been brought about by the unconscious inroads on their authority by the political executive.

Efficient administration is a result of various factors. Respect for authority, reverence for superiors, fear that undisciplined and laxity will be punished, an atmosphere of unquestioned obedience to, and respect for one's immediate superiors prevailing in the government hierarchy, all contribute to administration's efficiency. The installation of the political executive as the administrative head created a new situation. There was not a new head who unlike his predecessor was approachable. Influences could be brought to bear on him. The general belief that public administration is an art which any able-bodied citizen can easily master could be taken advantage of by instigating cases of supposed injustice which could be brought before him for redress over and above the head of the departmental hierarchy. Casteism and regional considerations did also play a part in the whole process of bringing about administrative deterioration. The foreign administrator could afford to keep himself aloof from all these factors because he was not answerable to anybody. The new political heads for the very opposite reason, could not entirely escape the contaminating influence of these factors. Thus, came about a situation where administrative authority became eroded. There was a tendency to look not to one's immediate superior for redressal of grievances or for promotion but to approach the minister directly for these purposes. A situation was created in which one's confidence that merit and hard work alone were the avenues of promotion came to be shattered and replaced by a tendency to approach the highest quarters for securing these rewards of service. This is the explanation given by the services for the present situation with which the administration is faded.

Two other factors contributed to the worsening of the administrative atmosphere. The first was the human failure to appreciate and understand seemingly unpalatable advice. Officers who were reputed for outspokenness were gradually relegated to insignificant positions with the result that, increasingly, palatable advice came to be delivered. Free and frank advice, if unpalatable, was withheld. We have reason to believe that, over a period of time, this tendency has been very much on the increase. Some of the Chief Ministers feel that they could never be sure that the advice they were getting was really the opinion of their secretaries or was being tendered under the belief that it would be liked. Secondly, officials working in the field carried the impression that their future prospects come to be affected by the stream of information about them, communicated to the chief minister of the state by the local bosses. This led to erosion of self-confidence of the administrators and depending on the personality of the officer concerned, there was a tendency to subordinate integrity and impartiality to the demands of political exigencies as desired by the local leaders in power in the district. Thus, interference over the administrative head in service matter, incapacity to tolerate unpalatable advice and a feeling in the districts that the view of the local bosses about them was a determining factor affecting their future have continuously resulted in a general fall in the standards of administration.

It is not our concern to apportion blame of this result. What is more necessary is to draw correct lesson from past experience and devise ways and means to secure improvements in the future.

If our analysis of the present administrative situation is correct, what concrete steps can be taken to see:

(i) that the ideal conditions prevail between the Minister and his Secretary and Department head;

(ii) that the services are encouraged to offer advice undeterred by the fear that it may not be liked;

(iii) that in the field administration, they are able to maintain impartiality and honesty and are not haunted by the fear of tales being carried about them, which may affect their prospects;

(iv) that a new confidence is created amongst them that their prospectus depend entirely on their hard work, honesty and merit and need no other proper support.

One of the suggestions is that there should be written code defining the political executive civil servant relationship in clear terms so that there is no scope for ambiguity. This will enable the civil servants to refer to the code and thus any pressure being exerted on them. The code will also enable departmental action to be taken against them for violating the code. This remedy might be useful and tried at the lower levels of the administration. It may help a BDC in the case of a Panchayat Samiti or the CEC in case of Zila Parishad in pointing out the appropriate sphere of his action, and may help to introduce greater efficiency in the working of these institutions. But at higher levels it is not likely to work, not be conducive to the growth of harmonious relationship. Here the trouble arises not from any lack of knowledge of what is right or wrong, but from a failure of the human factor which is likely to induce an encroachment on what are essentially service matters, by virtue of the unquestioned final authority vested in the political executive. It is not always sufficiently realised that the administration is a delicate instrument having a tone and optimum functioning capacity and any improper interference at any level with this instrument is apt to throw it out of gear and adversely affect its efficiency. Once the hold of the Secretary over the administration is loosened, once it is known that things can be done through his political chief that have not been possible to be done through him, an unconscious process starts which may well land the political chief in considerable difficulty by the Secretary refusing to take further responsibility and referring all cases to him for orders.

It should be realised, however, that the absolute authority of the Minister over the personnel in his departments is ultimately to secure the National wealth through the democratic form of administration. It is through him that there must be a common loyalty of the minister and the service. The services should never be used for any lesser ends and it is their duty to point out this clearly when circumstances demand it. On the other hand, it is not unusual to notice a "touch me not attitude" particularly when the minister is temperamentally weak and unable to assert himself. At times the undoubted co-ordinating authority of the Prime Minister or the Chief Minister may be so extended as to commit, inroads on ministerial responsibility. A variety of such conditions and circumstances will need appropriate action on the part of the either which is impossible to indicate in a general way some of the important considerations which should regulate this relationship:

1. Both of them should clearly and sympathetically appreciate the role of the other, and attempt at a maximum accommodations of each other's view.

2. On the part of the political executive there should be

   (a) A proper understanding of the administrative functions and recognition of its professional nature.

   (b) As little interference as possible in service matters e.g., postings, transfer promotions etc. Discouraging officers of the department to see him personally for redress of service grievances.

   (c) No requests for departures from declared and approved policies to suit individual cases either as a result of political considerations, or other considerations, which cannot be reduced to general principles of action.

On the Parts of the Services

(a) There must be a sincere and honest attempt to find out what the political head wants and make the necessary adjustment in policies and procedures to suit his wishes.

(b) A readiness to fall in with his political chief in all matters, unless strong grounds indicate a different course. In such a case he should politely indicate his dissent and if he is overruled in writing he should willingly carry out his order.

(c) The minister usually has a department and it frequently happens that the heads of the department and the secretary are different individuals; frequently they differ on the advice they give. In such a cases the best course is for personal discussion with both, frequently in each other's presence, and no secretary should consider such action as any encroachment on his personal relationship with his minister.

In our opinion it should be one of the important duties of the chief minister in the state and the Prime Minister at the centre to see that proper relationship between the political executive and the civil service develops and continues to grow. In case, certain stresses and strains are apparent immediate remedial action should be taken. Any delay is likely to vitiate the atmosphere so badly that till it persists it may adversely affect the working of the whole department.

As a measure to avoid such a situation developing, it is suggested that it should be open to either side, that is, the political executive or his secretary to ask for a change. This option should be strictly limited to the level of secretary. Those in the lower ranges in the hierarchy must be fully responsible to the secretary. If a minister considers that a change is necessary at a lower level, he should tell the secretary and the change should be effected through him. A request for change from either side should not be considered as a reflection on the capacity of the person, to pull on with the other; it should be granted as a matter of course as soon as it is made. We do not consider that a necessary corollary to such a request should be made to ask for a successor by name. The new appointment must be made in accordance with the normal procedure because if this salutary principle is not kept in view it may give rise to favouritism and groupism in administration.

The menace, of casteism and regionalism has gained momentum particularly in some states. These attitudes seem to have got tacit recognition and support. On the ground that the realities of a situation must be recognised, and that the only way to do so, is to provide for an appropriate balance between the different castes, in regional administration. This is not only allowing the spirit of casteism and regionalism full sway and recognition but the surest way of perpetuating it by giving it official sanction. It can not be emphasised that in the present situation in our country, fissiparous tendencies likely to be encouraged by such recognition. The only sure way of combating casteism is to scotch out of all traces of it wherever found, not to encourage them particularly in the services. There have been complaints made by highly placed officers of feelings of injustice being harboured by them on the ground of postings, promotions and transfers taking place on account of caste and regional considerations. It is necessary to secure the services and administrators that no account will be taken of these factors in relation to service matters, except as a matter of deliberate policy of providing weightage in recruitment

Training of Political Executives

The above discussion clearly shows that the political executive has to have a combination of qualities which are relatively rare. At these levels the person concerned requires well developed executive ability as well as developed qualities of political leadership. It is one of the weaknesses of a democracy that the choice of a political executive is based on factors not necessarily related to his capacities and personality. This is all the more so in those countries where the democratic institutions are yet to strike their roots in the soil and which are passing through critical periods of rapid social and economic change. To add to these difficulties, the nation seems to have shifted in the course of four decades info a situation which demands a programme of moral regeneration in all walks of national life. There has developed a general tendency to work less and ask for more. The task of the political leadership is, therefore, the most important, the most exacting and the most unenviable.

Thus, we would like to invite attention to the fact that there are no arrangements for providing an administrative background to persons selected to perform the duties of a political executive. His development as an executive is left entirely to chance and individual initiative. A proper initiation appears to be necessary in the context of our administrative situation where relationship have not yet crystallised and problems facing any department are much too complex.

It is true that there can be substitute for experience, but there are certain areas in which a long process of actual experience can be substituted by properly designed institutional programmes. Such programmes in the limited field of community development and co-operation which have served well both officials and non-officials for quite some time. The Yugoslav practice of having a full-fledged programme of orientation for their newly elected political executives may be of relevance. No one can assume office before successful completing these programmes. Formalisation to this extent is neither necessary nor desirable in our democratic set up. But a well conceived and purposeful programme would be of immense value. It is therefore, suggested that a programme either under the age is of the parliament on some academic institution may be down up.

The Zila Parishads and Panchayat Samitis can play an important role in the process of buildings up leadership. They should provide opportunities for constructive work both to the new comers to political life and to others returning from higher levels. Active participation by the political leader and to others returning from higher levels. Active participation by the political leaders at these levels would give them a better understanding of the administrative problems and an opportunity to come in closer touch with the realities of life, specially for those coming from urban and upper class background. The rising stature of presidential and other positions in Zila Parishad is already in evidence in Maharashtra and Gujarat. This is a healthy sign and should provide the necessary ground for development of political executives for the highest tiers in Government.

9

Centre–State Relations

"The distribution of power is an essential features of federalism. The object for which a federation is formed involves a division of authority between the Central Government and the separate states. The tendency of federation limit on every side the action of the government and to split up the strength of the State among coordinate and independent authorities is specially noticeable because it forms the essential distinction between a federal system, and a unitary system of government" (A.V. Dicey). In fact the basic principle of federalism is that the legislative executive and financial authority is divided between the Centre and the State not by any law passed by the Centre but by Constitution itself. This is what Indian Constitution does. To understand the basic nature of the Indian federation the constitutional provision have been discussed thoroughly.

Legislative Relations : The Constitution of India makes two fold distribution of legislative powers:

(a) with respect of territory; and

(b) with respect of subject-matter.

Territorial Jurisdiction : As regards territory, Article 245 (1) provides that subject to the provisions of this constitution, Parliament may make laws for the whole or any part of the territory of India. According to the Article 245 (2) a law made by Parliament shall not deemal to be invalid on the ground that it has extraterritorial operation i.e. outside the territory of India.

The legislative powers of the Parliament and State Legislature is subject to the provisions of the constitution viz. (1) the scheme of distribution of powers; (2) Fundamental Rights, (3) other provisions of the constitution.

Theory of Territorial Nexus : The legislature of state may make laws for the whole or any part of the state. This means that state laws would be void if it has extraterritorial operation. However, there is one exception to his general rule. A State law of extraterritorial nature will be valid if there is sufficient nexus between the object and the State.

Distribution of Legislative Powers Subject Matter : As has been pointed out at the outset, a federal system postulates a distribution of powers between the centre and the states. The present constitution adopts the method followed by the Government of India Act, 1935, and divides the powers between the Union and the States in three lists; the Union list, the State list and the concurrent list. The Union list consists of 97 subjects mentioned in the Union list are of national importance i.e., defence foreign affairs, banking, currency and coins etc. State list consists of 56 subjects these are of local importance, such as, public order, police, local government, health, sanitation, agriculture, forest fisheries, education etc. The states have exclusive powers to made laws on subjects mentioned in the state list.

Concurrent list consists of 47 subjects. Both centre and states can make laws on the subjects mentioned in the concurrent list. But in case of conflict between the Central and the State law on concurrent subjects, the central law will prevail. The concurrent list, thus, in the words of M.V. Pylee, is "a twilight gone, as it were, for both the Union and the States are competent to legislate in this field , without coming into conflict."

The Residuary Powers : Article 248 vests residuary powers in the Parliament. It says that Parliament has exclusive power to make any law with respect to any matter not enumerated in the concurrent list or the state list. Entry 9.7 in the union list also lays down that Parliament has exclusive power to make laws with respect to any matter not mentioned in the state or concurrent list.

Principles of Interpretation of List : The Supreme Court has evolved the following principles of interpretation in order to determine the respective power of the Union and the States under the three lists:

Predominance of Union List : The opening word of Article 246 (i) notwithstanding anything in clause (2) and (3) and the opening words of clause (3) subject to clause (1) and (2) expressly secure the predominance of the Union list over the State list and the Concurrent list and that of the Concurrent list over the State list.

Each Entry to be Interpreted Broadly : Subject to the overriding predominance of the Union list entry in the various lists should be interpreted broadly. See the cases of Calcutta Gas Ltd. v. State of West-Bengal and Union of India v. H.S. Million and International Tourism Corp. V. State of Haryana.

Pith and Substance : Within their respective spheres, the Union and the State legislatures are made supreme and they should not encroach into the sphere reserved to the other. If a law passed by one encroaches upon the field of other then court will apply the doctrine of pith and substance to determine whether the legislature concerned was competent to make such laws. See cases of State of Bombay v. F.N. Balsara and Ishwari Khetal Sugar Mills v. State of U.P.

Colourable Legislation : Colourability is bound up with incompetency and not tainted with bad faith or evil motive. A thing is colourable which in appearance only and not in reality, what is purports to be.

Thus the whole doctrine of colourable legislation is based upon the maxim that you can't do indirectly what you can't do directly". In these cases the court will look in the true nature and character of the legislation and for that its objects purpose or design to make laws on a subject is relevant and not its motive. If the legislature has power to make laws, motive, in making the laws is irrelevant."

State of Bihar v. Kameshwar Singh is the only case where a law has been declared invalid on the ground of Colourable Legislation. In this case, the Bihar Land Reforms Act 1950, was held void on the ground that though apparently it purports to lay down principle for determining compensation yet in reality it did not lay down any such principle and thus indirectly sought to deprive the petitioner of any compensation.

Repugnancy between a Central and State Law : Article 254 (1) says that if any provision of law made by the Legislature of the State is repugnant to any provision of a law made by Parliament which is competent to enact or to any provision of existing law with respect to one of the matters enumerated in the concurrent list then the law made by Parliament, whether passed before or after the law made by legislature of such state or as the case may be, the existing law shall prevail and the law made by the legislature of the State shall, to the extent of the repugnancy be void. According to Fazal A.R. the repugnancy would arise between the two statutes in the following situation:

1. It must be shown that there is clear and direct inconsistency between the two enactment which is irreconcilable, so that they can't stand together or operate in the same field.

2. There can be no repeal by implication unless the inconsistency appears on the face of the two statutes.

3. Where there two statutes occupy a particular field, but there is room or possibility of both the statutes operating the same field without coming in, to collusion with each other, no repugnancy results.

4. Where there is no inconsistency but a statue occupying the same field seeks to create distinct and separate offences, no question *of* repugnancy arises and both the statues continue to operate in the same field.

Parliament's Powers to Legislate on State Subjects (Articles 249, 250, 252,253 and 256) : Though in normal times the distribution of powers must be strictly maintained and neither the state nor the centre can encroach upon the sphere allotted to the other by the constitution yet in certain exceptional circumstances the above system of distribution is either suspended or the power of the Union Parliament are extended over the subjects mentioned in the state list. The exceptional circumstances are:

Power of Parliament to Legislate in the National Interest : According to the article 249 if the Rajya Sabha passes a bill supported by 2/3 by the members present and voting that is necessary or expedient in the national interest that Parliament should make laws with respect to any matter enumerated within state laws then it shall be lawful for the Parliament to make laws for the whole or any part of the territory of India so long as the, resolution remains in force. Such a resolution normally lasts for a year but it can be renewed as many time as it is necessary. These laws of Parliament will however, cease to have effect on the expiration of the period of six months after resolution has ceased to operate.

During a Proclamation of Emergency : According to Article 250 while the proclamation of Emergency is in operation the Parliament shall have power to make laws for the whole of India or any part of the country with respect to all matters in the state list. Such a law however shall cease to have effect on the expiration of six months after the proclamation of emergency has ceased to operate.

Parliament's Power to Legislate with the Consent of the State : According to Article 52 if the legislature of two or more states pass resolution to the effect that it is desirable to have a law passed by Parliament on any matter in the state list, it shall be lawful for Parliament to make laws regulating that matter. Any other state may adopt such a law by passing a resolution to that effect. Such law can only be amended or repealed by the act of the Parliament.

Parliament Power to Legislate for Giving Effect to Treaties and International Agreements : Article 253 empowers the Parliament to make any law for the whole or any part of the territory of India for implementing treaties and international agreement and conventions. But laws enacted for the enforcement of treaties will be subject to the constitutional limits, that is, such a law cannot infringe fundamental rights.

In Case of Failure of Constitutional Machinery in a State : Under article 256 Parliament is empowered to make laws with respect to all matters in the state list when the Parliament declares that the Government of the State can't be carried on in accordance with the provisions of the Constitution.

Centre's Control Over State Legislation : In addition to the Parliaments power to legislate directly on the state subjects under the foregoing Articles, the constitution also provides for the centre's consent before a Bill passed by a state legislature can become a Law. The following articles give centre a control over state legislation.

Article 31 (3) provided that a state law providing for compulsory acquisition of private property shall have no effect unless it has received the consent on the President.

Articles 200 directs the Governor of a State to reserve a Bill passed by a State legislature for the consideration of the President if in his opinion, if passed in to law, would derogate the power of the High Court so as to endanger the position which the court is designed to fulfil under the constitution. The object of the article is to preserve the dignity of the court which may be affected by the State law.

Article 288 (2) authorises a state to tax in respect of water or electricity stored, generated consumed, distributed or sold by any authority established by law made by Parliament. But it makes it clear that no such law shall be valid unless it has been reserved for the consideration of the President and has received his assent.

Article 304 (b) authorises a state legislature to impose reasonable restriction on the freedom of trade, commerce and intercourse within the state in the "public interest". But such law can't be introduced in the State legislature without the previous sanction of the President. This provision is intended to ensure the free flow of trade and commerce which may be hampered by unreasonable restriction imposed by a state law. In this case, Supreme Court struck down a law on the ground that it was passed without centre's consent.

Administrative Relations between Union and States

Articles, from 256 to 263 of the Indian Constitution deal with the administrative relations between the Union and the constituent units. It is no denying the fact that the Constitution of India gives a dominant position to the Centre over the States. Therefore, it is rightly remarked that "India is a unitary state with subsidiary federal principles rather than a federal state with subsidiary unitary principles." This dominant position of the Centre is reflected by the power of federal legislature to create new States, to alter existing boundaries of the States, to legislate for whole of India, to declare emergency, to appoint governors of the States, to distribute revenue resources and to regulate All-India Services etc.

However, despite these provisions the Centre must largely depend on states for the implementation of its policies and laws. Hence to ensure that the States through their actions or inactions do not undermine the efficacy of the policies and laws of the Centre, certain administrative control over the states has been given to the Centre by the Constitution which may now be noted-.

1. Article 256 lays down that the executive power of the State shall be so exercised as to ensure compliance with the laws made by Parliament and any existing laws which apply to that state, and the executive power of

the Union shall extend to the giving of such direction to a state as may appear to the Government of India to be necessary for that purpose.

Article 256 thus imposes a constitutional duty on the states to exercise their executive power in such a way as to ensure compliance with the Central laws applicable to states and for this purpose Centre can give directions to the state governments.

2. Article 257 further gives power and authority to the Centre to issue directions to the states on the following matters:

   (a) the manner in which executive power of the state shall be exercised as not to impede the exercise of executive power of the Union.

   (b) the construction of means of communications declared to be of national or military importance.

   (c) measures to be taken for the protection of Railways in the states.

If the states do not follow the directions of the Centre then President of India can impose President's Rule on the defaulter state under Article 356 of the Constitution and can assume all the powers of the states. However, if there is any additional financial burden on the state in this behalf it shall be born by the Centre as may be agreed.

3. Article 258 gives authority to the Union to confer certain powers on the State. Clause (1) empowers Union to entrust its executive power to a State. However, such delegation has to be with the consent of the state government. In the same manner Clause (2) empowers Union to use state executive machinery for the enforcement of Union laws and for this purpose, Parliament may confer powers and impose duties on the officers and authorities of the states. It may be

noted that for such empowerment consent of state government as required under clause (1) is not necessary. Clause (3) makes provision for compensating the states for any extra-financial cost as may be agreed upon. However, in case of disagreement extra cost shall be determined by an arbitrator appointed by the Chief Justice of India.

4. Article 258-A which was inserted by the Constitution (Seventh Amendment) Act, 1956 takes of practical difficulty faced in execution of certain developmental projects of the states. As explained earlier Articles 258 (1) empowered the Union to delegate its executive powers to the officers of the states but vice versa was not allowed. This provision removes this lacuna and empowers Governor of a State to entrust state functions to the officers of the Centre.

5. Article 260 deals with jurisdiction of the Union in relation to territories outside India. Therefore, if by any agreement, grant, usage or political sufferance Union has assumed jurisdiction of any state outside India, it can exercise its legislative, executive and judicial functions.

6. Article 261 has certain provisions which are called "full-faith and credit" provisions. It declares that full faith and credit shall be given to public act, shall include all valid legislative and executive acts. The term "public record" shall include all official books, registers, records made by the public servant in discharge of his public duties. It shall further include public records of private documents such as private property, deeds which are registered. However, the general rule laid down in Clause (1) is subject to legislative power of the Parliament and the Parliament may lay down rules relating to the mode of proof and the effects of it in other states.

Clause (3) provides for the execution of final civil court judgements given by a state civil court in other states. Subject to the provisions of Civil Procedure Code, final judgement of Civil Courts shall be executed throughout the territory of India without the necessity of any fresh suit upon the judgement. However, this provision does not apply to the enforcement of penal laws of other states.

7. So far we have discussed general provision regarding Centre-State administrative relations. However, Article 262 and 263 make some special provisions in this behalf. We are all aware that water disputes between the states has special significance because of the agriculture and energy requirements of various states. Recent Cauvery water dispute between Karnataka and Tamil Nadu regarding sharing of Cauvery river water testifies this fact. Article 262 authorises Parliament to make law for the adjudication of any dispute or complaint with respect to the use, distribution or control of the water of any inter-state river or river valley. Clause (2) further empowers the Parliament to create a separate authority for the adjudication of such inter-state water disputes to the exclusion of the Supreme Court of India. In exercise of this power the Parliament has passed Water Dispute Act, 1956 which empowers Central Government to establish a tribunal on, a complaint from a state government regarding water dispute with another state in relation to a inter-state river or valley. Such tribunal shall consist of one man only to be nominated by the Chief Justice of India from amongst present judges or have been judges of the Supreme Court or High Courts. The decision of the tribunal shall be final and binding. The idea-behind the adjudication of inter-state water disputes through a tribunal was to ensure that the matter is decided not only on the basis of private property norms but on public interest norms.

However, the binding character of the award of the tribunal has created some doubts, therefore, the President of India has referred this aspect of the matter which arose from Cauvery water dispute for the advice of the Supreme Court of India under Article 194 of the Constitution on July 26, 1991.

8. In order to ensure proper coordination between States, Article 263 makes provisions for the establishment of an inter-state Council. The duties of the Council shall be:

   (a) to enquire and advice in inter-state disputes.

   (b) to investigate and discuss matters of common interest.

   (c) to make recommendations for better coordination of policy and action.

Such a council shall be established by the President who shall define its organisation, nature and procedure.

It may be noted that Supreme court of India has power to decide inter-state disputes in exercise of its original jurisfiction but experience has shown that sometimes disputes of non-legal nature may arise between the states or centre and states where strict legal approach in the resolution of such disputes may not be desirable. For deciding such disputes and to ensure better goodwill and understanding mutual appreciation of problems of others, the provisions of the establishment of Council is a welcome step. The need for such a coordination often arises in the fields of agriculture forestry, irrigation education and public health etc. where the cooperation of state government is necessary. Therefore, unless there is some inter-government consultative forum such co-ordination is difficult. Hence the need for a inter-state council.

It is to be noted that State Reorganisation Act 1956 has set up five Zonal Councils for this purpose of proper co-ordination between states and between Centre and the States.

1. Northern Zone Council for Jammu and Kashmir, Punjab, Haryana, Rajasthan, Himachal Pradesh, Union Territory of Delhi and Chandigarh.

2. Central Zone Council for Uttar Pradesh and Madhya Pradesh.

3. Eastern Zone Council for Bihar, West Bengal and Orissa.

4. Western Zone Council for Gujarat, Goa, Maharashtra and Union Territories of Dadar and Nagar Haveli.

5. Southern Zone Council for Andhra Pradesh, Tamil Nadu, Karnataka, Kerala and Pondicherry.

Each Council consists of Home Minister of the Centre, Chief Ministers of the State and two other ministers nominated by the Governor of .the State concerned. Union Home Minister is the ex-officio Chairman. Each Council has advisers from Planning Commission and is aided by Chief Secretaries of the concerned States. These councils are designed to promote better cooperation and coordination between the States and the Union and the States.

Plain reading of Article 263 suggests that Council need not be a permanent body. It may be ad hoc body brought into existence for the purpose of dealing with any of the matters referred for its consideration. It may be noted that the creation of Inter-State Council would not oust the jurisdiction of the Supreme Court under Article 131 which invests the Court with the original jurisdiction in matters of dispute between states and between states and centre.

Separate Councils may be set up to deal with separate matters. Therefore, it has led to the establishment of the Central Council for Health in 1952 and The Central Council for Local Self-government in 1954. The purpose of these councils is to consider and recommend broad lines of policy in regard to all matters concerning Health and Local Self-Government including possible areas of cooperation between the states and the centre.

Co-ordination among States

Though a federal constitution involves the sovereignty of the units within their respective territorial limits it is not possible for them to remain in complete isolation from each other and the very exercise of internal sovereignty by the units require its recognition by the co-ordination of other units of the federation. This co-ordination between the States and the Centre is called co-operative federation.

Inter-State Council

Article 263 provides for the establishment of Inter-State Councils to effect co-ordination between the states. This inter-State Council is appointed by the President of India, if it appears to him that public interest would be reserved by its establishment. The inter-state council is generally charged with the duty of :

1. Inquiring into and advising upon disputes which may arise between states.
2. Investigating the discussing subjects in which some or all of the states of the Union and one or more of states have common interest.
3. Making recommendation on any subject and for the better co-ordination of the policy and action with respect to that subject.

It consists of all Chief Ministers with the Prime Minister as its Chairman. These councils have been established for the promotion of co-operation and for making efforts to solve common problems of the member states. They are to encourage Inter State (operation for successful implementation of development projects and also act as advisory body in matter of common interest particularly in respect of economic and social planning.

Sarkaria Commission of Centre-State Relations has also strongly recommended for the establishment on an Inter-State Councils to effect co-ordination between states.

Financial Relations

It is indeed a hard fact that if the legislative and administrative authority of the constituent units, are to be maintained they must be autonomous financially. However, this principle of federation has not been fully implemented in any of the existing federations of the world. In India the scheme of distribution of sources of revenue between the centre and the states is based on the scheme laid down in the Government of India Act 1935.

Framers of Constitution desired that the scheme of financial relation be flexible and adaptable to varying needs and renewable periodically in the light of the experience of central resources, the states needs, and available data. For this they recommended for the appointment of Finance Commission under article 280. The Constitution of India thus introduces a unique element of flexibility while tackling the problems of distribution of public revenues. "No other federal constitution makes such elaborate provision as the constitution of India has respect to the relationship between the Union and the states in the financial field. In fact by providing for the establishment of financial commission for the purpose of allocation and readjusting the receipts from certain sources, the Constitution has made an original contribution in this extremely complicated aspect of Federal relationship" Prof M.V. Pulse.

Taxation only by Authority of Law

Article 265 says that no tax can be levied or collected except by authority of law. No tax can be imposed by an executive order. Law imposing tax must be valid law. (Article 276 (2) 285 etc.) It applies only in respect of taxes not in respect of fees, service rendered etc.

Double Taxation not Prohibited under Article 265 : There is nothing in Article 265 which prohibits the legislature to impose a tax twice on a thing.

Distribution of Revenue between the Union and the States: Article 268 provides the scheme of the distribution of revenue between the Union and the States. The States possess exclusive jurisdiction over taxes enumerated in the State list. The Union is entitled to the proceeds of the taxes in the Union list. The Concurrent list includes not taxes, however, it is to be noted that while the proceeds of the taxes within the State lists are entirely retained by the States proceeds of some of the taxes in the Union list may be allowed wholly or partially to the states. The constitution mentions following categories of the Union taxes which are wholly or partially assigned to the state.

Duties Levied by the Union but Collected and Appropriated by the States : According to the Article 268 stamps duties and duties of excise on medicinal and toilet preparations mentioned in the Union list shall be levied by the Central Government. These are collected by the States within which such duties are leviable. The proceeds are assigned to the States.

Taxes Levied and Collected by the Union and Assign to the States: According to the Article 269 the following duties and taxes are levied and collected by the Union but the net proceeds are distributed among the States in such a manner as prescribed by the Parliament by Law.

(a) duties in respect of succession to property other than agricultural land.

(b) estate duty in respect of property other than agricultural land.

(c) terminal taxes on goods or passenger carried by railway, air and sea.

(d) taxes on railway fares and freights.

(e) taxes other than stamp duties on transactions in stock exchanges and future markets.

(f) taxes on the sale or purchase of the newspapers and advertisements published therein.

(g) taxes on the sale or purchase of goods in the course of inter-state commerce and trade.

Taxes Levied and Collected by the Union but Distributed between the Union and States : According to Article 270, taxes on income other than agriculture income and corporation tax shall be levied and collected by the Union and is distributed between the Union and the States.

Taxes Levied and Collected by the Union may be Distributed between the Union and States : Article 272, provides that the Union duties excise other than those on medicinal and toilet preparations as mentioned in the Union list are levied and collected by the Union. But Parliament by law also provide its distribution between Union and States.

Taxes for the Purposes of Union : Article 271 provides that if Parliament at any time increase any of the duties or taxes mentioned in Article 269, 270 by imposing a surcharge the whole proceeds of any such surcharge shall form part of the consolidated fund of India.

Grants in Aid : The Constitution provides for three kinds of grants-in-aid to the states from the Union resources. Under Article 273 grants-in-aid to Assam, Bihar, West Bengal in lieu of export duty on the Jute products for ten years from the date of commencement of out Constitution.

(i) Article 275 Parliament by law can provide to those states as social grants which undertakes schemes of the developments for the welfare of SC/ST.

(ii) Under Article 282 without passing laws for purposes like Hospitals and Schools.

Taxes for the Purpose of States : Article of 276, 277 are saving provisions. These provisions save the authority of the state to levy taxes, on subjects, now forming part of the Union list, immediately before the commencement of the Constitution. Thus taxes which are being levied by a state or a municipality or other local authority, notwithstanding that those taxes are mentioned in the Union list continue to be levied by those authorities until Parliament by law makes contrary provisions. Article 276 empowers the states to impose taxes on professions, trades, calling and employment for the benefit of the state or any local authority. But the provision of Article 277 does not extend to taxes levied under a law passed after the constitution came into force.

Restrictions of Taxing Power of States

On the Sale or Purchase of Goods : The States like the Union, has power to levy tax on the sale and purchase of goods, other than newspapers Art. 286, however, imposes the following restrictions on the state's power to impose tax on goods.

(i) Sale or Purchase of goods which takes place outside the State : Article 286 (1) (b) prohibits a state to impose a tax on the sale or purchase of goods which takes place outside the state.

(ii) Sale or Purchase of goods in the course of Import-Export : Article 286 (i) (b) prohibits the States to impose a tax on the sale or purchase of goods which takes place in the course of import of goods in to or export of the goods out of the territory of India. Parliament is empowered to lay down the principle for determining when a sale or purchase takes place in the course of import into or export from India.

(iii) Sale or Purchase in the course of inter-state trade or commerce : A State can't impose a tax on the sale or purchase of goods which takes place in the course of inter-state trade and commerce. Constitutional sixth amendment now vests exclusive power in the Parliament to impose tax in this regard.

(iv) Goods of Special Importance in the inter-state trade or commerce : Article 286 (3) prohibits a state to impose a tax on sale and purchase of goods declared by Parliament's law "Special Importance" to inter-state trade and commerce. Section 14 of the Central Sales Tax Act, 1956, specifies a number of goods of special importance.

(v) Tax on the sale or purchase of goods in the course of inter-state trade or commerce specified in sub-clause (b) (c) (d) of clause 29 of Article 366: 46th Amendements of Indian constitution 1982, has amended clause (3) of Article 286 which enables the Parliament to impose restriction in this regard. A state law can't impose a tax on (a) the transfer of goods involved in the execution of a works contract, (b) the delivery of goods or hire-purchase on any system of payments in instalments (c) the transfer of the right to use any goods for any purpose for cash, deferred payment or other valuable consideration. Such transfer or delivery is deemed to be a sale or purchase of goods and therefore state laws imposing taxes on such sale or purchase of goods shall be subject to such restrictions or conditions as may be specified by Parliament by law (by amending the Central Sales Tax Act).

Finance Commission

Article 280 provides for the establishment of a Finance Commission. President of India is empowered to constitute Finance Commission at the expiration of every fifth year. Parliament may by law prescribe qualification for appointment of members of the commission and the manner in which they shall be selected.

In exercise of the power under Article 80 (i) Parliament has passed the Finance Act, 1951. It provides that the Chairman shall be selected from amongst persons who have had experience in public affairs or should possess knowledge and experience as a Judge of High Court or qualified to be for the same, have special knowledge of finance and accounts of government and have special knowledge of economics.

Duties of Finance Commission : To make recommendation to the President as to :

(a) the distribution between the Union and the State of the net proceeds of taxes which are to be or may be divided between them under the chapter and the allocation between the States of the respective shares of such proceeds.

(b) principle which should govern the grants-in-aid of the revenues of the states out of the Consolidated Funds of India.

(c) any other matters referred to the Commission by the President.

Article 281 provides that every recommendation by the commission has to be placed before the Parliament.

Inter-State Tax Immunities : In India like Canada the doctrine of mutual exemption from taxation is applied in a restricted sense. Its scope has been deemed by the constitutional provision. The rule of mutual exemption from taxation has been recognised by Article 285 and Article 289 of the Indian Constitution.

Article 285 Exemption of Union Property from State Taxation.

Article 287 prohibits a state from imposing tax on consumption of electricity supplied to the Government of India or utilized for construction, maintenance or operation of any railways unless Parliament by law otherwise provides. Article 289, Exemption of State property or income from Union Taxation.

Borrowing Power (Article 292-293) in Article 292 gives the Union unlimited power to borrow money from consolidated fund of India.

Article 293, permits a state, subject to any limits fixed by the state legislature, to borrow money within the territory of India. Article 293 provides that states can't borrow money from outside countries. Government of India may itself extend a loan to the State under law passed by Parliament. So long as such a loan or any part there of remains outstanding no fresh loan can be raised by the State without the consent of the central government. [Article 293 (4)].

Centre-State Relations

The main characteristics of a federal constitution is the distribution of powers, between the Central and the regional governments. But the scheme of the distribution of powers between the centre and state it appears that the framer have opted of a stronger Centre. The reason for this was obvious, Article 245, 246 contain the scheme of distribution of legislative powers. There are three lists, the Union State and Concurrent list. The residuary powers are vested in the Union. On a subject on the concurrent list both the Centre and the State have power to make laws, but in case of conflict between the two, the law made by the Centre shall in the end prevail upon the state laws. Under Articles 249,250,253 and 256, the Union Parliament is empowered to legislate on any matter in the state list.

To conclude we can say that our constitution makers have structured this relationship towards centralising manner which was justified at that moment. To study the efficacy of centre-state relationship and recommendations in this regard Sarkaria Commission was setup by the then Prime Minister Late (Mrs.) Indira Gandhi. Here we will discuss recommendations given by this commission. The Commission has submitted its report to the Government. It has rejected the demand for curtailing the powers of the centre saying that a strong centre is necessary to preserve the unity and integrity of the country. The Commission's view is that there is no need for drastic changes in the constitution. In its view the fundamental provision of the constitution have done reasonably well and withstood the stresses and strains of heterogeneous society.

In financial sphere also, the Commission has not suggested for major changes in the basic schemes of the constitution. It has, however, favoured amendments to provide for sharing of corporation tax and levy of consignment tax on advertisements and broadcasting.

The Commission has made out a strong case for inter-state councils under the Article 263. The recommendations of Sarkaria Commission are well balanced and in accordance with the spirit underlying the various provisions of the constitution of ensuring unity and integrity of the country.

10

District Administration

District administration is one of the most important characteristics of administrative system and has been one of its oldest institutions. Shri S.S. Khera had defined district administration as the total function of the Government the district." District administration as we know it today is a British creation. It dates back to the year 1792, when the East India Company had assumed diwani functions. It had appointed collectors to scrutinize the revenue collection and to preside in the court. Gradually district collector's authority and power increased and before long he became the pivot of the district administration, representing the provincial government in its totality. So the pattern of district administration in India is based on the tradition of age old territorial organisation.

Despite the change in government that took place in India after independence, the structure of district level administration has remained relatively unchanged. What is most surprising about this continuity is that the administrative system, which initially was established as an essential element of colonialism, remains almost intact. The only difference is that the old Indian Civil Service (ICS) has been replaced by the indigenous Indian Administrative Service (IAS).

With the rapid expansion of the scope and activities due to the acceptance of the concept of welfare state after independence, the emphasis in administration has shifted from police functions and revenue collection to planned development. Thus since independence, efforts have been made to adapt this office to the existence of planned development and social change in a democratic framework. The district administration is no longer the custodian of law and order and administration of justice alone but it also expected of it that it should strive for the development of the district and create situation where people have a feeling that they are living in a welfare state. S.S. Khera has explained the purpose, position and the role of the district administration as "the total management of public affairs within this Units. " The fact of matter is that the activities and role of the district administration cover a wide and varied range.

With the advent of Panchayati Raj, the district administration has undergone a complete change. There are now two sectors of administration in the district : State and Panchayati Raj. While the Panchayati Raj bodies are by and large, charged with developmental work, the state is left with the regulatory functions like revenue, law and order etc. So a district is the basic unit of local administration in India. Great importance is attached to its administration. Each district is under the charge of a District Magistrate who is known by different names in different states such as District Collectors, Deputy Commissioner, District Officer. But he is customarily referred to as the Collector.

Before the introduction of responsible government, the Collector or District Magistrate was for most of the people king or ruler in his district. His power and prestige suffered when elected representative of the people acquired control over the governments of the province, later called the State, because the legislators and office bearers of the party in power became rivals to approach the ministers and high officials of the State.

The district collector now is the symbol of the state government although he is primarily the head of revenue administration. The ultimate responsibility for maintaining law and order in the district also rests with him. There are various Heads of Department of the District who are responsible for the executing of various projects and/or actual administration of specific services.

The Functions

The functions of the district administration are:

(a) to maintain law and order in the district.

(b) to collect and assess the taxes.

(c) to implement the land legislation.

(d) to take up development work.

(e) to ensure that justice shall be done and that rule of law shall prevail.

(f) to take immediate actions in case of natural calamity, disaster, famine etc., and

(g) to exercise miscellaneous functions on behalf of the State Government.

The two operationally significant forces dominating district executive administration in our country could unmistakably be identified as the district officer, on the one hand and, various district heads of the state government's executive departments like PWD, irrigation, agriculture, animal husbandry, cooperatives, education, forests, police, prisons, excise, taxation, industries, fisheries, social welfare, public health, engineering, medical and health, etc., on the other. Both are forces to be reckoned with. The former is the chief representative of the State government in the district and has variously been described as "Annadata", "Maa-bap" 'representative and agent of government, 'general manager of all government activities', 'eyes and ears, and sometimes arms, of the government', 'the kingpin of administration', 'the Keystone of arch of district administration', 'the Captain and sometimes 'non-playing of the team', 'the first citizen in the district', 'the supreme head of the district administration' and more recently and in more benevolent terms like friend, philosopher and guide, 'advisor, educator and helpers', 'the fulerum of grassroot democracy 'the main spring of development', and the director of the Rath of Lord Jaganath (the Rath of Panchayati Raj).

The district officer is supposed to play the leadership role in district administration as he is the leader of all the department's other than judiciary at district level. Besides, the district level officers have their own departmental divisional, or regional level officers and heads of the departments who too exercise supervision and control over them. This clearly underscores the fact that the State Government department's district level officers are subject to a duality of control of the district level officer and the other one of their departmental superiors.

The powers and functions or duties of the District Collectors are manifold, but the Revenue function is oldest and perhaps one of the most important one. Presently in most of the States, the Deputy Commissioner continues to be the ultimate head of revenue. His responsibilities toward revenue administration are given below:

Revenue Administration

Under various Revenue and Land Reforms act, the role of District Collector is of a great importance. As Collector he is responsible for the collection of revenue and he hears appeals in revenue cases against the decision of tehsildars and other subordinate collectors. He functions as Commissioner under certain scheme under which he exercises the Revisional powers in cases of allotment made to the landless and eligible persons. He ensures collection of land revenue. He reports to the government any damages to crops due to natural calamities and sends remission and suspension statement of land revenue to the Government. In case of calamities he has to ensure prompt supply of relief (including taccavi loans wherever possible). He ensures submission of correct agricultural statistical data to the state government for onward transmission to the government of India, thereby enabling Central and State Governments to have a stock about likely output of food grains. He is responsible to keep the land records correct and upto date yearly for which he is supposed to inspect subordinate offices personally or through other revenue officers. He is supposed to ensure proper compliance of rules regarding rehabilitation of oustees by his subordinate Revenue Officers in letter and spirit. He is responsible to check all encroachments on government lands and in private lands along side the motorable roads. As collector, he has to safeguard the interests of right holders of natural waters and to prevent people interfering with settled rights of irrigation in Revenue Estates. He has to keep close watch over agricultural land being converted into non-agricultural public purposes unless otherwise warranted. The collector when at the Headquarters has to verify the District Treasury balance in person and sign the account to be rendered to the A.G. He has to ensure that deposit registers are kept according to prescribed rule and that all necessary entries are made indicated without failing at the time of the transaction. He has to satisfy himself by periodical examination that the actual stock of cash, opium stamps and securities is kept under joint lock and key and corresponds with the book balance.

The Important Unit of District Administration

- The Judiciary
- The Police
- Revenue administration including the S.D.O. and tehsildar
- Public Health
- District Education Officers
- Publicity Officer and organisation and management of Co-operative Societies.
- Officers of Local Bodies like the Executive Officer D.D.O., etc.

District Collector no longer devotes major part of his attention to land revenue since the acceptance of the recommendation of M.T. Raju Committee in 1967. An IAS officer is now appointed under his control to look after the revenue administration. However, his responsibility to the government through the board of revenue remains intact. Under the Raju Committee report, however, his direct responsibility which was formerly confined to regulatory departments has been replaced by that of development departments.

District Collector's Role

The functions of the collector or Deputy Commissioner may be summarised as:

1. Land Revenue
2. Magisterial
3. Development
4. General Administration
5. Emergency
6. *Miscellaneous :* such as small saving campaigns, visits of VIPs, interviewing people, publicity and public relations, attending meetings and conferences and any other work entrusted by the Government.
7. *As Returning Officer:* The Collector is the Returning Officer for elections to Parliamentary and Vidhan Sabha and has the responsibility for co-ordination of the election work on the district level.
8. *As District Census Officer :* As the district Census Officer, the Collector is responsible for conducting of census operations once in ten years.

In addition to the above, he continues to perform other multifarious duties. It is perhaps not possible to compile a totally complete list of the duties, functions and activities of the Collector.

In fact, function not specifically allotted to any officer by any department but which none the less are required to be performed at the district level, devolve naturally on the collector. He has to collect information in regard to matters including parliamentary questions concerning this district. To the above list may be, added the following functions:

1. Work relating to Civil defence.
2. Responsibilities in the field of agricultural production.
3. Collection of loans, donations and subscriptions.
4. Role as the public relations officer of the Government.
5. Responsibilities in the field of municipal administration.
6. A natural leader in an emergency such as floods, famine, earthquake internal and external aggression etc.
7. Liaison with military authorities and welfare of members of the armed forces-both serving and retired.

As for the role of the collector as the District Development Office, his most noteworthy function is that of a co-ordinator. No doubt he has been vested with certain independent functional and financial powers in regard to certain programmes of development but these are not in themselves very important and could well have been discharged by any other senior officer subordinate to the collector. But as a coordinator he alone can function effectively, in spite of having no direct administrative control over district level officers of various departments because by traditions and standing his place as a leader of the district team is accepted by all in natural course. Need for coordination both vertical and horizontal, has become all the more important in the context of Panchayati Raj. Panchayati Raj as a system was indeed a change of revolutionary character in our administrative system.

For the first time in our history a hierarchical system of local government was introduced at the village, block and the district levels which was not only charged with the task of providing certain welfare services and amenities but also with a wide range of extension services, which elsewhere are normally operated directly by technical departments or universities. With the introduction of Panchayati Raj the work load of the collector in respect of the development programmes was no doubt reduced because of the transfer of many these programmes to Panchayati Raj bodies. However, his responsibility as a co-ordinator has increased. The role of the District Officer as a co-ordinator, in the circumstances, demands on the incumbent's personality. Some District Officers have been extremely successful in carrying the technical officers with them but some, on the other hand, fell out with the technical officers. It is necessary that District Officer who is an officer of sufficient maturity and experience, to command respect of the technical officers. The District Officer in his relationship with technical officers is first among equals. He should therefore, be very restrained and tactful in his relationship with technical officers who are generally sensitive in their dealings with the District Officer (DO).

The technical officers have the feeling that they stand to gain by their co-operation with the District Officer. There may be situations when young and inexperienced DOs have to deal with very senior and experienced technical heads. The DO is the highest functionary of the state government i.e. the district and the effectiveness of the state government depends very much on the leadership and respect which DO is able to command from his fellow officers. It is in this context that the government's policy regarding the choice and posting of DO assumes importance. However, this sensitive issue does not get attention it deserves. The present day arrangement of having Deputy Commissioner with only four or five years service has ruined district administration. This is quite the opposite of the old ICS officers of British days when one could find DCs with more than 20 years service. The West Bengal Committee on Administrative Reforms has also recommended that DCs must be IAS officers of at least 10 years service.

Deputy Commissioner plays an important role as an intermediary between the people and the government and also between the departments. He has to keep himself informed about the happening in the district right from the village level upwards. A large number of people belonging to different sections of the community meet him everyday with their difficulties and grievances through personal contacts, petitions, field visits and meetings.

The collector heads the public distribution system and is directly responsible for the distribution of controlled and essential commodities. He grants wholesale licenses for trading in food grains and other essential commodities. He is the head of the rationing system in the district and expected to control black-marketing and ensure timely and equitable distribution of essential and controlled commodities. In the days of scarcity, availability of wheat, sugar, cooking oil, cement, etc. affect the people most and the success and reputation of the collector depends very much on how successfully he is able to supervise the distribution of these essential commodities. It is the public distribution system. Such vigil is necessary to keep the public distribution system responsive to the needs of the people.

All this obviously entails and enormous amount of work for the District Collector. The position of the collector is under strain. An effort was made in 1948-49 by the Bombay Committee on Reorganization of district Revenue Offices to analyse the collector's load and the analysis found that there is certainly too much burden and heavy pressure on the work load of District Collector. Similarly, the Madras District Revenue Administration Enquiry Committee (1955) analysed the work load of the collector that collector has to work from early morning till late at night, even to cope with his normal work. The collector is thus an over-worked official. Inevitably some of the work remains neglected and some only superficially attended to. It is, therefore, in the interest of the efficiency of this office that he be provided relief by:

1. Reducing the size of the district;

2. Relieving him some of his work and living him adequate staff facilities;
3. Separation of development functions;
4. Reducing the number of committees over which he has to present to preside.
5. Doing away with time wasting protocol duties which he has at present to perform.

Arrangements, therefore, must be devised to afford him relief within the framework of the existing size of the district. The Statesmen to have taken home this point and have adopted measures without disturbing the boundaries of district. In the first place, the gradual implementation by states of the constitutional provision urging separation of judiciary from the executive has been relieving the Collector of what is essentially judicial case work. Secondly, consequent upon the emergence of Panchayati Raj development work in the district has been transferred to the popularly elected three tier system, which has to this extent, reduced the collector's direct involvement. Maharashtra and Gujarat have each separated the Collector from development work by putting the latter under the charge of a Chief Executive Officer/ District Development Officer who is a full time functionary drawn from the Indian Administrative Service. And lastly states have adopted definite measures to provide him relief although the precise arrangement has varied from state to state.

An Agent of Change

Traditionally the governmental attitude towards the role of the district officer is that he is ultimately responsible for everything that occurs in his district. However, the thrust of the government since independence has shifted from law and order to developmental activities. In actual practice the district officer is expected to take the lead in bringing about social and economic change.

Economic development is measured by increasing production in both the agricultural and industrial sectors. There are a number of factors related to increased productivity, including extension of electric power, better roads, increased irrigational facilities as well as availability of fertilisers. An important element in economic development is availability of credit for rural population. With nationalization the Government has put pressure on bankers to open branches in rural areas. These branches are extending credit to small farmers for all kinds of agricultural improvements.

With the adoption of a constitution that contains dealing with social welfare, both the federal and state governments have pledged themselves to a programme of social and economic change. This pledge has been translated into programmes of redistribution of land to landless, housing for houseless, education for all, medical assistance to the poor, and protecting the civil and political rights of all minority groups, From the perspective of the state and federal governments, it is the district officer who is responsible for implementation of all programmes of economic and social change.

It is apparent that significant shifts have taken place in the role of the district officer from colonial time to the present. Much of the power formerly associated with this position has declined. Whereas a major addition to the role has been the responsibility for economic and social development.

In most cases while district officers recognised development as a major goal, they failed to carry it out effectively because of their preoccupation with maintenance of law and order. There are a number of reasons for their failure—the lack of commitment being the most important. Other obstacles are short tenure in district, the ad hoc nature of the office, and individual differences in ability and motivation. The red tape and political interference has eroded the spirit of the development programmes and hamper the people's progress as well as poses big threat for effectively functioning of district administration. Now a days what we have noticed that there is too much interference by the local politicians in the day to day administration at the district level, making District Officer ineffective and diverting his attention from development programmes. If the government is really interested in development of the rural people, it should check this undesirable political interference in the day to day administration. Our political structure encourages participation of politicians in carrying out social work. This practice prevents administrators from playing an independent role.

Lately, two patterns of district administration have emerged in India. One is the Maharashtra and Gujarat pattern whereby regulatory functions have completely been separated from development functions by an arrangement whereby (i) all district level officers of development departments have been placed under the administrative control of Zila Parishad: (ii) an IAS officer has been appointed as Chief Executive Officer of the Zila Parishad; and (iii) Administrative Control of all officials of Zila Parishad is exercised through him. The second pattern is the one that obtains in Tamil Nadu, Rajasthan and other States. In these States the Collector continues to look after both the regulatory functions and development functions. Both the patterns have worked fairly well though the pattern adopted by the State of Maharashtra and Gujarat has been giving greater opportunities to the elected representatives and has also helped in better co-ordination in development activities.

It has therefore, been suggested that at the district level the administration should be divided under three heads (i) Tax Collection (ii) Law and order and (iii) Development.

Integration and Decentralization

Recent changes have brought about an integrated approach to all developmental activities by bringing the departmental heads together in the State Development Board, with the Chief Secretary as its chairman and a similar board providing a link between the State and Panchayati Raj sectors with the collectors as its chairman at the district level. The system now fully weaves all agencies-state, district and panchayats concerned with developmental administration into an integrated one. This is further strengthened with the emergence of the collector as the state government personified. with powers of heads of development departments at district level. The system of Zila development board appears to be the logical outcome of democratic decentralization. With the enhanced powers and authority of the collector, the government has physically come down ad at district level and thus the delay in the decisions and instructions on the part of heads of departments is minimised to the possible extent. Secondly, the system seeks to keep district administration as a whole united by bringing both regulatory and development departments under the charge of the collector. This does not cause much strain, for he is relieved of direct responsibility of the non-development departments. This is an improvement on the scheme of bifurcation of regulatory and developmental activities in most of the States. Also, this arrangement is superior to the previous set-up when the district departments functioned in a rather disjoined and incoherent manner. Thirdly, the system is based on an assertion that the primary responsibility of the district elected council is deliberation and formulation of plans and schemes while the responsibility of the rural bureaucracy is their implementation and execution. Finally, by involving the revenue divisional officer in the actual implementation of plans, the integrated approach is extended to the level below the district also.

The district continues and shall continue to be the nodal point of the Indian administrative system where the policies and programmes of the government coverage and upbring directly upon the citizens. Unfortunately the public image of district administrator is currently at a low ebb partly because of the apathy of the administrators and partly due to the prevalence of absolute official procedures and practices.

It is not the case, however, that India has not given any attention to perform the district administration during its post independence period. There have been several expert reports on changes in the administrative structure, style, quality of personnel training e.g., Balwant Rai Mehta Report, ARC on District

Administration, Ashok Mehta Report, and other various committees and sub-committees which are appointed time to time to streamline the district administration. But despite all the experts reports and studies, we are exactly where we were in 1947 with regard to the chronic ailment of district administration. Unfortunately the district administration has become notorious for inefficiency, corruption, delay and lack of responsiveness to the needs of the members of the society. District administration under the leadership of District Officer will have to overcome these deficiencies before he is able to play his proper role in meeting new challenges and performing new tasks and functions. In any attempt of refashioning the administrative system, the reform of district administration should receive urgent attention. Apart from the structural and procedural reforms, the utmost importance should be given to the attitudinal reforms. There appears to be a strong need for attitudinal training to the district officers.

11

Municipal Bodies

The traditional form of urban local government for large cities has been the Municipal Corporation, the chief characteristics of which being the dichotomy between the deliberative and the executive wings. This model of Municipal Corporation has come in for a lot of criticism, the main being that it is a source of conflict between the deliberative and the executive wing and that such a municipal structure does not permit an effective control to be exercised by the representative of the people. The existence of an irresponsible chief executive affects the democratic principles as the chief executive is a salaried official. Hence, there was persistent demand for reforms.

The Indian Institute of Public Administration (IIPA) (1971) examined the various alternatives to municipal structural reforms in India, viz-a-viz, proposal for model legislation for Municipal Corporation. This was done on persistent demand made in the various sessions of the All India Council of Mayors and the Central Councils of Local Self-Government for structural reform of urban local bodies in the country. The IIPA considered several alternatives but could not come to any specific recommendations.

In 1980, the Union Ministry of works and housing appointed four Study Groups, one of which was for the purpose of examining the constitution. Powers and laws of urban local bodies and Municipal Corporation. It was a broad based Study Group consisting of elective elements at the Municipal level, the administrators having experience in the management of urban development and academic experts on the subjects. The terms of references were:

(a) To examine the organisational structure of various types of urban local authorities;

(b) To define the executive structure of Municipal Corporation in the context of suggestions regarding the Mayor-in-Council system;

(c) To consider the possibility of introducing uniform laws and regulations for different types of urban local bodies.

On the question of devising a suitable management structure, the recommendations of the Study Group revolved round the following basic ideas:

(i) Cities with a population of one million and over, and capital cities of the states to have the pattern of Mayor-in-Council.

(ii) Cities with population less than one million to have the pattern of Mayor-in-Standing Committee.

(iii) in the Mayor-in-Council form of Management Structure, there should be consultative committees for various subjects chaired by members of the mayoral cabinet.

(iv) In the Mayor-In-Standing Committee form of Management Structure there would be a graded committee system with the standing committee at the apex.

(v) Every corporation to have a statutory accounts committee on the lines of the Public Accounts Committee in the Parliament and State Legislatures, and it is to be chaired by a councillor drawn from the opposition group/party.

(vi) Large and medium sized municipalities to have the Chairman-in-Standing Committee form of Management Structure on the lines of the Mayor-in-Standing Committees.

(vii) Under the system of Mayor-in-Council, the Commissioner of the city corporation is to be appointed by the State Government in consultation with the mayor and withdrawn at his instance.

(viii) Municipal administration should be managed by a unified state wide municipal cadre of administrative and technical personnel.

The study Group's Arguments were in favour of the Mayor-in-Council form of management structure. Being an approximation (not exactly similar) to the cabinet form of government with which the country is, familiar, the Mayor-in-Council-form of Management Structure scores better over either strong mayor or council manager varieties. Moreover, as it gives enhanced importance to the political wing of the city government, this form of management is likely to attract talents better than those found so far in the service of city government.

The Mayor-in-Council system was also preferred by the All India Council of Mayors. No serious attempt was made in spite of the various recommendations at various quarter for structural change in the urban local bodies till 1980, when the West Bengal Legislative Assembly passed in May, 1930, the Calcutta Municipal Corporation Bill, 1980, adopting a Mayor-in-Council form of Municipal Government for the city of Calcutta. This system has very close resemblances to the cabinet system of government.

In this lesson, the various aspects of the Mayor-in-Council form of urban local Government, viz-a-viz., the Calcutta Municipal Corporation Act, 1980 would be discussed so as to familiarise the students with the main features of the Mayor-in-Council form of urban local Government.

Under the Calcutta Municipal Corporation Act, 1980, the three authorities of the Calcutta Municipal Corporation are:

(a) The Mayor

(b) The Mayor-in-Council and

(c) The Corporation (with its Borough Committees)

Mayor-in-Council

The Mayor-in-Council comprises of a Mayor to be elected by the councillors from amongst themselves and a deputy Mayor and not more than ten other elected members of the Corporation to be nominated by the Mayor (Sec. 8).

The deliberative wing is to be headed by a Chairman to be elected by the Councillors from amongst its elected members. Thus Mayor is no longer the head of the deliberative wing.

The executive powers of the Corporation which were earlier vested in the Municipal Commissioner are now to be exercised by the Mayor-in-Council (Sec. 32) which is to be collectively responsible to the Councillors (Sec. 8). The major instrument of ensuring the collective responsibility, however, is through the passing of a resolution by the Corporation in accordance with (Sec. 7) for removing the Mayor from office. The mains stress is, thus, on the accountability of the Mayor, even though a wide range of powers vests in Mayor-in-Council.

The Borough Committee members are expected to function under the general supervision and control of the Mayor-in-Council , however, the Committee-members as councillors would be free to discuss and raise any issue in the corporation.

The executive functionary would be the Mayor-in-Council , through the Commissioner, who would be answerable to the Corporation for its performance. The Corporation would have the power to remove the Mayor-in-Council by passing a no confidence resolution by a simple majority.

Under the present Act, the Mayor-in-Council enjoys a greater degree of influence on personnel matter even though the important positions are being manned by officers appointed by the State Government and enjoying its protection. The top echelons of the Corporation's organisation are statutory specified. The Municipal Commissioner, Joint Municipal Commissioner, the Controller of Municipal Finances and the Chief Municipal Auditor are to be appointed by the State Government in consultation with the Mayor-in-Council. Other officers are to be appointed by the Mayor-in-Council in consultation with the State Public Service Commission or by the State Government.

The Mayor-in-Council can be said to be the culmination of more than a century's old debate on the so-called dichotomy between administrative efficiency and popular representation. In terms of reconciling the earlier imbalances created due to the separation of the executive and the deliberative wings, with full executive powers vested in an individual appointed by the state government, the introduction of Mayor-in-Council system is a step forward in ensuring that power of decision-making in respect of implementing the various functions lies with the political executive, elected on the basis of popular representation.

Position of the Mayor

The Mayor as well as the Deputy Mayor is to be elected yearly from among the Councillors. There is provision for re-election too. Under the Act, Statutory position of these two officers has been provided in the Statutory Standing Committee and they have power of casting vote (for mayor only) in Committee decision.

The Mayor presides over the Mayor-in-Council (Sec. 34) and he is empowered to allocate the business to the member of the Council as he thinks fit (Sec. 33). He can remove from office any of the members in the council including the Deputy Mayor (Sec. 9) and he can fill any vacancy caused by the death, resignation and by removal of any member (Sec. 8). If a Mayor ceases to hold office, the newly elected Mayor constitutes his own Council (Sec. 9). The term of the Mayor and his Council is counterminus with the full term or the inexperienced term of the Corporation.

The Municipal Commissioner is to exercise his powers subject to the supervision and control of the Mayor (See. 38). The accountability of the Municipal Commissioner to the Mayor and not to the Mayor-in-Council is intended to strengthen his leadership as the Mayor is the Chief Executive and the leader of the team in the Mayor-in-Council.

Municipal Commissioner

Under Section 39 of the Act, it has been provided that the Municipal Commissioner shall be the principal executive officer of the Corporation, but subject to the supervision and control of the Mayor.

Sub-section (2) of Sec. 39 states that all officers and employees of the Corporation shall be subordinate to the Municipal Commissioner.

Section 14 of the 1980 Act provides that the State Government shall appoint the Municipal Commissioner from amongst persons who are or have been in the service of Government in consultation with the Mayor-in-Council if the State Government so directs, the Mayor-in-Council. If the State Government so directs, the Mayor-in-Council may appoint the Municipal Commissioner in consultation with the State Public Service Commission. The Act also provides that the Mayor-in-Council may with the prior approval of the State Government appoint a Municipal Commissioner from amongst officers who are or have been in the service of the Corporation. Thus there are three ways by which the Municipal Commissioner can be appointed.

Removal of the Municipal Commissioner : Section 14 (5) of the 1980 Act provides, "that in case of any such officer (which includes the Municipal Commissioner), if the Mayor-in-Council so decides, the State Government shall terminate the appointment of such officer."

The Act provides that the Municipal Secretary would be the custodian of all papers and documents connected with the proceedings of the Corporation and the Municipal Accounts Committee. Under the Act, it has also been provided that the Municipal Secretary would function under the supervision and control of the Municipal Commissioner.

As regards the financial powers of the Municipal Commissioner, the new Act (under Sec. 44) provides that the Municipal Commissioner is the sanctioning authority for amounts not exceeding five lakhs of rupees.

Under provision of Sec. 3-5 of the 1980 Act, it has been provided that the Municipal Commissioner would chair the meetings of the Municipal Streets Technical Committee and the Municipal Building Committee which involve besides other, representatives of the Calcutta Metropolitan Development Authority, Calcutta Police, Fire Services, etc. and sort out problems of coordination between various agencies involved in urban development work in Calcutta.

Basically the Mayor-in-Council system, as the Cabinet system of Government in the local body is described as a structural reform and is not an internal management reform. The major contribution of the Mayor-in-Council system of the city government will be to bring back political sanction to city administration according to Kalyan Biswas. The structural changes brought about under the Calcutta Municipal Corporation Act, 1980 represents a bold new experiment in the history of urban local Government in India. The extensive reorganisation of the political and administrative authority structure is expected to channelise substantially the institutional processes and behaviour for better performance of the Corporation.

According to M.K. Moitra, the major areas of critical concern, would be the Mayor-in-Council and Borough Committee relationship, the relationship between the Borough Committee and Borough Employees, viz-a-viz the Commissioner, the Mayor and the Mayor-in-Council.

The Authorities : All the Municipal Corporation Acts provide that Municipal Commissioner will be one of the municipal authorities. He is the chief executive functionary and heads of the executive wing of the Corporation. The special characteristics of the Municipal Corporation is the separation of the executive from the deliberative. The Commissioner is at the apex of the executive hierarchical pyramid and is responsible for carrying out all the policies passed by the deliberative wing of the Corporation.

The Municipal Commissioner is appointed by the Central Government in case of Delhi. The tenure of the Commissioner is specified in the Corporations Act. In case of Himachal Pradesh, the Commissioner holds office for a term of three years in the first instance. His term may be renewed for a term not exceeding three years. The Commissioner is usually appointed from amongst the Class I officer of the Government. His salary, allowances etc., are determined by the Government and is paid out of the Corporations funds. The Commissioner is granted leave of absence by the Government and whenever such a leave is granted to the Commissioner, the Government appoints another person to officiate as Commissioner in his place.

Sahib Singh and Swinder Singh in their book 'Local Government in India' state that the genesis of the office of Municipal Commissioner in India may be traced from the time the Municipal Corporation were first introduced in the presidency towns in the middle and the third quarter of the 19th century. The example of the Bombay pattern which differentiated between the executive and deliberative functions and placed the executive authority in the hands of a responsible officer of the State Government provided the basis for a similar experiment in many states under the controlling Acts. After the analysis of the various provisions of Municipal Corporation Acts and the practice being followed by the various states, they bring the following common facts about this institution:

1. The office of Municipal Commissioner is based on the philosophy of complete dichotomy between the legislative and executive functions.

2. The Commissioner is appointed by the State Government for a fixed term ranging from 3 to 5 years and he is the sole head of the executive wing.

3. He is a professional, high ranking senior administrator belonging to the IAS cadre.

4. The various statutes controlling the Corporations do not debar non-governmental personnel to be appointed as Commissioner. However, the practice is to appoint serving civil servants.

Functions of the Commissioner : The Commissioner is the head of the executive wing and has to execute the policies decided by the deliberative wing and its statutory committees. Besides enforcing the resolution of the Corporation he exercises control over the staff of the Corporation. Under the Corporation Act, many dutie, have been vested in the Commissioner. For this purpose, the Commissioner is assisted by subordinate officers and he is empowered to delegate any powers, duties or functions vested in him by the Act to any Municipal officer. He is responsible for the overall functioning of the various departments of the Corporation, like Health, Public Works, Roads and Buildings, etc. All the employees whether of the technical or general cadre are subordinate to him and he may prescribe duties and exercise control over the acts of all municipal employees as specified in the Act.

The Commissioner is vested with emergency powers too. The Acts provide that in case of an unforeseen event or natural calamity involving or likely to involve extensive damage to any property of the Corporation or danger to human life he can take such immediate action as he considers necessary and make a report forthwith to the Corporation of the action he has taken.

The functions which the Municipal Commissioner has to perform are specified in the Municipal Corporation Act. The HP Municipal Corporation Act prescribes the following functions which are to be performed by the Municipal Commissioner. Section 5 1 of the Act, lays down that save as otherwise provided in this

Act, the entire executive power for the purpose of carrying out the provisions of this Act and of any other Act for the time being in force which confers any power or imposes any duty on the Corporation, shall vest in the Commissioner who shall also:

1. Exercise all the powers and perform all the duties specifically conferred or imposed upon him under this Act or by any other laws for the time being in force;
2. Prescribe the duties of the exercise supervision and control over the Acts and proceedings of all officers and other corporation employees, and subject to any rules that may be made under Section 70, disposes of all questions relating to the service of the said officers and other employees and their pay, privileges, allowances and other conditions of service;
3. On the occurrence or threatened occurrence of any sudden accident or any unforeseen event or natural calamity involving or likely to involve extensive damages to any property of Corporation, or danger to human life, take such immediate action as he considers necessary and make a report forthwith to the Corporations of the action he has taken and the reasons for the same as also of the amount of cost, if any incurred or likely to be incurred in consequence of such action, which is not covered by a budget grant.

Section 52 of the Act empowers the Corporation to require Commissioner to produce documents and furnish returns, records estimates, statements, account or statistics concerning or connected with any matter pertaining to the administration of the Corporation's Act or the municipal government of the city. Every such requisition has to be complied with by the Commissioner without any unreasonable delay.

The Municipal Commissioner discharges all the duties that are specified in the Corporation Act and carries out the policies and resolutions, enunciated or adopted in the deliberative wing of the Corporation. The resolutions passed by the various Standing

Committees of the Corporation are also executed by the Municipal Commissioner.

The Commissioner participates in the deliberations of the deliberative wing and is often called upon to defend himself and his subordinates. He is to furnish all information required for deliberations. He has the right to speak but has no right to vote.

The powers of the execution of the work of the Corporation is conferred upon the Commissioner by the Act apart from this the Standing Committees may also delegate additional powers/ functions to the Commissioner. Thus, there are two sources of powers i.e., (i) those listed in the Act and (ii) those delegated by the Corporation/ Council and its standing committees.

Sources of Income for the Municipalities

Indirect Taxes : Octroi, terminal lay and tolls on roads and ferries etc. - ,

Direct Taxes : Tax on houses and lands, duty on transfer of properties, haisiyat tax, tax on professions, and trades, pilgrime tax, bazar tax and tax on dogs etc.

Service Levy: These are for the specific service discharged by the municipality and include water, light, conservancy tax etc.

Government grants, miscellaneous receipts, fines etc.

Financial Powers of the Municipal Commissioner : Important financial duties are also performed by the Commissioner. Some of the functions having financial implications are listed below:

1. The preparation of the budget estimate, i.e., the estimates of the income and expenditure of the Corporation.
2. The Commissioner can on behalf of the Corporation enter into contracts with other agencies, e.g. The Shimla Corporation Act empowers the Municipal Commissioner to enter into contracts on its behalf. But for

every contract involving an expenditure not exceeding twenty five thousand rupees or such higher amount, prior approval of the Corporation has to be obtained.

3. He is vested with powers to dispose of property of the Corporation in the manner prescribed.
4. The Municipal Commissioner can employ values to assist him in the valuation of land or building.
5. He can seize property vehicles and animals in case of non-payment of taxes.
6. He is empowered to prepare the assessment list of all lands and buildings in the city for the purpose of assessing tax to be levied by the Corporation. The Commissioner is authorised to amend the assessment list in the manner prescribed.
7. Power of remission or refund of tax also lies with the Commissioner in the manner prescribed.

Functions with Regard to the Procedure and Conduct of Corporations Meetings etc. : The Commissioner performs other important functions with regard to the Corporations meetings. The first meeting of the Corporation after the election is convened by the Municipal Commissioner. In case of Shimla Municipal Corporation, the first meeting, however, is convened by the Divisional Commissioner. After the elections and till the Corporation is constituted, the Commissioner exercises all powers and duties conferred and imposed upon the Corporation. For the meetings of the Corporation, the Commissioner prepares a list of all the questions admitted and circulates the same to the Councillors of the Corporation.

The Commissioner is the member of various Standing Committees and ad hoc committees and participates in its deliberation.

The Mayor is the head of the Deliberative wing and the Commissioner is the head of the Executive wing. The institutional roles of the Mayor and the Commissioner are distinctively different. The Commissioner as a senior civil servant is expected to faithfully implement the provisions and the resolutions passed by the Council. His business is not only to see that the provisions the law are upheld but also to prevent unlawful acts. Sometime, the Mayor in conjunction with the Council can create hurdles and delay or thwart the execution of work.

The conflict between the Commissioner and the Mayor are not uncommon. Conflict of egos often occur and the Mayor considers himself a representative of the people is often a shrewd politician but the Commissioner considers him a layman in administrative matters on account of his possessing professional expertise and wide administrative experience.

For the smooth working of the Corporation it is essential that the two act in unison and with mutual understanding. The Mayor heads the deliberative wing which performs the policy making functions and the Commissioner heads the executive wing and is responsible for the execution of policy. The employees of the Corporation are subordinate to him and he cannot allow his subordinates to direct their loyalties towards members of the deliberative wing and ignore the directions given or the administration corrective applied by him. The Mayor and the Councillors have their own ways of influencing, interfering the browbeating the subordinates. In such situations, the Municipal Commissioner has to act with lots of tact and patience. He cannot annoy the Mayor and the Councillors, if he does this at his risk as the Commissioner can be removed from the Corporation, if the deliberative wing passes a resolution to this effect. The Government then have no alternative but to recall the Commissioner and appoint another in his place.

Urban Bodies Consists of :

- Municipal Corporation
- Municipal Council or Board
- Small Town Committees

- Notified Area Committees
- Cantonment Boards

Except the last viz. the Cantonment Boards, all other local bodies are subject to the State Legislation with the result that local bodies in different States have a difference with regard to organisation, powers, functions and resources.

Commissioner and the Councillor

The relationship between the Commissioner and the Councillor is very delicate. The Commissioner is appointed by the State Government. He exercise powers and performs the duties conferred or imposed upon him by the Act. However, the Corporation, viz-a-viz, the Councillors wield control over him. The Government would have to recall a Commissioner at a special meeting of the Corporation a resolution is passed by a majority of not less than two-thirds of the total number of members. The Councillor has to strike a very delicate balance with Councillors. The Councillors are bound to interfere in the day-to-day working of the Corporation and may brow beat a Commissioner into taking wrong decision which would serve the Councillors, vested interest. This makes the job of the Commissioner very difficult. Tremendous tact and patience is required on the part of the Commissioner in carrying out the multifarious activities required of him and keeping the councillors satisfied amidst various conflicting interests.

Commissioner and the Standing Committees

The Commissioner as the chief executive of the Corporation has very close relationship with the Standing Committees. The Standing Committees which is primarily an operationally oriented body often finds the Commissioner standing in its way. The Commissioner armed as he is with vast administrative experience and disinclined to permit rash decisions is considered as an inhibiting factor in the functioning of the Standing Committees. Inevitably, therefore, the relationship between the Commissioner and the Standing Committee is one of the perpetual conflict and experience has shown that the relationship is far from harmonious.

The Commissioner is the pivot of the Corporation's activity holding a tremendously big charge and performing multifarious duties. He not only operationalises the many resolutions of the Corporation and its Standing Committees but also help the deliberative wing in chalking out new policies. Being the executive heads of the Corporation, he controls the subordinate staff and has to maintain discipline and efficiency among the staff so that the numerous duties of the Corporation is carried out effectively.

The Commissioner has to be a person of great tact and experience and in the day-to-day working of the Commissioner, he is subject to lot of pressure from various quarters especially from the Councillors by whom he can be removed if a resolution is passed by a majority vote as prescribed in the Corporations Act. The role of the Commissioner is vitally important in the civic body and needless to say, the success of the Corporation depends on the functioning of the Commissioner.

Committee System

In Urban areas, municipal bodies perform vital civic functions. The rapid pace of urbanisation with its growing population, increasing standards of living and rising expectations have increased the demand for more and better civic amenities. Not only are the demands on municipal administration growing, but they also require assistance and counsel in diverse fields with expertise in various arena of its activity. The Municipal Council comprising of elected people's representative is too large a body to meet often to transact the various functions listed in the Corporation's Act. Some matters are very urgent and have to be transacted without much delay and on a more continual basis, in such situations, the Standing Committees are called upon to perform the functions and matters of policy etc., only are put before the council.

Almost all the Municipal Corporation, Committee's Act make it obligatory on the part of the municipal bodies to set up certain committees. The Committees mentioned in the Act of the municipal body the Constitution of which is compulsory is known as

Statutory Committees. Apart from the statutory committee most of the Acts give powers to the Corporation to constitute special ad hoc committee.

Statutory Committees

The Statutory Committees are those which are constituted in accordance with the provisions of the Act. The composition, size, term functions and powers of these are specified in the Act. e.g., the Shimla Municipal Corporation Act provides for a Finance and Contract Committee. The Delhi Municipal Corporation Act provides for a Standing Committee and Committees in respect of public utility services like sewage disposal committee, education committee and rural committee. The Standing Committee according to the Delhi Municipal Corporation Act shall consist of fourteen members who shall be elected by the Councillors and elder men from among themselves at the first meeting of the Corporation after each general election or as soon as possible at any other meeting subsequent there to [Sec. 54(1)]. Other aspects of the Standing Committee i.e., its structure, powers, functions the role and powers, of the Chairman and the Deputy Chairman etc., all have been specified in the Act. Similarly, in Uttar Pradesh, Maha Palika Adhiniyam, 1959 makes provision for two Statutory Committees, i,e., an Executive Committee and a Development Committee. These have been examples of a few Statutory Committees.

The composition on the Statutory Committees vary from Corporation to Corporation. The term of the Committee also vary ranging from one year to three years. The Municipal Corporation of Shimla's Standing Committee consists of the Mayor, the Commissioner and such manner of elected members as may be decided by the Corporation. The Mayor and the Commissioner are the ex-officio Chairman and ex-officio Commissioner of the Committee respectively.

As regards the functions, the Standing Committees act as the Executive Committee of the Corporation. It exercises such powers and perform such function as are conferred upon it by the statute

The Standing Committee of the Delhi Municipal Corporation approves the form in which the budget of the Delhi Corporation is to be prepared and also recommends the budget to the Councils for approval. It is also empowered to reduce the amount of the budget grant or transfer any amount from one head to another in the budget. It grants leave of absence to the Municipal Commissioner. It makes appointment of certain categories of employees of the Corporation. It has access to all Municipal records, accounts and correspondence relating to the Corporation's work.

The various Corporation/Municipality acts of the different States provides for the constitution of non-statutory committees too. Non-statutory committees are those committees which are constituted by the council at its discretion. The various aspect of the non-statutory committee i.e., its composition, size, terms, functions and powers etc., determined by the Council. Ad hoc Committees are committees constituted for a specific purpose. The tenure of Ad hoc Committees may be fixed or may not be fixed. Special Committees are those committees which are constituted for some special purpose, its time limit i.e., its tenure ending when the functions is over. Its powers, functions, composition etc., are at the discretion of the Council which creates it. The Committees-Statutory non-statutory, ad hoc or special may also constitute sub-committees. Sub-committees are constituted when the work becomes unmanageable or heavy.

The Committees are a common feature of municipal administration. There are many advantages in having the committee system of municipal administration a reason which has given rise to multiplicity of committees. Along with the advantages, there are certain drawbacks too. The following paragraphs would bring about the two sides of the Committee system i.e. its advantage and its disadvantages.

Arguments in Favour of the Committee System : There are many arguments in favour of the Committee System in the Municipal Administration. Some of the merits of the Committee System are as follows:

1. Committees ensure that all business has been subjected to prior consideration. This process of predigestion, is of major importance in local government.
2. Committees share the complex range of municipal work dealing with the minute details of every service and enable the council to concentrate itself on policy matters.
3. Committees are constituted with councillors in accordance with their interest and specialisation. This leads to personal satisfaction to the members and allows them to make effective contribution to the work of the committee and to the civic committee as a whole.
4. The Council is unable to take all decision, one alternative is to transfer such decision-making power to an individual, to an official or elected member. But experience shows that wisdom of any one is open to doubt. It is here that the committees play important role.
5. The Committee enable powers to be shared.
6. At the Committee level the average councillor can get opportunity to participate effectively and thus can prove his worth and ability and thus make greater contribution to the locality.
7. Committees work in an informal atmosphere. Such an environment softens differentials in status and partisan opinion and at the same time officers nominated on the committee can intervene is discussion and offer advice.
8. The special knowledge of co-opted members of the Committee in beneficial.
9. The Committee system is a partnership of men and women of varied background and expertise in general matters because the members of the committee work in collaboration with the heads of the various departments.

10. The smaller size of committee make them more effective organs of deliberative wing for thoroughly discussing and understanding issue and problems.
11. The Committees relieve the Corporation/ Council of the work load, as large volume of decision on minor as well as major issues will otherwise be required to be taken to the Corporation/Council.
12. The Committee system ensures more effective control of the deliberative wing over the executive wing in matters of policy formulation and executive.
13. The use of committees generally permits matters to be discussed in privacy in an atmosphere where there can be greater possibilities of understanding amongst members of opposite groups with less fear of finding themselves politically committed, as it happens in the council's meetings.

Disadvantages of the Committee System : The Committee System has a number of disadvantage which tend to weaken the municipal administration. Some of the disadvantages of the Committee System are as follows:

1. More and more functions are being delegated to the Committees. Multiplicity of committees created problems for the various departments as they have not only to deal with the Corporation itself but have to make available their services to the various committees, thus increasing their work load and leading multiplicity and duplication of work. This impinges upon the effectiveness of the working of the Corporation/ Council as a whole.
2. When there is duplication or work, this leads to wastage of scarce resources and it is the citizen who has to bear all this in terms of poor services and higher taxes.
3. The position of the Municipal Commissioner is weakened considerably under the Committee system.

For each major department/work there is a correspon-ding committee and when the Committee has statutory powers, the department assumes as well becomes accountable to the respective committee. In such situations, the role of the Municipal Commissioner suffers a lot and he is not able to effectively coordinate the functioning of the executive wing of the Corporation.

4. With more and more functions and decision-making powers being delegated to the Committees, the role of the Municipal Corporation /Council has been reduced to a mere rectifying body and the meetings of the deliberative wing is becoming a mere formality in which the councillors do not show any keen interest as important decisions are mostly taken before there by the Committees.

5. Excessive use of Committee system have distorted the role of the deliberative wing as well as the executive wing than what was intended when these wings were separate. There is much intermingling of the work of these two wings resulting in conflicts. All this affects the proper functioning of the municipal body.

6. The Committee system demands too much of councillors time. The meetings of the committees are more frequent. When the members of the Committee get too much involved in the Committee's work, they tend to neglect their wards. The functions of the Corporation/Council's Councillor is that of projecting the problems and needs of the citizen in their respective wards and providing redressal of the grievances of the people. This vital function tends to be neglected when the councillors get involved in paperwork instead of field work. Maintaining contract with the people, the vital requisite to make any representative institution work democratically and responsibly suffers when the links with the people are severed.

The Committees and the Commissioner: The Commissioner is an appointee of the State Government (in case of Delhi it is the central government) and it is listed as one of the authorities of the Corporation. Similarly, the Statutory Committees are also listed as authorities of the Corporation. The Commissioner is the executive head of the Municipal Corporation. When the committees (which may be too many), thus creates the problem of power-sharing among the various committees and between the Committees and the Commissioner. The Committees do not allow the administrator to function effectively. The Committees come with direct contact with the municipal staff, have access to all papers and documents of the Corporation and in such cases the executive administrator, i.e., the Municipal Commissioner gets side tracked.

G.M. Allikarjanayya in a paper 'The Working of the Standing Committees' brings out the relationship and describes that the relationship between the Commissioner, and standing Committee is one of the perpetual conflict. The author states that the Standing Committees are primarily an operationally-oriented body, often finds the Commissioner standing in its way. The Commissioner armed as he is with vast administrative experience and disinclined to permit rash decision is considered as an inhibiting factor in the functioning of the Standing Committee.

The Committee System in local government is widely prevalent in India. The municipal bodies are rendering a wide range of services and the committees have become indispensable for administrative purpose. When the municipal body's membership is large, proper supervision as well as in-depth involvement of the municipal member is not possible. The number of services being performed by the municipal bodies has increased manifold and have become very complex. All these factors have necessitated the requirement for the committees. The Committees have been created for administrative convenience, the purpose of the committees make them more effective organs of deliberation. There are also many dysfunctional aspect of the Committee System. There is committee's fragmentation in municipal administration. There is often conflict between the Standing Committees and Municipal Commissioner and the role of the deliberative and the executive wings gets distorted. It also leads to politicisation of municipal staff. The meeting of the municipal bodies deliberative wing has been reduced to a mere formality etc. Thus, it is necessary that the committee system should be modelled in such a way that the working of the committee contribute towards the effectiveness and efficiency of the municipal administration.

12

Panchayati Raj

Panchayat in India have been the pulse beat of our democracy, the roots of the Republic since the ancient times. In the words of Sir Charles Metcalfe, "The village communities are little republics having nearly everything they want within themselves, and almost independent of any foreign relations. They seem to last where nothing else lasts. Dynasty after dynasty tumbles down revolution succeeds to revolution; but the village community remains the same."

The Panchayat served as the backbone of our democratic institutions around which the entire fabric of social and economic activity of the village rested. From Vedic times to the beginning of the British Rule these Panchayat looked after our villages and their requirements. With the advent of industrialisation, the village corporate life disintegrated. In the highly centralised British Rule the institution of Panchayat received a set back, though some efforts were made by the British to revive the centuries old rural institution.

Panchayati Raj in Ancient India

The subject of Local Self-Government in ancient India has both historical and practical importance. The story of Panchayat can be gathered from the numerous references with which Vedic literature is replete. A.S. Altekar has made a comprehensive study of early literature in this respect and in his book, "State and Government in ancient India brings out the various facts of Panchayats in India."

Local Government existed in India from time immemorial. There are indications in the early literature especially in the Vedas, in the Epics of Ramayana and Mahabharata, Upanishads and in the Jataka stories that there was a highly organised system of local government in ancient India. Kautilya's Arthasastra too gives a vivid picture of local government in the ancient times.

Altekar writes that since earliest times the village has been the pivot of administration in India. Villages were the real centres of social life and important units in the country's economy. They sustained the edifice of national culture, prosperity and administration.

The village government was usually carried under the supervision and direction of the village headman. In the Vedic literature he is referred to as the gramani. He figures frequently in the Jatakas. The Arthasastra attests to his important part in the administration, He was called *gramika* or grameyaka in northern India and *mununda* in the eastern Deccan in the early centuries of Christian era and *gramuki* or pattakila in Maharashtra, *gavunda* in Karnataka and *mahattaka* or mahantka in U.P. between 600 A.D. to 1200 A.D.

The headman had a very important role to play in the village administration. Defence of the village was one of the most important duty of the village headman. Collection of the government revenue, keeping records of rights and transfers of the village lands were other functions performed by him.

Village Assembly

The village Headman and other functionaries were guided in their work by the village public. All respectable householders of the village had an inherent right to become the members of the Primary Village Assembly. They were known as *mahattamas* in U.P., mahattaras in Maharashtra, *mahajanas* in Karnataka and *perumakkal* in Tamil country. The opinion of the village public was made known through the village elders who formed a kind of informal council. The village elders yielded power to set matters right if the village headman acted unreasonably or against the established customs. These village councils were known as the pancha-mandalis in Central India and gramajanapads in Bihar.

The village council or Panchayat consisting of the village elders performed many important functions. The settlement of the village disputes, imposing capital punishment upon the criminal was however left to higher authorities. The collection of land revenues was another responsibility fixed upon the village council. The ownership of the village waste lands were vested in the village Councils. In South India evidence has been found that shows that the village councils used to transact business as bankers as well. Organising works of public utility, providing relief in case of calamities like famines, construction, maintenance and repairs of irrigation tanks etc., was also the responsibility of the village council during the Chola period. Jatakas also mention about the village councils maintaining roads, providing drinking water, building public halls etc. The village council was also engaged in promoting the cultural interest of the village community.

Finances : The village council was entitled to spend a small percentage of the revenues collected in the village. Fines, donations, taxes and cesses etc., also were a sources of revenue.

Sub-committee : There are also indications in the early literature that the village administration work was carried out by sub-committees which consisted of village residents. The village residents got an opportunity to participate in their own affairs and thus the element of popular participation was there. Different sub-committees were constituted for carrying out different work.

Control over the Rural Local Bodies : Radhakumud Mookerji (Local Government in Ancient India, 1920) writing on the relations between the local and the central government points that the relations between the local and the central government have been systematically dealt with in the Arthashastra of Kautilya, in which has been well worked out the delimitation of the boundaries of the two administrative authorities. The province in Kaurava's system was made up of four divisions or districts each of which was placed under a *Sthanika*. Groups of five or ten villages were placed under the royal agent called *Gopa*. The duty of this agent seems to have been to supervise the working of the rural administrative machinery under the self-governing villages. The smallest village had about 100 families and the headman was known as *Adhyaksha,* the accountant as *Samkyuka,* the veterinary doctor as *Anikashta* and physician as *Chikitshak*. The Adhyaksha were under the Gopa and the Adhyaksha's responsibilities were defined very clearly.

Above the Gopa were the *Rajukas* at the district level. The Rajukas were responsible to survey land, settle land revenue. Vishayapati was the head of the district. In the urban centres, the city head was known as the Nagaradhyaksha.

Mookerji writes that the point of connection between the village and the central government was the taxation imposed upon the former by the latter. He writes that the extent of control exercised by the Central government over the village was determined by the necessity not merely of securing the revenue due from them but also maintaining a firm grip upon the sources of that revenue.

In spite of these controls and supervision especially in respect of revenue matters, the local bodies more or less wielded great independence and were more well knit bodies looking after the entire administration of the village. The relations between the Centre and the local bodies was smooth and healthy. Proper supervision was exercised by the higher officials and honest men ensured that the local bodies functioned properly.

Mughal Period

The Mughals had very little interest in the local governments and their interest was confined only to revenue and police. During the Mughal rule in India, the administration of the town was vested in an officer called *Kotwal*. The Kotwal was responsible for performing many municipal functions.

The Decline : According to S. Maheshwari, the impact of foreign invasion over India was disastrous for the survival and autonomy of the Panchayat. Gradually, towns developed as the centres of trade and politics and villages were cut off from the main stream of the social and political power. This process of decline and isolation was spread over several centuries.

British Period

Although local government flourished in India since time immemorial, the present form of local government in India is a British creation. When the Britishers came to India, Panchayat in most places were already dead as units of effective administration due to multifarious reasons. According to Dr. Kopardkar, the origin of the modern local self-government system owes much to Sir Josia Child who obtained a Charter from James II to set up a Corporation at Madras in 1642. The British regime did away with the indigenous foundations and the ancient local taxation system and new patterns were created.

S.R. Maheshwari divides the local government during the British rule into the following periods, each period characterised by a definite aim and purpose.

1687-1881 : Local government was viewed and utilised to collect central and provincial finances, and thus, to subserve imperial needs.

1882-1919 : Local government began to be viewed as self-government.

1920-1937 : Local government came within the jurisdiction of provinces and further, was transferred to popular control.

1938-1949 : Local government was in a state of repair and reconstruction.

The early years of British rule in India witnessed a highly centralised form of government during which the authority of the Panchayat was undermined. Important developments which took place during this period was the setting up of the Municipal Corporation in Madras in 1687, 1926, the Municipal Corporation was replaced by Mayor's court. In 1793, Municipal administration was established in three Presidency towns of Madras, Calcutta and Bombay. In 1842, the Bengal Act was passed.

The year 1870 is significant for local government in India as in 1870 Lord Mayo's famous resolution on decentralisation from the Centre to the provinces emphasised the desirability of associating Indians in Administration, and indicated the municipal government as the most promising field for this purpose. The resolution of 1870 was important not only in urban but also in rural areas.

Lord Ripon's Resolution : Lord Ripon has been regarded as the father of local self-government in modern India as Lord Ripon's Resolution of 18th May, 1882 laid the foundations of the system of local self-government as it exists today. The resolution of 1882 on Local self-government has been regarded as one of the greatest achievement of this Viceroyalty. The noteworthy features of 1882 Resolution of Lord Ripon is as follows:

1. The resolution laid down that at least two-third members of the municipalities be non-officials.
2. System of election-elected members and chairman.
3. The resolution viewed that the establishment of the local institution was necessary not only to provide civic facilities but also to create political awareness among the people of the country. It was to be an instrument of political and popular education.

4. Establishment of a new-work of rural bodies, a two tier system with district board and sub district boards based either upon the subdivision or the tehsil.

5. The district board was to act as the supervising and coordinating authority.

6. Taxes such as octroi house tax and professional tax were introduced and primary functions of construction, etc., were fixed.

The resolution of 1882 did not have the desired result and was significantly whittled by the provinces which enjoyed the freedom to interpret the resolution according to local conditions. The Royal Commission Decentralisation (1907) found that the developments of a quarter century since Ripon's Resolution were almost negligible.

The Government of India Act 1919 made local self-government a transferred subject and hence a responsibility of the popular ministry. The Act of 1935 established Provincial Autonomy and provided more opportunities for the development of the local institutions, but the village bodies, particularly remained weak and ineffective.

Post-independence Era

Recognising the importance of democratic institutions at the grass root level, the Indian Constitution laid down in Article 40 of Part IV of the Directive Principles of State Policy that the State shall take steps to organise Village Panchayats and endow them with such powers and authority as may be necessary to enable them to functions as units of self-government. The Panchayati Raj institutions, thus set up became a State subject under the Constitution and the State and the Union Territories were free to design the structure powers and functions of such bodies keeping in view their local situation.

The PRIs exist in almost all the States and UTs with considerable variation in structure, mode of elections etc. Presently, 195354, there are 2, 32,519 Grant Panchayat 4525 Block Panchayat Samities and 350 Zila Parishads in the country. The tenure of the elected bodies in these institutions varies from 3 to 5 years in different States. The hill States of Meghalaya, Nagaland, Mizoram and UT of Lakshadweep have no Panchayati Raj Institutions (PRIs) and the rural institutions are set up in accordance with the customs and traditions of the village.

The following events have been milestone in the development of Local-Self Government in India.

Balwantrai Mehta Committee

India with her history of thousand of years of civilisation is endowed of with glorious traditions. The institution of Panchayatas have been handed down from time immemorial and have been able to persist through the ages in spite of adverse political conditions. It has been able to survive the effects and changes of alien rule and many political uncertainties. Although local government, viz. Panchayat existed in India since the ancient times, in its present structure and style of functioning, it owes existence to the Team for the Study of Community Projects and National Extension Service. Also popularly known as the Balwantrai Mehta Committee after the name of its President, to whom goes the credit for the present system of rural local government in India.

In 1957, the Team for the Study of Community Projects and National Extension Services was appointed by Committee on Plan Projects in order to study and report on the Community Projects and National Extension Service. The Committee made a number of recommendations and envisaged a three tier system of rural local government i.e. Panchayat, Panchayat Samiti and Zila Parishad. Democratic decentralisation was the name given to this system Before this is discussed in detail later in this lesson, the Composition of the Committee and terms of reference are given.

Composition of the Committee

1.	Shri Balwantrai G. Mehta	Chairman
2.	Dr. S.D. Sharma Minister Madhya Pradesh	Member
3.	Thakur Phool Singh Deputy Minister, U.P.	Member
4.	Shri B.G. Rao (Formerly Chief Secretary) Govt. of Madhya Bahrat	Member
5.	G. Ramchandran (Coopted later on by the team)	Member

Terms of Reference : The terms of reference of the Committees were very wide and comprehensive. It was asked to study and report on the Community Projects and National Extension Service with a view to ensuring economy and efficiency generally and with specific reference to the following aspects:

1. The content of the programme and the priorities as assigned to different fields of activity within it.

2. The arrangements for the execution of programme with special reference to:

   (a) Intensification of activities in the sphere of agricultural production;

   (b) Co-ordination between

   (i) Different ministries/departments at the centre.

   (ii) The centre and the states.

   (iii) The different agencies with the Community Projects Administration and other State Government organisations and departments.

(c) The organisational structure and methods of work with a view to securing a greater speed in the despatch of business.

3. The assessment of the requirements of personnel for community projects and national extension service and examination of existing training facilities in order to meet the growing requirements of personnel for extending the coverage of the programme.

4. The assessment of the extent to which the movement has succeeded in utilizing local initiative and in creating institutions to ensure continuity in the process of improving economic and social conditions in rural areas.

5. The methods adopted for reporting upon the results attained by the community projects and national extension service.

6. Any other recommendation that the Team may like to make in order to ensure economy and efficiency in the working of the community projects and the national extensions service.

The Mehta Committee soon set to work and between 21 st February and 4th August, 1957, it visited 58 selected blocks in 13 states and also availed of the opportunity of discussions with persons belonging to different categories, directly or indirectly connected with the community development work. There were available reports and records on the working to the movement.

The recommendations and conclusion based on observations and studies of the team were sent to the State Government and later in September and first half of October, 1957, the team held discussion with the State Government's Report was then finalised and signed on November-24, 1957 with a short note of dissent by Shri, B.G. Rao. The report presented in three volumes was broadly accepted by the National Development Council and the National Development Council communicated the accepted recommendations of the Mehta Committee to the States for implementation in the middle of 1958 and action to be taken was left to the State Government.

Recommendations of the Committee : Balwantrai Committee in its report recommended a scheme of democratic decentralisation as a measure remedial to the failure of the community development programme. The main findings of the Committee were:

1. The community development and national extension service programme had failed to evoke popular initiative.

2. Local bodies at a level higher than the Panchayat had generated but little enthusiasm in the community development programme.

3. Even the Panchayat had not come into the field of community development in any significant way.

The Committee has observed in this respect So long as we do not discover or create representative and democratic institution which will supply the local interest, supervision and a care necessary to ensure the expenditure of money upon local objects confirms with the needs and wishes of the locality, invest it with adequate power and assign to it appropriate finances, we will never be able to evoke local interest and excite local initiative in the filed of development."

The Committee recommended decentralisation of responsibility and power to levels below the State and devolution of power to a body which when created will have the entire charge of all development work within its jurisdiction. Democratic decentralisation was the name given to the local government process and the concept of democratic decentralisation as envisaged by the Balwantrai Mehta Committee was essentially in rural context. The Committee felt that democratic decentralisation would evoke people's initiative and mobilise their voluntary and spontaneous participation and the report offered a blue print for Panchayati Raj which was to serve as the institutional framework of democratic decentralisation in rural India. Democratic Decentralisation envisaged by Balwantrai Mehta Committee is popularly known as 'Panchayati Raj (rechristened on the suggestion of Jawaharlal Nehru).

The Committee envisaged a three-tier system of rural local government, namely Village Panchayat at the village level, the Panchayat Samiti at the block level and the Zila Parishad at the district level.

The Panchayat

Balwantrai Committee suggested a three-tier scheme of democratic decentralisation with Panchayat at the base. The village Panchayat should be constituted on an elective basis. The Committee also suggested for the co-option of two women members and one member each from the scheduled tribes.

Functions : The Committee suggested the following compulsory functions for the Panchayati Raj viz-a-viz:

(i) Provision of water supply for domestic use

(ii) Sanitation

(iii) Maintenance of public streets, drains etc.

(iv) Lighting of the village streets

(v) Land management

(vi) Maintenance of records relating to cattle

(vii) Relief to distress

(viii) Maintenance of Panchayat roads, culverts, bridges etc.

(xi) Supervision of primary schools

(x) Welfare of backward classes and

(xi) Collection and maintenance of statistics

The Committee did not make a distinction between civic amenities and development functions. According to them 'development work' includes: agriculture, animal husbandry, cooperation, minor irrigation works, village industries, primary education, local communications, sanitation, health and medical relief, local amenities and similar subjects. The Village Panchayat was to act as the agent of the Panchayat Samiti in execution of any scheme of development or other activities. The Committee emphasized the desirability of using the Village Panchayat as an agency for the Collection of land revenue.

Finance : As regards the resources of the Village Panchayat the Committee suggested the following main resources:

1. Property or house tax.
2. Tax on markets, bazars etc.
3. Tax on carriages, carts, bicycles, boats and pack animals.
4. Octroi or terminal tax.
5. Conservancy tax.
6. Water rate.
7. Lighting.
8. Income from cattle ponds.
9. Fees to be charged for registration of animals sold within the local area.
10. Grants from the Panchayat Samiti.

The Committee was of the view that the resources of the Panchayat are necessarily inelastic and every effort should be made to assist them to add to them.

Panchayat Samiti

The intermediate tier in the Panchayati Raj system of rural local government in India is the Panchayat Samiti. The Balwant

Rai Committee suggested that the Panchayat Samiti should form the most important unit in the three-tier scheme which should have a jurisdiction co-extensive with a development block.

The Committee recommended that the members of the Panchayat Samiti should be indirectly elected by the village Panchayat and should include two women members and one member each from the scheduled castes and scheduled tribes as co-opted members (in case their population exceeds five percent of the total population). It further recommended that the number of seats equal to 10 percent of the number of elected seats may be filled by representatives of directors of co-operatives functioning within the block either by co-option or by election. The Panchayat Samiti should have an elective Chairman. Members of all the Panchayat in the block should be elected from amongst themselves of members of the Panchayat Samiti. The tenure of the Panchayat Samiti should be five years.

Functions : The Committee felt that the Panchayat Samiti would be the primary unit to deal with development activities as Panchayat would be too small to form a viable unit for the purpose. The Panchayat Samiti would act as the sole authority for all development programme which are of exclusive interest of the area and would cover agriculture, animal husbandry, cooperation minor irrigation, village industry, primary education etc.

Finances : Balwantrai Mehta Committee recommended the following sources of income to be assigned to the Panchayat Samiti:

1. A percentage of land revenue collected within the block area.
2. Cess on land revenue, water rate etc.
3. Tax on professions and trades.
4. Surcharge on duty on the transfer of immovable property.
5. Rents and profits accruing from property.

6. Tolls and leases of roads and bridges.
7. Pilgrim tax.
8. Primary education cess.
9. Proceeds from fairs and markets.
10. Grants from the Government.

The Committee recommended that the income from their own sources of the Panchayat Samiti could be further augmented by adequate grants-in-aid from the State Government conditionally or unconditionally or on a matching basis with due regard to economy.

Control Over the Panchayat Samiti : The Committee was of the view that Panchayat Samiti should function in freedom from interference by the Government and that it must not be cramped by too much control by the Government or Government agencies.

As regards guidance, the report stressed that the 'Panchayat Samiti will need guidance in technical as well as administrative matter; but this guidance should, under no circumstances, result in excessive regulation or control; nor should such guidance or advice be considered as interference.'

Zila Parishad

The third tier of the scheme of democratic decentralisation of the Balwantrai Committee is the Zila Parishad, and it constitute the apex in the Panchayati Raj system of rural local government. The Committee suggested the Zila Parishad at the district level with a view to ensuring necessary co-ordination between the Panchayat Samitis in the district, as the district continues to be the unit of administration and the unit of co-ordination of the functions of all departments functioning within the area (i.e. the district).

The Committee suggested that the Zila Parishad should consist of the Presidents of the Panchayat Samitis in the district, all the MLAs and MPs representing the district and district level officers. The Collector should act as the Chairman of the Zila Parishad and one of his officers should be its Secretary. The Committee also recommended that the Zila Parishad should have a Standing Committee for Finance and Services.

Functions of Zila Parishad : The Committee recommended the following functions of the Zila Parishad:

1. Examination and approval of the budget of the Panchayat Samiti.
2. Distribution of funds between the various blocks.
3. Co-ordination and consolidation of the block plans.
4. Channelising the demands of the Panchayat Samitis for funds for special purposes.
5. General supervision of the activities of the Panchayat Samiti.

The Committee had visualised the Zila Parishad mainly as a supervisory and co-ordinating body. To quote; "We do not contemplate that this Parishad will have executive functions; that ways lies danger to the initiative and therefore the effectiveness of the Panchayat Samitis in their early, Years".

Stimulated by the recommendations of the Study learn a number of States enacted legislation with regard to the rural local bodies on the pattern of the board outline suggested by the Team in Rajasthan and Andhra Pradesh were the pioneering States in bringing legislation for introduction of Panchayati Raj as early as October and November 1959 respectively. The State Governments have adopted different patterns of Panchayati Raj suitable to the local conditions and the PRI vary from State to State in size, number, terms of officer. The note worthy contribution of the Balwantrai Committee in the post-independence era is that Panchayat came into existence all over the country. The basic philosophy behind Balwantrai Mehta Committee's democratic decentralisation (Panchayati Raj) was to evoke people's participation, it had in mind decentralisation and democracy.

It was realised that Panchayati Raj Institutions have not followed in the India still. The recommendations of the Study Team for effective administrative decentralisation, democratic decentralisation of political and administrative powers have not taken place. Time and again it has been felt that these institutions must be strengthened and the appointment of the Ashok Mehta Committee in 1977 marked the second phase of Panchayati Raj in the post- independence era. To improve the functioning of Panchayati Raj, another Committee was set up by Janta Party Government.

Ashok Mehta Committee

The functioning of Panchayati Raj institutions in many States reveal that these institutions have been reduced to an extremely peripheral status. Efforts have been made time and again to revitalise and revive these age old institutions. When the Janata Government came into power at the Centre in 1977, a fresh effort was made to put some vigour and vitality in the Panchayati Raj system. The Ashok Mehta Committee was set up by the Janata Government in 1977 and it has marked a turning point in the concept and practice of Panchayati Raj.

The Committee made a detailed study of the PRIs and consulted a large number of experts and produced a very good report making certain revolutionary recommendations including statutory provision of assured financial resources to the PRI at the village, block and district level along with control of the governmental machinery to implement the programme. The Janata Government at the Centre was short-lived and with its departure lessened the zeal for the implementation for these recommendations. However, some State Governments had adopted some of the recommendations to suit their situations.

West Bengal took the initiative in 1978 to give a new life to its Panchayat on the lines of the Ashok Mehta Committees. Karnataka followed the pattern recommended by the Ashok Mehta Committee by enacting the Karnataka Zila Parishads. Taluk Panchayat Samiti, Mandal and Nyaya Panchayats Act, 1983 which received the President's assent on July 10, 1985. After elections, framing of rules and making various administrative arrangements these units at various levels became operational in April, 1987.

Andhra Pradesh passed the Andhra Pradesh Mandal Praja Parishads, Zila Praja Parishads and Zila Adhivrudhi Sameeksha Mandals etc. Act in 1986 by repealing the Andhra Pradesh Panchayat Samitis and Zila Parishads Act, 1959. This Act came into force with effect from January, 14, 1987.

Jammu and Kashmir introduced the new Bill in April, 1988 repealing the Jammu & Kashmir Panchayati Raj Act, 1968.

We shall briefly attempt to mention some of the important features of the Ashoka Mehta Committee Report in this section. Before it, however, the terms of reference of the Ashok Mehta Committee is given:

Terms of References : The terms of reference of the Committee, inter alia, required it to examine the working of the Panchayati Raj institutions in regard to mobilisation of resources as also planning and implementation of the scheme for rural development in all objective and optimal manner, and in looking after the interest of the weaker sections of the society. The Committee was also required to

(a) examine the methods of constituting the PRIs, including the system of elections, and to assess their effect on the performance of the Panchayati Raj system.

(b) suggest the role of the Panchayati Raj institutions and the objectives, which could be attained through them, for integrated rural development in the future.

(c) suggest measures for reorganising the PR system and removing the shortcomings and defects with a view to enable these institutions to fulfil their future role, and

(d) recommend the form and content of the relationship that should exist between the Panchayati Raj institutions, the officials administrative machinery, and the co-operative and voluntary institutions involved in rural development.

Recommendations of Ashoka Mehta Committee : The Ashok Mehta Committee made a number of recommendations on the various aspect of the Panchayati Raj Institutions, i.e. on the list institutional structural and functions contours of the PRIs.

The Committee felt that the institutional structural and functional contours of Panchayati Raj have to be in conformity not only with the accelerating pace of development but also with its strategies and policies. The Committee was of the view that on account of growth of the span, spatial scatter and the complexities of the development activities, as also significant changes in the strategies, the context of institution-buildings in rural India has undergone a change since the submission of the report of the Balwantrai Mehta Study Team in 1957.

Transfer of Power : The Committee recommended to transfer substantial quantum of powers from the State Government to the local bodies of distribution of powers between the Union and the States which would require a detailed but separate consideration. In order to achieve requisite status as well as continued functioning, the Committee felt that some provision in the Constitution deserves a careful consideration by the government.

The main recommendations of the Ashok Mehta Committee are as under:

Structure of the PRI : The Committee recommended a two tier structure a district level Zila Parishad and a Mandal Panchayat. The Mandal Panchayat would cover a population of 15,0000 to 20,000 and would also facilitate the forgiving of necessary linkages with schemes for development of local points and growth centres and would ensure efficient management of the growing rural-urban linkages. In tribal areas Mandal Panchayat may be formed with smaller population.

1. The directly elected elements must preponderate over the others at all levels. In the elections, the scheduled

castes and scheduled tribes should get representation on the basis of their population.

2. The Chairman of Zila Parishad will be elected indirectly.
3. The President of the Mandal Panchayat may, however, be elected directly or indirectly as the States may desire.
4. The term of all the elected tiers should be four years and as far as possible, election to all these bodies should be held simultaneously.
5. The Zila Parishad should consists of six types of the members:
   (a) Members elected from suitably demarcated electoral divisions.
   (b) Presidents of the Panchayat Samitis on an ex-officio basis.
   (c) Nominees of bigger municipalities.
   (d) Nominees of district level cooperative federation.
   (e) Two women who have secured the highest number of votes in the Zila Parishad elections to be made members. In case no women comes forward then 2 women be co-opted.
   (f) Two co-opted members—one with special interest in rural development and the other drawn from University/College teachers.
6. The Zila Parishad would function through a number of committees. The composition of these committees would be on the basis of proportional representation so as to ensure representation to all sections and shades of opinion.
7. All members of the Zila Parishad and MLAs, MLC and MPs from the concerned district shall constitute the Planning Committee.

Composition of the Mandal Panchayats

The Mandal Panchayat would consist of the following categories of members:

1. Fifteen members directly elected on village-cum-population basis.
2. Representatives of farmer's service societies.
3. Two women securing the highest votes in Mandal Panchayat elections and if none contested, two women may be co-opted.

Village Committee

The Committee was of the view that the Gram Sabha has an important role in activating the democratic process at the grass roots and deserves genuine encouragement. The Committee recommended that village committees should be constituted and should consist of

(a) Members elected to Mandal Panchayat from the respective electoral unit.

(b) Members elected to the Zila Parishad from the respective electoral units.

(c) Representative of small and marginal framers.

The Village Committee would be presided over by the member of Mandal Panchayat elected from the village.

Functions of the PRIS

1. The Committee was not in favour of drawing out a list of functions in an all India perspective since it felt that this would not have much operational relevance due to the fact that local priorities in all development programmes vary from region to region. The Committee, therefore, favoured a decentralised approach in this respect so that the States and the Union Territories

could have adequate scope for evolving their own list of functional priorities.

2. The Committee recommended that all the development functions relating the district which are being discharged by the State Government should have to be placed under the Zila Parishads. Functions which cut across district boundaries like University education, medium irrigation projects etc. should not be transferred to the Zila Parishads.
3. Planning was considered one of the most important functions which should be entrusted to the Zila Parishads as the Committee felt that merely entrusting the development functions to Panchayati Raj Institutions would remain incomplete unless all the PRIs are vested with the authority to take their own decisions and plan according to their own requirements.

Functions of Mandal Panchayat : As regards the functions of the Mandal Panchayat the Committee recommended that the Mandal Panchayat would be responsible for implementation of the schemes and projects assigned by the Zila Parishads. It recommended that the Mandal Panchayat would:

(a) Play a promotional role in activating community action.

(b) Build up organisation and project formulation.

(c) Would play an increasing role in the sphere of municipal and welfare functions.

(d) The Mandal Panchayat shall continue to perform the functions conventionally assigned to them under various statutes.

(e) The Committee was of the view that in due course of time, the Mandal Panchayat will have to become base-level organisation for project implementation and as such they would not only take over the functions of the block, but higher level technical expertise will be made available to lower levels.

The Committee felt that there was a need for a genuine decentralisation accompanied by corresponding resources. It recommended purposive work allocation and transfer of money component along with the functions assigned to them for implementation.

The Committee recommended that there should be full time Executive Officer of the Mandal Panchayat as they would be handling not only the developmental work but also the municipal and welfare functions. 'The development departments staff at the field level, i.e. the extension officers, stockmen, etc. should move to the Mandal Panchayat level.

Control Over the PRIS : The State Government should not supersede the PRIs on the partisan ground and if suppression becomes necessary these should be replaced by an elected body within six months.

The State Government should not postpone elections of PRIs.

PRI election should be conducted by the Chief Election Officer of the State in consultation with the Chief Election Commissioner.

The State Government should also arrange for periodical independent evaluation of the working of Panchayati Raj Institution by independent agencies including educational institutions with the universities playing an important part.

Minister for Panchayati Raj

The Committee felt that on account of increase in the volume of development work and their growing complexity, it would be necessary to constantly study the developmental requirements and mould the structures and functions of the State level Departments, so there should be a Minister for Panchayati Raj. The Committee recommended that the main task of the Minister for Panchayati Raj would be as follows:

(a) Enactment of PRI legislation.

(b) Elections of PRIs.

(c) Training of elected office bearers.

(d) Promotion of audit of Panchayati Raj account.

(e) Review of PRIs activities for report to the State Legislature and

(f) Promotion of camp training of elected members of PRIs.

Nyaya Panchayats

The Ashoka Mehta Committee was of the view that the working of Nyaya Panchayat has shown mixed results, in most cases they remained inactive. The administration of justice on a decentralised basis has its merits, but the functioning of the existing Nyaya Panchayat have not been able to elicit popular satisfaction.

The Committee was of the view that Nyaya Panchayat should be kept as separate bodies and should not be mixed with the people elected for development of Panchayat.

Members of Nyaya Panchayats : The Committee was in favour of a combination of qualified judge to preside over a bench of a separately elected Nyaya Panchayats.

The elected Nyaya Panchayats will not be entitled to seek re-election; they should serve in an area other than that from which they have been elected.

Political Parties and PRIS

The Ashok Mehta Committee favoured the participation of political parties in PRIs elections. It was of the view that this would ensure clearer orientation towards development programme and facilitate healthier linkages with higher level political process. Direct elections coupled with programme-based contests, would offer great scope to weaker sections for availing of the opportunities offered by the political system.

Finances of PRIS

1. The taxation powers to be given in the PRIs should be limited and specific and must not operate inequiously.

2. Incentives can be offered for optional taxes realised. These may take the shape of award of prizes or provision of matching grants.

3. The Committee recommended the complete transfer of land revenue to PRIs in a phased manner over a period of five years taking into account the buoyancy of other taxes.

4. The PRIs should levy fees/taxes for service for lighting, sanitation, water supply etc.

5. The power to impose taxes should not be divorced from the responsibility for their collection, therefore the Committee recommended the officials of the PRIs to themselves collect the taxes.

6. The Committee also recommended that the Mandal Panchayat should be granted a permanent annual grant of not less than Rs. 2.50 per capital. This should be apart from the taxation powers and other transfers effected.

7. The Committee was of the view that the PRIs should be given compulsory powers of taxation and that the PRIs should mobilise enough resources of its own apart from the budgetary devolution from the state Governments.

8. The Committee recommended that the every state should endeavour to present consolidated finance of PRIs to the Legislature.

The Committee also recommended that the State Governments should consider the establishment of a Committee of the Legislature to be specifically concerned with the financial and physical performance of PRI bodies. Along with the consolidated finance accounts, the State Governments should also lay on the table of the Legislature, an administrative report on PRIs.

Miscellaneous Recommendations

1. Apart from these recommendations, the Committee also made a number of recommendations on the human resources development and stressed (training for official) for elected representatives and also recommended combined courses for both officials and elected representatives together.

2. The Committee stressed the importance of the role of the voluntary agencies in mobilising people's support for PRIs and recommended its strengthening and encouragement to supplement the efforts of the PRIs.

3. The PRIs should undertake the promotional and co-ordination work like motivation and organisation of co-operatives.

4. As regards the Urban-rural relationship, integration of rural-urban areas in a balanced reciprocity of economic and social growth can be achieved by linking up the rural areas with urban focal points.

The Report (AMC) gives an insight into working of the PRIs in India. Some States like West Bengal, Andhra Pradesh J&K etc. remodelled the PRIs in their States in the light of the recommendations of the Ashoka Mehta Committees Report, the success of its working remains to be seen in due sources of time.

Recommendations of the Committee to Review the Existing Administrative Arrangements for Rural Development and Poverty Alleviation Programme (CAARD)

A Committee to Review the Existing Administrative Arrangements for Rural Development and Poverty Alleviation Programmes popularly known as CAARD was constituted under the Chairmanship of Shri GVK Rao which submitted its report in 1985.

The GVK Rao Committee (CAARD) pointed out that the decline in the status and authority of Panchayati Raj Institutions may be attributed to the reluctance of political leadership at State level to share power with district leadership.

The Committee pointed out that past experience clearly indicates that the government machinery (bureaucracy) alone cannot be assigned the responsibility for achieving economic development and social justice. On the other hand, there is some evidence that wherever the Panchayati Raj bodies have been actively involved, the implementation of rural development programmes have been quite easy and conducive.

The Committee stressed the need of involving the people and their representatives effectively in drawing up programmes of rural development and their implementation and that the Panchayati Raj institutions have to be energised and given all the support needed so that they can become effective organisations for handling people's problems.

PRI and Planning : The Committee recommended that the Panchayati Raj Institutions at the district level and below should be assigned important role in respect of planning implementation and monitoring of rural development programmes. The Committee was of the view that the district should be the basic unit for policy planning and programme implementation. It recommended that the Zila Parishad should become the principal body for management of all development programme which can be handled at the level.

The Committee recommended that a post of District Development Commissioner (DDC) be created to look after and co-ordinate all the developmental activities in the district.

The Committee suggested that the District Development Commissioner may be made the Chief Executive of the Zila Parishad in those States where the Panchayati Raj institution hold the responsibility for planning and implementation of various development programmes and, in those states where there is no Zila Parishads, the DDC could function as Chairman and Chief Executive of the District Development Council.

The Committee was of the view that the some of the planning functions at the State level may have to be transferred to the district level for effective decentralised district planning and it also recommended the introduction of the concept of district budget.

The President of the Zila Parishad should be directly elected for a term co-terminus with the Zila-Parishad, or for one year each on the Mayoral pattern.

Sub-committees : The CAARD recommended that the work of the Zila Parishad should be done by a number of Sub-committees, elected on the basis of the proportional representation so that participatory democracy could be developed and encouraged.

13

The Planning

Planning simply refers to the systematic approach to achieve the predetermined objectives. Dimock & Dimock have defined planning in the following terms

Planning is "the use of rational design as contrasted with chance the reaching of a decision before a line of action is taken instead of improving after the action has started."

Planning is the process of devising a basis for a course of future action.

"Planning is the process of determining the objectives of administrative effort and of devising the means calculated to achieve them. "

Planning makes it necessary for other organisations to undertake certain more functions:

"A governmental system created to maintain order, administer justice, regulate international relations, defend the nation, and impose and collect taxes for the expense of these activities, is not equipped for the positive task of guiding and controlling the conservation, development and utilization of the national resources of integrating its economic and social life. It has become increasingly clear that decisions taken in a moment of crisis, or from a purely departmental point of view, or under organized pressure from some particular interest, or on traditional lines, or with a wholly inadequate knowledge of the material facts and probable consequences, are not good enough. "

Thus planning is an integrated effort of the following inter-linked steps:

Object Determination : The object of planning is decided at the first hand. For this purpose data is collected from various sources : Primary and Secondary, both to deal with all the aspects of the problem. It involves extensive examination of the various alternatives before taking the final decision. Object Determination is a political function because it is a matter of policy.

Selection of the Best Course of Action: After testing the various alternatives methods, it becomes imperative to choose the best of all the alternatives. The best course of action is implemented and follow up programme starts from here.

Determination of Various Ways and Means : After determining the objectives to be achieved the next step in the planning process is to find out the various ways in which the objects may be realised. Here various suggested methods are tested to find out the most suitable method to achieve the target. Sometimes all alternatives may be tested through actual operation.

The Characteristics

Planning is Regional and Dynamic Process : Planning devised in the past has its inseparable link with the present. The chain of planning never stops unless it fulfils its aim and object. It is the outcome of rational intellect, and thus it never proceeds to achieve futile aims. To quote Pfiffner and Presthus in this context.

Planning is rational because its demands a systematic analysis of several possible means and ends, followed by a selection of those means though best used to the designated end.

Planning is Flexible According to the Necessities : Though planning is not the matter of daily change, yet it is not changeable always. It is desirable that flexibility must be inherent in the planning process. It must have the capacity to absorb all the changing contingencies of the time.

Planning is Comprehensively Integrated Progress : Planning is not restricted to any particular place or subject. It includes many subjects concerned with the development of the nation and society.

Planning is Basically a Staff Function: Planning is undertaken; though in very small amount at all the levels of the organisation. It is also necessary for the personnel working at different levels of plan implementation to be aware of the planning. Thus, primarily, it is a staff function.

Planning is the Synthesis of Various Programmes : Planning covers varied programmes which touch the interest of the human beings. It covers agriculture trade, industry, road and transport, fisheries, education, health, welfare etc. Planning process is the synthesis whole of these varied programmes.

Planning Process

The process of planning essentially means the applications in a comprehensive manner of scientific methods in dealing with problems of economic development and keeping in view the interrelations of different sectors as well as the needs of the future.

India has tried to evolve a procedure of economic planning which is not too rigid or centralised and yet able to mobilise the willing cooperation of the people for a balanced programme of rapid economic development. The procedure evolved falls somewhere in between broad economic policy making as in a country like the U.K. and the detailed economic planning as in a country like USSR. The nearest parallel to it in Western Europe is the French system.

Planning in India is influenced by its institutions. We have a federal system of government. The Constitution clearly divides the authority between the Centre and the State. We have the private and public sectors. The private sector, however, is also influenced by the government through its fiscal and monetary policies and control.

In India we have multi-level planning, i.e., the plans are prepared at the National, State and District levels. The starting point of the whole process of plan formulation in the mandate given through the National Development Council to the Planning Commission setting out the contours and objectives within which the plan would be formulated.

The mechanics of plan process show a continuous contact between the Centre and the State and the final outcome is quite in a nature of consensus through the literative process.

There are a number of agencies involved in the planning process. The agencies involved at the Central level are the Planning Commission, the National Development Council, the Union Ministries and Departments have their own planning cells for preparing detailed plans. The Plan Finance Division of the Union Finance Ministry is closely associated with the planning process. Some of the other ministries dealing with the economic and social development sectors also participate in the process of planning of State Plan schemes. Reserve Bank of India, Life Insurance Corporation, and a number of financial research and assistance channelising agencies under the overall control of the government of India, the Central Statistical Organisation and the National Sample Survey Organisation participate in the process of Planning.

At the state level, the State Cabinet, the Secretariat, the Finance Department, the Planning Secretary, State Planning Board, District Planning Board, the various heads of Departments and officials, from the district level department, Directorate of Economic and Statistics, Research Institutions, Finance Corporations, Universities and Voluntary Agencies participate in the process of planning.

In India, the planning exercise is taken up for preparing perspective plans, medium term and annual plans. A perspective plan is usually prepared for ten to fifteen years. In the Planning

Commission, perspective plans are prepared by the Perspective Planning Division.

Five Year Plans are an example of medium term planning. These plans are prepared in the light of the perspective plans. This is a rational approach to planning which takes into consideration the changing socio-economic technical and political conditions in the country, thus giving flexibility to perspective planning.

Annual plan is an instrument of adjustments and revision and a means to operationalize the medium term plans, i.e., the Five Year Plans and the Annual Plans are prepared within the framework of Five Year Plans and allow for changes to be made according to the changing complexion and needs of the country.

Formulating Five Year Plan

The process of formulation of a Five Year Plan is spread over a period of two to three years and involves a good deal of horizontal and vertical interaction. This process is divided into the following stages

(i) Background studies, analysis of constraints on development and evolution of perspective.

(ii) Preparation of Approach Paper, setting up of Working Groups/Study Groups both at the Centre and in the States for sectoral and other studies.

(iii) Issuing of guidelines by Planning Commission based on the approved Approach Paper, both to the Union Ministries/Departments and to the State Government for the preparation of detailed plans including assessment of financial resources.

(iv) Detailed estimation of financial resources.

(v) Preparation of detailed sectoral plans and formulation of the Draft Five Year Plan.

(vi) Consideration of the Draft Five Year Plan at various forms, academic institutions and expert groups.

Planning Commission also organises special meetings with leaders of political parties, academicians, representatives of industry and agriculture, trade union leaders and the like.

(vii) Approval of the Draft Plan by the National Development Council.

The Procedure : The first step in the process of formulating a Five Year Plan is the preparation of a paper on 'Approach to the Plan'. While undertaking work in this connection, Working Groups are also set up for reviewing the progress in the implementation of the current Five Year Plan and making detailed recommendations regarding programme, projects schemes and policies as well as outlays and targets for the various sectors and sub-sectors. Members of the Working Groups are drawn from officials in the Planning Commission, Central Ministers/Departments, other institutions, State Governments and experts in the field. As many as 149 Working Groups were set up in connection with the Ninth Plan. These included a Group for Study of Financial Resources for the seventh Five Year Plan as well as a Group for Study of Potential as well as the Instruments for Domestic Resources Mobilization.

The Approach Paper is prepared on the basis of the preliminary exercise undertaken in the Planning Commission in regard to possible major parameters of growth over the long-term perspective period, as well as during the Five Year Plan period, experience of the past projected requirements, likely availability of resources and such information as become available as a result of the work undertaken by the various Working Groups. Views of the Central Ministries, State Governments, Consultative Committee of Members of Parliament, Panel of Economists, experts and cross-section of the public are also taken into account. Objectives, strategies, policies and programme thrusts are enunciated in this paper. The paper is considered by the National Development Council and after approval by the Council, it is placed before the Parliament.

While initiating work on the Approach at the national level, the State governments are also advised to take preliminary steps for formulating their approach and set up Working Groups wherever considered necessary. After the Approach Paper is approved by the National Development Council, the Planning Commission addresses the Central Ministries and State Governments for undertaking the exercise of formulating detailed proposals for the plan. Suitable guidelines are indicated for this purpose.

Separately, the Financial Resources Division of the Planning Commission requests the State Governments to furnish detailed estimates of resources for the Plan. For the Centre, the estimates of resources are finalised by the Working Groups for Study of Financial Resources, which includes, inter alia, representative of the Planning Commission, Ministry of Finance and Reserve Bank.

Detailed discussions are held with each State Government to prepare mutually agreed estimates of resources for its Plan. The estimates of Central assistance, market borrowing and additional resource mobilisation by the State taken at this stage are tentative. After the resources discussion with a state, its Plan proposal are discussed in various sectoral Working Groups at a one day meeting. For the 9th Plan, 26 sectoral Working Groups were set up. Each Working Group was presided over by the Adviser of the concerned Subject Division of the Planning Commission and had in it representative of the concerned Central Ministries/Department bodies and the concerned Department of the State Governments. The Working Group took stock of the progress, problems and future requirements and made detailed scheme-wise recommendations of the Ninth Plan.

The recommendations of all the Working Groups on the proposals of a State are considered by the Concerned State Plan Adviser. He takes a view on these recommendations in the light of his informal discussions with the State and Central Officers and also his knowledge of the development activities in the State. He prepares a report making detailed recommendations covering the programmes, targets and outlays. This report forms the basis of discussion between the Planning Commission and the State Government for finalising the Plan of the State concerned. The final position regarding the State's own resources, including market borrowing and additional resource mobilisation, Central assistance, size of the State plan and programme content emerges after discussion.

In the case of Central Plan, the procedure adopted for the Ninth Plan was that the Division concerned prepared a Status paper taking into account the recommendations of the concerned. Working Group/Working Groups, Ministry's proposals and its own assessment of the development programme that was considered feasible and necessary. This status paper constituted the basis of discussion between the Planning Commission and the Secretary of the concerned Central Ministry/Department. It is the light of the discussions with the Ministries and the anticipated availability of the total resources for the Central plan, the Planning Commission took a view on the development programme of each Ministry Department.

In the process of finalising the Plan, the Planning Commission also consults the consultative committee of members of Parliament, panel of economists, representatives of industry, labour and agriculturists, social scientists and other experts. The views expressed in the Parliament and at other forms are also taken into account.

The Central and State Plans, together with the scheme of financing for these, as finally approved, are incorporated in the Five Year Plan. After approval by the Union Cabinet, the Plan is brought up before the National Development Council. After the Council has approved the Plan, it is brought up for consideration by the Parliament.

The procedure for the formulation of the Annual Plan is the same as for the Five Year Plan in the case of the State.

Annual plan for any particular year is just not started on a clean state. The Annual draft is initiated-within the frame work of the approved Five Year Plans and is built up within the range of normal plan schemes and the parameter suggested. The importance of the Annual plan lies in the fact that the Five Years

Plans are operationalised through them. Another factor which enhances its importance is the fact that both the Central and State Governments operate through the mechanism of annual budgets, thus the annual planning process and the annual budgeting process were more or less simultaneous and a co-ordinated. For effective implementation of the Five Year Plan, the Annual Plans are framed with the objective of ensuring year by year progress of achieving the Five Year Plan targets.

After the budget is passed by the Legislative Assembly and communicated to the respective heads of the Department, the money started flowing in for the development projects schemes of the approved plan documents.

The plan process is an on-going process, once the finances are made available and the work starts, the progress of the work is watched closely by the Heads of the Departments. Annual and mid-term reviews of the various projects and programmes are undertaken. Monitoring is done. Post and concurrent evaluation of the Plan schemes is also undertaken, which further become papers for the background studies.

Taking an overall view from the institutional and functional aspects planning both at the formulation and execution stages involve many agencies which interact at a number of levels. This interrelationship between the various agencies is presented in Chart.

An Appraisal

The Process of Planning as is exercised in India is under a lot of criticism. Some of the drawbacks are given below:

1. A general complaint of the State Governments is that they are required to adhere to unduly rigid and detailed Union directives mainly because of their dependence on the Union Government for plan funds.

2. The States are not given due opportunity to participate in the national planning according to their needs and priorities.

3. There is too detailed scrutiny by the Planning Commission and other Central Organisation of States Plan proposals.

4. The Centrally Sponsored Schemes have made deep inroads into State sphere of activity and have affected their initiative and priorities.

5. States crucial dependence on Central assistance for the Plan and the mechanism of earmarking of outlays has restricted their manoeuvrability allocate resources among development heads.

6. That there is the formulation, scrutiny and finalisation of the State Plans of the Planning Commission.

Suggestions : Some of the suggestions to make plan formulation effective are as follows:

1. The States should set up State Finance Commission to suggest measures for mobilising resources in the State and make recommendations for distribution of finances to the district and lower levels. In this way independence of the Centre would be lessened. The Sarkaria Commission had also recommended the setting up of the State Finance Commission.

2. The review and evaluation part of the planning process is weak. Evaluation of both the qualitative and the quantitative aspects of the plan needs to be examined.

3. There is need to sufficiently strengthen the planing machinery at various levels. This suggestion was offered by the ARC in 1967. Other recommendations of the ARC included.

(i) Allowing greater freedom to the States to formulate details of their plans within the broad guidelines given by the Planning Commission and approved by the National Development Council.

(ii) Restructuring of the Working Groups and representation of States on them.

(iii) A more effective role for the National Development Council as a forum for arriving at consensus and its guiding economic policies.

(iv) Putting of limits on the Centrally sponsored scheme.

(v) Decentralization of the planning process so that the plans are more area specific and people specific. The recent announcement by the Government to allow states to use 40 percent of their plan outlays according to their own properties is a welcome move towards decentralised planning.

A national plan is a charter of action which holds out hope and describes the effort that the national has to put in. It is a blue print to ensure better and very satisfying levels of living. The formulation of the plans in India is a complex process as planning is a cooperative process of shared action between the Union and States. There are various levels of planning in India. As such the constraints at the various level needs to be removed so as to make planning exercise effective and purposeful.

National Development Council

Planning in India has emerged as a comprehensive area of government function. In a large country like ours, with dual polity and administration, planning involves a continuous and wide ranging interaction between the Centre and the States. Entry 20 of List III (Concurrent List) relates to Economic and Social planning and we have a multi-level planning framework.

The National Development Council was set up in August, 1952, on the suggestions of the Planning Commission and is regarded as the most significant step for promoting understanding and consultation between the Union and State Governments on planning and common economic policies. The main objective of the National Development Council was to strengthen and mobilise the efforts and resources of the nation in support of the plans to promote common economic policies in all vital spheres and to secure the balanced and rapid development of all parts of the country. The claim for popular democratic sanction behind the plan rests on the ground that this body comprises mainly of the elected representatives of the people at large as well as on the ground that a wide scope is given for public discussion of the plan in its draft form.

Function of the National Development Council : The Administrative Reforms Commission, in its report on the Machinery for Planning, dealt with the role and functions of the National Development Council and made a number of recommendations. The Government considered the recommendations of the Commission and decided to reconstitute the National Development Council as well as redefine its functions. Hence *vide* Cabinet Resolution No. 65/15/C F-67 dated 7th October, 1967 the redefined functions of the National Development Council areas follows:

1. To prescribe guidelines for the formulation of the National Plan, including the assessment of resources for the plan;
2. To consider the National Plan as formulated by the Planning Commission;
3. To consider important questions of social and economic policy affecting national development;
4. To review the working of the plan from time to time and to recommend such measures as are necessary for achieving the aims and target set out in the National Plan, including measures to secure the active participation and co-operation of the people, improve, the efficiency of the administrative services, ensure the fullest development of the less advanced regions and sections of the community and through sacrifice borne equally by all citizens, build up resources for national development.

Composition of the National Development Council : Initially, the National Development Council was composed of the Prime Minister of India, the Chief Ministers of all States and the Members of the Planning Commission. On the recommendations of the Administrative Reforms Commission, the Council was reconstituted and now composes of the Prime Minister, all Union Cabinet Ministers, Chief Ministers of all States and Union Territories and the Members of the Planning Commission. Delhi Administration is represented in the Council by the Lt. Governor and the Chief Executive Councillor and the remaining Union Territories by their respective Administrator. Other Union Ministers and State Ministers can also be invited to participate in the deliberations of the Council.

The Resolution of 7th October, 1967 stated that the Council may appoint, from time to time, suitable sub-committees or panels.

The Cabinet Resolution further stated that the meeting of the National Development Council is to be held at least twice a year and the council if need shall meet as often as may be necessary. Its Standing Committees/panels however shall meet frequently. The inclusion of the Chief Ministers of the State has strengthened the bound between the Union and the States, thus ensuring co-operation of the States in plan formulation and plan implementation. The advice given by the National Development Council at the various stages of plan formulation carries great weightage as the Council consist of policy makers in power. Prior approval of the National Development Council is necessary before it is presented to the Parliament for consideration. Thus, the Council has acquired a unique position and have been responsible for giving the Indian plans a truly national character.

Commission on the Centre State Relations (Sarkaria Commission) and the Role of National Development Council: The Commission on Centre-State relations constituted under the Chairmanship of Justice R.S. Sarkaria in 1983 examined among other matters, the subject of Planning as it covers inter-governmental relations viz-a-viz social and economic development. The Sarkaria Commission while examining the work of the National Development Council, its role and composition pointed out that there has not been any marked improvements in the Council's functioning, even after its reconstitution in 1967. Some of the deficiencies which came to the notice of the Sarkaria Commission are enumerated below:

(i) The National Development Council meets only at the initiative of the Planning Commission which determines its agenda.

(ii) The Council has been approving the Approach Paper and the Draft Plans but has not been keeping track of the progress of the Plan. Consideration of other questions affecting national development which is one of its stated functions has been infrequent and insufficient.

(iii) The frequency and duration of its meetings are very inadequate.

(iv) The Planning Commission has not always put before the Council alternative sets of perspectives, strategies and targets along with the assumptions made to enable it to decide among the choices available.

(v) The conferencing procedure consists of the speeches made by the Chief Ministers with very little of mutual discussion.

(vi) The summing up of deliberations often does not reflect the variety of views.

(vii) The time given to States for crystallising their view is often insufficient.

(viii) The Standing Committees and the Special Committees are not formed or convened on regular basis for in-depth analysis and consideration of issues.

The Commission was of the view that as a result of the above deficiencies formalism rather than systematic and effective participation in foreign consensus and commitment of national policies is observed to have been the dominant feature of the National Development Council's working. It has not been able to guide the Planning Commission in identifying the feasible alternatives so that a choice can be made from among them and has not made critical appraisal of the working of the plan and of the policies affecting national development. This has also given rise to such complaints, as made by a Chief Minister that, plan strategies and policies have not been put to sufficient debate and informed consideration and have been rather hurriedly put through.

The Commission after examining the working of the National Development Council and carefully considering the various views and suggestions of the State Government and others made a number of recommendations with regards to the status, role of the National Development Council. Some of the important suggestions and recommendations of the Commission to make the working of the National Development Council affective are given below:

The Commission was of the view that the National Development Council should be made to function more effectively and emerge as the highest political level inter-governmental body for giving directions and thrust to planned development of the country. Being the supreme inter-government body for all matters relating to socio-economic development, it is necessary that the National Development Council should be renamed and reconstituted as the National Economic and Development Council by Presidential Order under the provisions of Article 263 so as to have direct moorings in the Constitution. The provisions of the clause (b) and (c) are wide enough to encompass the functions of the National Development Council. The National Economic Development Council (NEDC) thus constituted will, while retaining adequate flexibility have a measure of authority with formalised status having the constitutional sanction of Article 263.

The Commission did not suggest any major change in the composition and broad charter of work of the NEDC. It was of the view that the suggested change in name to National Economic Development Council' will help make explicit what is already implicit in the present charter of the National Development Council that along with developmental issues it has to consider and advise on relevant economic issues also. The Commission was of the opinion that in the interest of healthier Union-State relations, it is necessary that this should be explicit and the NEDC or its Standing Committees should meet regularly to consider important economic issues of national significance in addition to the usual development issues.

The Commission further stated that while the role of NEDC will be advisory, it hoped that healthy conventions will develop to the effect that the advice given and decision taken at this forms will be respected. The representation by Union Ministers and State's Chief Ministers with Prime Minister as the Chairman, on this forum, given constitutional status under Article 263 would be a sufficient guarantee for the commitment to its decisions. It need not have technical experts as its members. But it may obtain technical experts advice from the Union and the State Governments and also from other sources whenever necessary. It should formulate its own procedure to enable it to discharge its responsibilities.

The Commission felt that the NDC is a too large body which has not been able to pay collective attention to the detail of the matter. To meet this problem, it should have a Standing Committee, as mentioned earlier.

The Commission recommended that a Standing Committee of the NEDC should be constituted consisting of the following:

1. The Prime Minister
2. The Finance Minister
3. Three other Union Minister nominated by the Prime Minister
4. Deputy Chairman of the Planning Commission
5. Governor, Reserve Bank of India

6. Six Chief Ministers, one from each zone selected by rotation or consensus.

The Standing Committee should also be constituted under Article 263 along with NEDC. It should devise its own procedures for effective functioning. All matters concerning the NEDC will also be considered by the Standing Committee which may decide the agenda for the meeting. The NEDC may, however, set up other commission or sub-committee to advise it on the Standing Committee on special issues.

Other important recommendations of the Commission on the National Development Council viz-a-viz- planning process are as under :

(i) NEDC should be involved in the formulation of the Plan right from the beginning. Selection of the structure and setting up the various Working Groups should done under the guidance of the Standing Committee of the NEDC.

(ii) The draft Approach Paper should be circulated to the States at least two months in advance of the meeting of the NEDC to consider the same. It should contact all relevant data, alternate strategic, etc.

(iii) A preparatory meeting should be held by the Planning Commission, with all Deputy Chairman and/or Secretaries of the State Development Boards two week prior to the NEDC to consider the Approach Paper Draft for Five Year Plan for sidentifying the main issue and firming up the agenda for the meeting of the NEDC.

(iv) Deliberation in the NEDC should be so structured as to facilitate meaningful discussions on each item of the agenda. Sufficient time should be available for the same, so that, after the general statement by the Prime Minister and the Chief Ministers, there is enough time to discussing individual items of the agenda. Minutes of the discussion in the NEDC should be recorded item wise. It will help provide more time for discussion, prepared general statements of Chief Ministers are circulated before hand and the Chief Ministers read out of a brief summary.

The various recommendations of the Commission on Centre-State relations on the National Development Council an active consideration and implementation to make the function of the National Development Council really effective and meaningful as the role of National Development Council in the planning process is of paramount importance. The National Development Council is the apex institution for arriving at consensus among the Union and the State on various matters relating to planning and socio-economic development. Although the National Development Council is not a statutory body and its very composition gives it a unique character and its recommendation are treated with reverence by the Union and the State Governments. It imparts a national character to the entire process of planning.

Planning Commission

In almost all the progressive countries of the world, the scope of governmental activity, in relations to the social and economic life of the people has greatly increased as a result of strong reaction against the philosophy of Laissez faire. Modern governments have at least two main functions to perform— to maintain law and order and to promote economic development. Economic development is very high on the agenda of government activities of third world countries. One of the methods of achieving economic development and social justice is the system of economic planning.

India opted planning in the fifties as the vehicle of its development though its interest in it date back to 1876 when Dababhai Naoroji published his paper on Poverty of India. Indian leaders had urged the necessity of coordinated action in the economic field as a means to the economic development of the country. As the struggle for national independence progressed, its social and economic aims became more definite. Much useful programme in the field of national planning was adopted by the

National Planning Committee which was set up in 1938 by the Indian National Congress with Pt. Jawahar Lal Nehru as its chairman. The work of this committee was, however, unfortunately interrupted due to the outbreak of the Second World War. Towards the end of 1946, the Advisory Planning Board which was set up by the Interim Government of India, recommended the appointment of a Planning Commission to devote continuous attention to the whole field of economic development and to suggest means and methods to rebuild the shattered economy of the country. Accordingly, on 15 March, 1950 a Planning Commission was set up by a resolution by the Government of India to formulate and secure the execution of plans for the most effective and balanced utilisation of the country's resources.

The Planning Commission under the Chairmanship of the Prime Minister commenced work on 28 March, 1950. The objectives of India's planning and its social premises derive from the Directive Principles of State Policy set fourth in the constitution. Among these Directive Principles were the state shall strive to promote the welfare of the people securing and protecting as effectively as it may, a social order in which justice-social, economic and political shall form all the institutions of national life.

Further that:

"The State shall, in particular, direct its policy towards securing:

(a) that the citizens, men and women equally, have the right to an adequate means of livelihood.

(b) that the ownership control of material resources of the community are so distributed as best to sub-serve the common good.

(c) that the operation of the economic system does not result in the concentration of wealth and means of production to the common detriment.

Since 1950, each Plan has marked an important phase in India's economic history for the realization of above objectives.

The Planning Commission and the National Development Council are involved in the formation of the Five Year Plan. The Planning Commission is the supreme organ of planning of India. In the machinery and procedure for planning, the Planning Commission naturally occupies the most important position but it has neither constitutional nor even statutory authority. Two features marked the birth of this institution. First it was placed outside the conventional Ministeries and departments with a view to preventing it from failing into runts, and what is more, felicitating development of supra-departmental view. Secondly, a commission type of organisation was deliberately preferred to provide requisite flexibility in evolving appropriate internal organisation in response to emerging needs, and also to build up brains-trust.

The Planning Commission is essentially a staff agency, its main function being advisory and coordinating rather than executive. Free from day-to-day administrative and executive work the planning commission is in a position to devote itself almost entirely to the formulation of the Plan and evaluation of the progress achieved in the execution of each stage of the plan. Under its terms of reference, the Planning Commission performs the following functions.

(a) make an assessment of the material capital and human resources of the country, including technical personnel, and investigate the possibilities of augmenting such of these resources as are found to be deficient in relation to the nation's requirements;

(b) formulate a plan for the most effective and balanced utilization of the country's resources;

(c) one determination of priorities, define the stages in which the Plan should be carried out and propose the allocation of resources for the due completion of each stage;

(d) indicate the factors which are tending to retard economic development, and determine the conditions which, in view of the current social and political situation, should be established for the successful implementation of the plan;

(e) determine the nature of the machinery which will be necessary for securing successful implementation of each stage of the Plan in all its aspects.

(f) appraise from time to time the progress achieved in the execution of each stage of the plan and recommend the adjustments of policy and measures that such appraisal may shown to be necessary and

(g) make such interim or ancillary recommendations as appear to it to be appropriate either for facilitating the discharge of the duties assigned to it, or on a considera-tion of the prevailing economic conditions, current policies, measures and development programmes: or on an examination of such specific problem as may be referred to it for advice by central or state government for facilitating the discharge of the duties assigned to it. Another functions have been added to the Commission:

(i) problems of planning.

(ii) formulation of the development plans of Central and State governments.

(iii) Planning of industrial development.

(iv) perspective planning.

(v) public co-operation in national development.

(vi) publication of the journal Yojana.

It is thus clear that the Planning Commission was established as a staff agency to prepare national plans for economic development within the framework of a federal government, a parliamentary democracy, and a welfare state. The Commission was to suggest, co-ordinate, evaluate policies and programmes, although the final responsibility to the people's representatives and to the people remained with the political institution. Although the States had no Planning Commission of similar status, they have special planning departments and State Naming Boards to do the planning work. Since 1957, the emerging Panchayati Raj institution in the villages, the blocks and districts are increasingly associated with the formulation and implementation of plan within the range of responsibilities assigned to them.

Organisation of Planning Commission : The organisation of the Planning Commission facilities its role as an 'advisory body' functioning at the highest policy level without, however, being involved in the responsibilities of day-to-day administration. The organisation and composition of this institution has undergone far-reaching changes since its inception in 1950. The Prime Minister of India has been from the beginning the Chairman of the Planning Commission and has participated and given direction to the thinking on all major issues of policy. The office of Deputy Chairman of the Planning Commission is distinct from that of Minister of Planning. On the recommendation of the Administrative Reforms Commission, the Planning Commission has been reconstituted.

The Planning Commission was reconstituted in August 1967, on the lines suggested by the ARC, except that the Prime Minister continued to be the Chairman of the Commission and the Union Finance Minister its part time member. After its reorganisation, it has seven members, two of these are·important ministers, viz., the Prime Minister and the Minister of Finance. Five were full time members who are eminent public men, administrators and technical experts. The present composition of the Planning Commission is of only four full time members and three ex-officio members viz., the Prime Minister, the Finance Minister and the Planning Minister. The Deputy Chairman in addition to looking after the day-to-day work of the commission is responsible for plan coordination, plan evaluation, administration and servicing.

Eminent economists of the country have suggested that an expert in the economic affairs should be a whole time deputy Chairman and the political wing can be represented by the Prime Minister, who is always the Chairman of the Commission. It was suggested that both the Chairman and Deputy Chairman need not to be political leaders. The Planning Commission should be some kind of an expert body, and its deputy Chairman should be an expert. In the past at one time Congress government appointed an eminent economists (Dr. D.R. Gadgil) as deputy chairman of the Commission.

Although the full time members are not ministers as such, but they enjoy the status of Ministers and are invited to attend meetings of the cabinet when subjects with which they are directly concerned are taken up for consideration. The four full time members of the Commission are in charge of one each of the four following groups:

(a) Industry, Labour, Transport and Power Group; (b) Agriculture and Rural Development Group; (c) Perspective Planning Group and (d) Education Scientific Research and Social Services Group. The staff of the Commission comprises a number of technical as well as administrative officers and is headed by a Secretary.

Secretariat Organisation : The Planning Commission functions through a Series of division and sections, each headed by a senior officer designated usually as advisor or Chief or Joint Secretary. Some of the divisions are headed by middle grade officers known as Directors who work generally in association with other senior officials. The office of the Planning Commission consists of three types of branches, viz., (1) General Branches (2) Subject Branches (3) House Keeping Branches. The work in the first two types of branches is primarily technical; of the third administrative or secretariat branch.

The general branches either, carry out studies relating to the plans as a whole rather than to any particular sector, or co-ordinate work of the various subject branches. There are twelve general branches in the Planning Commission, Viz, Perspective Planning, Statistics and surveys; Economic Socio-Economic Research, Plan Coordination, Programme Administration, Multi Level Planning, Employment and Mass Power Planning, Monitoring and Information, Project Appraisal, Scientific Research and Plan Information and Publicity.

Among the general branch, the Perspective Planning Branch is responsible for the formulation of long period projections and plans, while the other branches primarily concern themselves with work relating to the five years or annual plans. One of the responsibilities of the Programme Administration Branch is to assist the Advisors in their day-to-day work regarding the coordination of the planning efforts of the States with those of the Central Government.

There are fourteen subjects branches viz., Agriculture Land Reforms, Irrigation, Power, Transport, Communications, Education, Employment and Manpower, Health and Family Planning, Housing and Urban Development, Industry and Minerals, Village and Small Industries, Social Planning and Social Welfare. The subject branches have their counterparts in the various ministries and the state Government and are responsible for collecting, processing and analysing all relevant informations required for the formulation, processing and evaluation of the policies and programme included in the plan. They also organize various research studies which are deemed necessary for the purpose of planning in their respective fields either on their own or through competent technical organisation in the country.

The main house-keeping branches are Administrations General Co-ordination, and Organisation and Methods. They are staffed mainly by administrative or secretariat personnel.

The plan evaluation work is carried out in the Programme Evaluation Organisation. The organisation is administratively under the Planning Commission but in all technical matters it is guided by the Programme Evaluation Board. The Programme Evaluation Organisation is headed by a Chief Director. While much of the detailed technical work in connection with planning is thus done in the Working groups, there is need, especially in an economy of the size and complexity of India to consult on general policy, from time to time, other knowledgeable people also, especially non-official experts, at various stages of formulation as well as implementation of the plans. These consultation have necessarily to be at different level technical, administrative and political. They not only elicit valuable advice and being fresh views to bear on official thinking but also help increasing the plan as a greater public understanding and give it a national character. Attempt is made to have such consultations through a number of standing bodies variously known as Council Panels, Advisory Committees and Consultative Committees.

The National Planning Council comprises seventeen members in addition to the full-time members of the Planning Commission covers the entire field of Planning. In addition, there are eight Panels, consisting of both officials and non-officials having special knowledge and experience in the relevant field to provide technical advice on matters for which these are appointed, viz., as scientist and economists, on Agriculture, Land Reforms, Health, Ayurveda, Education, Housing and Regional Development.

There are also seven advisory committees viz., on Irrigation; Flood control and Power Projects; Policy and Co-ordination; Co-ordination Committee for Planning Forums; Rural Industries Planning Committee, National Advisory Committee on Public Co-operation, and Committee on Land Reforms.

The other important advisory bodies functioning in the Planning Commission are (a) Committee on Plan Project and (b) Research Programme Committee. The Committee on Plan Projects was established in 1956, with the Union Home Minister as Chairman. The Union Minister of Finance is also a member of the committee. In additions, the Prime Minister as Chairman of National Development Council, nominates two Chief Ministers of States as Members of the Committee for each class of Projects. The Union Minister concerned with the Project or a class of projects under investigation is also a member of the Committee.

In short, the Planning Commission has adopted an organisation which reflects its experts character. Its internal organisation is built around two hierarchies which may be called as the administrative and technical ones. The administrative hierarchy has the Secretary of the Planning Commission at the top under him Joint Secretaries, Deputy Secretaries, Under Secretaries and other lower staff. These functionaries carry out the normal administrative tasks necessary in an organisation. The technical hierarchy, on the other hand, begins with advisors who report directly to their respective members depending upon the allocation of work among them. The technical hierarchy is manned by experts, such as economists, engineers, statisticians etc. through some of the Advisors may be drawn from a generalist administrative service like the IAS also. The majority of the experts are the economists. The Planning Commission is today the single largest employer of the Indian Economic Service. The functionaries on the administrative side are drawn from the IAS and other non-technical centre services like, the Indian Audit and Accounts Service, Indian Revenue, Central Secretariat Service, etc. All taken together the Planning Commission has a staff of about 1150 out of which 450 are officers others being clerical and lower category staff.

Role of the Planning Commission : For a country like India the Planning Commission occupies a key position. In some ways, Planning Commission is a unique institution, and in the sphere of governmental organisation, there has hardly been recent development comparable in its practical importance or in its general significance, from the point of view of the 'Science of Public Administration', to the growth of Planning Commission. It is mainly a staff agency of the Government of India and acts as nerve centre of national planning. Although it has neither constitutional status nor statutory authority yet it has come to exercise significant influence over the formulation of public policies even in matters other than that of economic development, That is why Commission has been sometimes called a parallel cabinet and sometimes a super cabinet.

While the Planning Commission itself often takes the initiative in suggesting new policies or programmes one of its main function is to co-ordinate policies or programmes originating from other agencies of Government. It seems to perform to its functions through arranging a large number of consultation between various interested agencies by making the fullest use of knowledge and experience available with them for the purpose of formulations as well as evaluation of the Plan. One notable achievement of the

Planning Commission is that it has developed the process of planning into great cooperative endeavour and in this process conventions and formal understanding play no less an important role than formal legislation and order.

But the gap between planning and the implementation of the plans, between promise and performance, between slogans and operational policies during the last decade in particular, has undermined the credibility of planning. The very relevance and effectiveness of planning and the usefulness of the Planning Commission in India's socio-economic and political system have begun to be doubled many quarters. Such doubts are not in the same class as the protest of the conventional right wing opinion against any kind of planning at all of the angry denunciation at one time (heard late in fifties, the early sixties), when economic development made its most impressive gains in India that the Planning Commission was assuming the role of a "SUPER CABINET".

The Planning Commission had passed through turbulent time in the last ten years and the plans drawn by it have been a major casualty of political uncertainties, pressures and changes. The authority and prestige of the Commission has been greatly eroded in this process and it has gradually lost the key role it placed in policy making and enforcement of planning discipline at a time when development planning was making some headway during the Second and Third Five Years Plans. A body such as the Planning Commission can only function by securing a broad national consensus behind the aims and objective of development planning. It has, therefore, to be an advisory body with technical competence of a high order capable of presenting rational and considered choice to the government and the nation. The Planning has been reconstituted in 1977 after the formulation of Janta Govt. at the centre. But since the Janta Government could not last long, no healthy traditions in matters of planning could develop. There has been the gross violation of the planning discipline and total disregard for planned parameters and priorities. The Planners have been gradually pushed out of any reckoning in the planning process by the Union ministers. The state governments, on their part have tended more and more to look upon the Planning Commission as a Central instrument of interference and control.

The fact to be reckoned which indeed is that attempts have been made over the years to reduce the Planning Commission to the position of a Central government department. The Planning Commission as earlier known, thus ceased to exist.

Criticism : The Planning Commission may be subjected to the following criticism:

1. Inclusion of the Prime Minister in the Commission has made it in a way an extension of the cabinet. This has entailed a certain measure of constitutional impropriety. ARC has also pointed out this criticism.

2. It is a staff organisation being divorced from operational responsibilities. It has shown an increasing tendency to wander further away from realities particularly about limitations of resources and performance. It is, according to many a starryeyed organisation manned by persons who are fanatically applying textbook maxims.

3. Flexibility in regard to organisational development has been abused in practice. The Commission is itself a vision of Parkinson's Law. The number of personnel in the Planning Commission is around 1150.

4. There is excessive centralization of functions viz-a-viz Central Ministries and the State Governments. In addition to causing delay it undermines the sense of responsibility of the latter.

5. It has not manifested the quality or the vigour of a truly brains trust organisation.

6. Interrelationships between planning and economic welfare has made Planning Commission also an agency of economic co-ordination. But policy making in economic affairs is the primary responsibility of the

Ministry of Finance (Department of Economic Affairs). There is thus a measure of overlapping of functions, which needs to be straightened out.

The Administrative Reforms Commission examined the functions, compositions etc. of the Planning Commission and made the following recommendations:

1. The statement of the functions of the Planning Commission set out in the Government of India Resolution of March 1950, appointing the commission should with right modifications, continue to be the basis for its working. Its role should be confined to the formulation of the plans, the long term perspective plan: the five year plan and the annual plan and the evaluation of the plan performance. It should cause to involve itself in executive functions and decisions.
2. The Commission should submit an annual reports to the Parliament on plan performance.
3. The Planning Commission should be a non-statutory advisory body having close, relation with Union Government.
4. The Prime Minister has to be closely associated with the working of the Commission without being its Chairman. The Prime Minister may attend the meetings of the Commission or address it whenever he considers it necessary. The Prime Minister will preside over the meetings of the Commission.
5. The Finance Minister will also be closely associated with the working of the Commission. He will not be a member of the Commission.
6. Ministers should not be appointed as members of the Commission.
7. The number of members should not exceed seven. They will be selected on the basis of their expertise and

experience. The members may, as at present, have the status of Minister of State and the Chairman will have the status of a Cabinet Minister.

8. The members may be appointed for a fixed terms of five years. But in order to preserve continuity, the term of one or two members may be extended by a year or so. Reappointment, however, may be made only in exceptional cases.

9. A location of work may be made among the members keeping in view their special knowledge and expertise. Decision on important questions should be taken by the Commission as a whole and not by individual members.

10. The Commission should have a highly qualified persons without being tied down to any specific cadre of service as is Secretary. Its procedures should be streamlined, simplified and based on officer-orientation. The functioning of the Commission should be so organized as to provide for the triple need of analysis, thinking and planning.

11. The cabinet as a whole, and not its sub-committee should finally decide the proposals referred to it by the Commission.

The temptation to make the commission yet another place, for providing berths to out of work politicians or run it as department in the government should be avoided. Many of the weaknesses and the distortions in the planning process can be rectified if the original concept of the Planning Commission is maintained, the Commission is made a non-partisan expert advisory body with the Prime Minister as its Chairman. The latter will provide a link with the government as well as ensure that political commitments receive due attention in development planning.

Planning Machinery at the State Level

At the state level there is no Planning Commission but there is a State Planning Department which is directly under the Chief Minister. The department keeps close touch with Central Planning Commission and the various departments of the state, co-ordinating their programmes for development and formulating the development plan for the state as a whole. The plan prepared by it is put first to the Council of Ministers of the State, then to a State Development Board or Planning Advisory Committee which usually consists of State Ministers and important non-official representatives and finally to the State Legislatures. The suggestions made by the Planning Commission are generally kept in view, otherwise the procedure of Planning at the State level is practically similar to that at the Centre.

Planning Board for States Envisaged : The Planning Commission has suggested to State Governments that every one of them should establish a State Planning Board.

These Boards, it has been suggested, could be set up, more or less, on the lines of the Planning Commission and they could assist the State Governments in the formulation of the main policies and solution of the basic problems of implementation.

These Boards, in the view of the Planning Commission, could have the Chief Ministers of the States as their Chairman and could also include the State Finance Ministers as members. Like the Central Planning Commission, the State Boards could each have two or three full-time members who possess special experience and knowledge of planning economic problems.

The States have been also given the hint that the Statistical Bureaus in the states could function in close association with the State Planning Boards which could gradually develop their own expertise on planning.

Case of Boards : The Planning Commission seems to be of the view that State Planning Boards would be able to tackle planning problems more comprehensively than individual departments of State Governments who are mainly concerned with the implementation of specific projects, and solution of particular problems. The State Planning Boards it is felt, could also assess the proposals of individual departments and help them to plan in a more systematic way and with better perspective. The State Planning Boards could also co-ordinate the developmental scheme of the State better.

The information of the State Boards, in the opinion of the Planning Commission, will also facilitate improvement in the quality of planning and help in the evolution of more flexible procedures on matters like central assistance and annual planning.

It is also felt that the State Planning Boards could contribute much in bringing about closer collaboration between the Planning Commission and the States in drawing up the plan for long term development.

Planning at District and Block Levels

Below the State level an attempt is made to undertake the work of planning at the District and Block levels. This is done jointly by the officers of the various development departments and the members of the District Councils or Block Councils and/or the non-official representatives. The District Collectors and the Block Development Officers are responsible for co-ordination at the district and block level respectively.

Planning at Village Level

An experiment is being made to carry the process of planning to the village level. The village plan is to be prepared by the Village Panchayat or Council and Co-operatives with the help of the development and the extension staff at the block and the village levels.

14

Rural Development

India lives in the villages. It is rural development in the broad sense of the term that holds the key to all economic progress, industrial or agrarian, urban or rural. Poverty has remained the challenges in India's development efforts, the eradication in which is the supreme objective of all development efforts and has the widest incidence, and in fact, its source in rural areas.

Special Programmes

Rural poverty in its multi-dimensions and mass concentration has continuously engaged the attention of the government and a number of official programme of poverty alleviation have been tailored and administered to attack poverty in its different facts. These wide ranging schemes starting from the pre-independence era and including the path breaking comprehensive Community Development Programmes and other sectoral schemes for special target groups in the post- independence era worked with varying degree of success.

India is made up of villages and the majority of the Indian population live in the villages. The development of India, therefore depends upon the upliftment of the rural areas. Some of the major rural development programmes currently being implemented in India are being discussed in this part.

Integrated Rural Development Programme (IRDP) : Integrated Rural Development Programme was introduced in 1976 as it was found that problems of poverty, unemployment and underemployment in rural areas are unlikely to be solved through ad hoc and isolated sectoral programmes which were being implemented. Integrated Rural Development as a concept embraces a very ranging and comprehensive set of activities pertaining to all aspects of rural economy and covering rural people in their entirety including cultivators, landless labourers, rural artisans etc. The strategy of integrated rural development lays special emphasis on optimal utilisation of local resources—human technological and natural with the help of science and technology and an even more active involvement of people in all stages of its formulation and implementation.

Integrated Rural Development Programme is a major instrument of the strategy to alleviate rural poverty. It aims at the total development of the rural areas by linking special programmes and activities in a single strategy for developing various facts of rural society. It is, in fact, a package of programmes embracing all aspects of rural problem viz. agriculture, rural industrialization, provision of infrastructure and services like health, nutrition, education, literacy and basic amenities.

The objective of the IRDP programmes is to enable selected families in rural areas to cross the poverty line. This is achieved by providing productive assets and inputs to the target group. The assets which could be in the primary, secondary and tertiary sector, are provided through financial assistance in the form of subsidy by the Government and term credit advanced by financial institutions. The programme is implemented in all the blocks (if the country assistance is given to the rural families of the target group annual income below the cut off line of Rs. 4,800. The poverty line income having line income is identified at Rs. 6.400/.

The programme of asset-endowment under IRDP was designed to develop self-employment ventures in a variety of activities like semi-culture, animal husbandry and land-based activities in the primary, sector, weaving handicraft, etc. in the secondary sector, service and business activities in the tertiary sector. With a view to diversify the occupational structure, it had been stipulated at least 33 percent of the beneficiary coverage should as far as possible, be in the secondary and tertiary sectors. The assets provided to the selected household are financed through a mix of Government subsidies and institutional credit on average subsidy credit ratio of 1:2. The capital cost of the assets are subsidised to the extent of 25 percent for small farmers, 33-1/3 percent for marginal farmers, agricultural labourers and rural artisans and 50 percent for the scheduled tribes. A family could receive upto Rs. 3,000/- by way of subsidy in drought prone areas, the limit of subsidy ceiling was Rs. 4,000/- while for tribal families/ beneficiaries it was Rs. 5,000/-.

The Programme Evaluation Organisation of the Planning Commission, RBI, NABARD, Institute of Financial and Management Research and a number of other institutions have conducted studies in respect of IRDP. Some of the significant issues brought out by these studies are as follows:

1. The financial allocations and physical targets under the programme were determined on a uniform basis per block, without regard to the incidence of poverty, or even the size of population, which in some cases also resulted in the selection of ineligible families.
2. The extent of wrong identification was quite high at around 15-20 percent. The main reasons for wrong identification were (a) reliance on lists of households identified under the SFDA where the identification was based on land holding rather than income; (b) non-involvement of people's institutions in the survey and selection process; (c) better bank ability of those having an asset base; and (d) collusion between the government functionaries and vested interest in some cases.

3. There have also been complaints of outright leakages through corruption and malpractices which however, have not been quantified by any of the studies. Some of the factors which could have promoted this are: (a) non-involvement and lack of awareness among the beneficiaries; (b) methodology of administration of subsidy; and (c) insufficient investment in terms of project cost norms resulting in purchase of substandard assets.

4. The selection of schemes under the programme has shown an overwhelming bias towards animal husbandry more particularly much cattle, while this activity has considerable employment and income generation potential, this was vitiated by (a) the shortage of good quality animals, (b) artificial increase in prices of animals and (c) absence of linkages and support structures for feed, health cover and marketing. On the other hand, the predominance of this activity can be explained by factors such as familiarity of the beneficiaries and block functionaries alike and absence of expertise in projectisation respect to secondary and tertiary activities.

5. A major problem has been found to lie in the absence of backward and forward linkages. It appears that no real steps have been taken to provide institutional support for the supply of raw materials and more particularly for marketing. .

6. Inadequacy of banking infrastructure in certain areas particularly in the North-East, has affected credit flow adversely, shortages of staff, almost everywhere, have resulted in insufficient security and delayed disposal of loan applications and absence of supervision and follow up insistence on security in spite of instructions to the contrary has resulted in the exclusion of the poorer among the target group.

7. Another weakness of IRDP which has been discovered during the implementation is non-adoption of the cluster or group approach.

8. An important bottleneck has also been found to lie in administrative weaknesses both in terms of the qualified staff required at the block and district levels and in respect of vertical and horizontal co-ordination and integration between different departments.

Although there have been many shortcomings in the programme, there have been strong positive features also. It has resulted in substantial additional income of a large number of beneficiaries and the creation of assets also. Some of the important components of the IRDP are also being discussed in lesson.

Training of Rural Youth

The scheme of training rural youth for self-employment is a component of IRDR. The Scheme of Training Rural Youth for Self-Employment was started on 15th August 1979 with the objective of providing technical skills to rural youths to enable them to take up self-employment in the broad fields of agricultural and allied activities.

The target group of TRYSEM comprises rural youths between the ages of 18 and 35 from families living below the poverty line. The scheme lays down that a minimum of 30 percent of the trained youths should belong to Scheduled Caste and Scheduled Tribe Communities and a minimum of 3.1-3.1 percent of the rural youths trained should be women.

Training under TRYSEM is to be need-based. It is provided at institutions such as Industrial Training Institutes (ITIs) Polytechniques and Institutes run by voluntary agencies or master craftsmen who function from their own places of work. The training is imparted in a vocation of the choice of the Youth. Under the scheme the trainees get a stipend upto Rs. 150/- per month for a period of one year. If he gets training outside his village, he will be given Rs. 250/- per month. The institution/master-craftsman is also given an amount of Rs. 500/- per trainee for raw material. A kit costing Rs. 600/- is also provided to the trainees. The expenditure under the scheme is met out of IRDP.

Development of Women and Children in Rural Area (DWCRA)

The programme of development of women and children in rural areas, a sub-scheme of IRDP, is designed exclusively for the women members of rural household below the poverty line to provide them suitable avenues of income generation according to their skills and local conditions. The scheme was launched in 1982-83 as a pilot projects in 50 blocks of the country. The programme is now being implemented in 161 districts of States and Union Territories. The scheme was started for those women who were not in a position to take advantage of schemes under the IRD Programmes.

The main aim of the programme is to increase the income of the rural women of target groups by taking up income generating activities such as bamboo work, dairy development, carpet weaving, shawl making, beekeeping, handicraft, spinning, weaving, fish vending, broom and rope making, bread making, pickle making, candle making and baking.

The programme is funded by the Centre, State and UNICEF dually. Beside, UNICEF provides funds for training of officials, non-officials and also provides programme input viz. equipment to groups, child care facilities etc.

Jawahar Rozgar Yojana

Jawahar Rozgar Yojana was announced by the Government of India on April 28, 1989, to be implemented and administered by Village Panchayats all over the country. The then existing wage employment programmes viz. National Rural Employment Programme (NREP) and Rural Landless Employment Guarantee Programme (RLEGP) were merged with this Yojana.

The scheme aims to give employment to at least one member of each poor rural family for 50 to 100 days in a years, in the vicinity of places of their residences. It is also expected that some integrated schemes will be introduced to provide employment among nomadic tribes. 15 percent of total resources transferred to the village panchayats will be exclusively used for the benefit of the Schedule Castes and Scheduled Tribes. The State Government is to supply some model schemes to the village Pradhans for their guidance and 30 percent of the beneficiaries are to be women.

80 percent of the total finances of the JRY will be borne by the Central Government and the rest 20 percent will be borne by the States. The funds will be allotted to State and Union Territories in proportion to the number of persons living below the poverty line. The devolution of these funds to districts will be determined in terms of criteria of backwardness such as the share of scheduled caste and scheduled tribe with total population of the district the share of agricultural labour to total labour and the level of agricultural productivity. It has also been decided to give specific consideration to such areas as the hills, deserts and the islands.

The criteria for the distribution of resources to Village Panchayat from the districts will be on the basis of population of each village panchayat. If the population of the village panchayat is less than 1000, then, it will be assumed 1000 for the allocation of funds. At the district level the funds are allocated to the District Rural Development Agencies and Zila Parishads. The Districts Rural Development Agencies and Zila Parishads are expected to devolve the funds to the Panchayats within one month of the receipt of the money. The diversion of the funds from one district to another as well as from one village panchayat to another is not permitted under this scheme. However, if the common interest of two districts or villages exists in a particular programme, then, the pooling of the resources can be allowed.

Under this scheme the village panchayat is the pivot around which the scheme revolves. The panchayat can hold the balance to select and implement the programme which will benefit the rural community. The block authority will not interfere in the working of the panchayat. However, the block authority may assist the village panchayats in technical scrutiny of the programme.

Types of Work

As poverty is the product of economic social, political, cultural and environmental factors, a package of programmes which affects the above mentioned factors is required to mitigate the poverty. Keeping this aspect in mind the following programmes have been envisaged for the JRY—Construction of roads, houses for individual members, SC/ST, rural banks, community services such as Panchayat ghars, aganwari, primary school, water conservation, flood, and drought control, irrigation facilities, construction of institutional sanitary latrines etc.

The main objective of the programme is generation of larger employment opportunities for the unemployed population of rural population, the unemployed and underemployed persons, both men and women in the rural areas and creation of productive community assets for the direct and continuing benefits to the poverty groups. As already stated the expenditure under this programme is shared by the Centre and the States on 80:20 sharing basis. The allocation of funds to the States is made on the basis of incidence of poverty and from States to Districts, the allocation is made on the basis of number of agricultural labourers to main workers, percentage of SC/ST population of rural population.

Accelerated Rural Drinking Water Supply Programme (ARDWSP)

Rural Water Supply is basically a state subject. The Government of India, however accords top priority to this programme through the Accelerated Rural Water Supply Programme. The National Drinking Water Mission was launched in 1986 to give a sense of urgency to the task of covering all villages by 1990, which however has not been fulfilled.

Antyodaya Programme

Antyodaya means upliftment of the poorest of the poor. The programmed envisages to improve the lot of the poorest people by adopting a micro approach with family as a unity in the development programme. Efforts under this programme is concentrated on the economic development of the poorest families in the rural area and their welfare. The scheme of Antyodaya was launched first by the Rajasthan Government on October 2nd, 1977. During the time of Janta regime, many State Governments launched the Antyodaya Programme. But a change of Government subsequently the scheme was also scrapped in the States.

The Himachal Pradesh State Government reintroduced the Antyodaya Programme from the year 1990-91 and under it decided to provide subsidy to Non-SC/ST Antodaya families at par with SC/ST under IRDP. Since the programme IRDP is being implemented in the state on 50:50 sharing basis and the Government of India provides 50% subsidy only to SC/ST families and 25% to 33% subsidy to general categories, it was decided that the Non-SC/ST families identified under Antyodaya will also be provided subsidy at per with the SC/ST. Under IRDP the State Government will provide the additional funds to fill up the gap between 30% and 50% subsidy limit for different economic assets/ programme for increasing the income of the identified Antyodaya families.

Integrated Child Development Service (ICDS)

Among the nation's most precious resources are its children the architects of its future. The proper case of children must, there be a high priority for any country. The Integrated Child Development Services (ICDS) scheme was one of the major programme taken up in 1975-76 in the central sector on an experimental basis. It was started in thirty three rural/tribal blocks and some urban slums, for providing children from poor families with the basic services of health, supplementary nutrition and non-formal pre-school education for a better start in life. On the basis of the positive results of these experimental projects, the pace of expansion of this programme was accelerated in the Sixth Plan.

The major programmes of ICDS seeks to lay a solid foundation for the development of the nation's human resource by providing an integrated package of early childhood services. These consist of (i) supplementary nutrition, (ii) immunisation, (iii) health check-up, (iv) referral services, (v) nutrition and health education and (vi) non-formal education to children below 6 years and pregnant and nursing mothers in most backward/rural/tribal blocks and urban slums. ICDS activities centre around the anganwadi where children upto six years as well as pregnant women and nursing mothers are given a daily cooked meal to improve their nutritional status. The ICDS is one of the most comprehensive scheme for child development in the country. It recognizes the essential links between good nutrition and health care, education and proper child care by the mother. For women and children from poverty-stricken families in rural, urban and tribal areas, the ICDS beings hope of a better life and a way of breaking out of the various circle of poverty, ill health and illiteracy.

Drought Prone Areas Programme

Drought Prone Areas Programme is under operation in the arid and semi-arid parts of the country where environment is degraded due to soil erosion, loss of vegetation cover, water stress etc. The programme aims at restoration of ecological balance on a long term basis through harmonious development of land and water resources.

Integrated Rural Energy Planning Programme (IREPP)

On the basis of the sixth plan experience of Pilot Projects, IREP Programme which was found successful, the IREPP was fully activated in all the States and Union Territories during the Seventh Plan. The IREP programme consists of the following components:

(a) Developing institutional mechanism in the State/UTs

(b) Training

(c) Project preparation

(d) Project implementation

(e) Provision of financial incentives

(f) Monitoring

These components are funded through Central and States financial outlays for IREPP. The Central financial component is utilised for setting up institutional mechanism through funds for staff support and their training and monitoring of the programme. The State financial component would be utilised for project preparation project implementation and for provision of financial incentives to users and manufacturers for IREP projects.

Desert Development Programme (DDP)

In certain parts of the country ecological balance has been so severely upset that conditions of extreme aridity, shifting sand, scanty vegetation and severe wind erosion prevail. For controlling, the process of desertification and restoration of ecological balance, the Desert Development Programme was launched in these areas. The main activities covered are sand-dune stabilisation shelter belt plantation, conversion of surface water, recharge of ground water squatters, efficient water resource management, afforestation grassland and pasture development and horticulture.

Land Reforms Programme (LRP)

Land Reforms measures have been perceived as an integral part of the strategy for rural development with focus on disengaging the rural poor from exploitative agrarian relations. In the context of the scattered nature of land holdings, redistribution of land constitutes an important step in social and economic upliftment of the weaker sections. Various land reform measures have been pursued since Independence to provide access for the landless rural poor to land.

Agricultural Marketing Programme (AMP)

The Agricultural Marketing Programme envisages, among other things, regulation of agricultural markets, grading and standardisation of agricultural and allied commodities, assistance for setting up of rural godowns, market research and planning and training of personnel.

Thus we see that a number of programmes have been introduced for the development of rural areas. However, any strategy of development can succeed only with the help of an active participation of the population for which such a strategy had been conceived and put forth. Such participation of the people has to be organized, continuous and active for the continued success of the various programmes.

15

Personnel Administration

Personnel Administration is the totality of concern with the human resources of organization. It is one of the organisation's major linkages with its environment. It applies in microcosm the values, the ethics, the philosophy of that environment, and it in turn influences the environment. To whatever extent this is true in any organisation, it is all the more true in the public service simply because of its size and its relationship to the whole people. Personnel administration is that branch of administration which is responsible, on a staff basis for concentrating on those aspects of operation which one primarily deals with the relationship of management to employees and employees to employees and with the development of individual and group. It is the process of attracting, holding and motivating people involving all managers-line and staff.

Personnel Administration is the planning, organizing, directing and controlling of the procurement, development, compensation, integration, maintenance and separation of much resources to the end that individual, organizational and societal objectives are accomplished. Edwards Flipps States.

Personnel Administration is something of state of mind. It is an attitude compounded by understanding both the forces which shape manpower, needs, supply and problems and at the same time, the importance of human will and personality. It is kind of continual educational process for employer and employee alike. It is management's conscience as well as its privilege; it is employee's obligation as well as their right. It is enlightenment in the fusing of organisational goals with individual needs.

Prof. Jucius has defined Personnel Administration : "The field of management which has to do with planning, organising, directing and controlling various operative functions of procuring, developing, maintaining and utilising a labour force, such that the: (a) objectives, for which the organization is established are attained economically and effectively; (b) objectives of all lands of personnel are served to the highest, possible degree; and (c) objectives of the community are duly considered and served". According to this definition, Personnel Administration is concerned with the managerial (planning, organising, directing and controlling) and operative (procurement, development, maintenance and utilisation) functions, with a view to attaining the organisational goals economically and effectively and meeting the individual and social goal.

Personnel Administration is basically concerned with people at work and their relationship with each other. The Institute of Personnel Management U.K. has defined personnel management as follows:

"Personnel Management is part of management function which is concerned with people at work and with their relationship within an enterprise. Its aim is to bring together and develop into an effective organisation the men and women who make up an enterprise and having regard to the well-being of an individual and of working groups, to enable to make their best contribution to its success."

Personnel examines what is, can be or should be done to make people more productive and more satisfied with their work. The contributions of the personnel functions to organisational effectiveness are reflected in the objectives pursued by personnel specialised and departments:

1. To provide the enterprise with well-trained and well-motivated employees.
2. To use the work force efficiently and effectively.
3. To develop and maintain a quality of work life that makes employment in the enterprise a desirable personnel and social situation.
4. Personnel consists of numerous activities, including employment recruitment, selection, and orientation.
5. Career development and counselling, performance evaluation, and training and development.
6. Compensation and protection.
7. Labour relations.
8. Equal Employment opportunity programmes.
9. Discipline, control and evaluation of the personnel function.

In particular, Personnel Administration is concerned with the development and application of policies governing the following factors:

1. Manpower planning, recruitment, selection, placement and termination.
2. Education and training and career development.
3. Term of employment and methods and standard of remuneration.
4. Working conditions and employee's services.
5. Formal and informal communication and consultation, both through the representatives of employer and employees and at all levels throughout the enterprises.

6. Negotiation application of agreement on wages and working conditions.

Personnel Administration in India, as it is interpreted, discussed and practised, is largely static, legalistic and ritualistic. Assisting top management in realising the last concept of statemanship is the central task and fundamental purpose of dynamic personnel Administration. There are three fundamental concepts of dynamic personnel administration recognised in contemporary time. First is the concept of the development of people to their fullest potentialities.

Personnel Administration is a live responsibility but also a staff function in Administration. It is a basic management responsibility, permeating all levels and types of administration in all organisation, private or public. Personnel specialists help line managers by providing advice, counsel, services and various types of controls to help administration secure consistent administration of personnel policies which serve individual needs and further organizational objectives.

The Scope

The personnel function occupies a paradoxical position in public administration. The well performed personnel function probably touches on or is involved in a wider range of activities, than any other organisational function. The hopes, aspirations, fears, problems and apathies, actions, balance, creativity and innovativeness of people determine the ultimate success or failure of the organisation. The basic functions of Personnel Administration in an organisation are as follows:

1. Placing the right man on the right job.
2. Starting new employees in the organization.
3. Training men for jobs that are new to him.
4. Improving job performance of each man.

5. Gaining creative co-operation and developing smooth working relationship.

6. Interpreting policies and procedures.

7. Controlling labour costs.

8. Creating and maintaining a high level of developmental morale.

9. Protecting health and physical condition of employees.

Personnel Administration in India can now boast of sophisticated training courses including sensitivity and grid systems, management by objective system, performance appraisal technical the application of behavioural science and groups dynamic, and knowledge of such other modern administration practices.

Emerging Role

In view of the imposing challenges confronting the human resources in organization, a final challenge is axiomatic increasing effectiveness of the human resources, function in helping solve the people problems confronting business. The focus of the personnel function has to be On process helping evolve less formal process that line administration can use to better manage people. Thrust, is, to be on process orientation. The personnel function has to assure that human resources strategies are developed and that they are linked to and supportive of organisational goals and strategies.

Research Organisation

This is to include:

- Audit of current practices and manpower utilisation.
- Experimentation of innovative ideas.
- Evaluation of personnel programmes.
- Computerisation of manpower information system for increasing quality and efficiency.

Developing Personnel Policies

- Modification of human resources system to have the growth and development expectation of employees.
- Policies to become more sensitive to organisation's internal needs have long range perspective.
- Consistency and fairness in implementation and interpretation.

16

The Recruitment

Recruitment of personnel for the Civil Services is one of the crucial task of modern government and lies at the heart of problem of personnel administration. The main test of any machinery of recruitment lies in the ability to recruit the right type of persons for the right jobs. Today every nation is paying more and more attention to the problem of recruitment of civil service personnel. There is a desire that only intelligent, vigorous and persons with initiative and farsightedness should be picked up as civil servants.

A very important problem of the public, personnel is that of recruitment. Recruitment deals with efforts to find out and induce suitable candidates to compete for appointment to the Public Service. A bad policy of recruitment can wreak the entire personnel programme. Recruitment is selection by competent authority for trial appointment to a post in a service. This is perhaps the most important aspect of personnel administration.

Concept and Meaning

Recruitment is of considerable importance to administrative organisations, for it is crucial to a strong and efficient public service.

It is the cornerstone of the whole public personnel structure. It has a specific meaning and according to Dimock, "It means securing the right people for particular jobs and it may take the form of advertising for large groups of employees or tracking out a highly skilled individual for specific work."

The term 'Recruitment' has no precise meaning. According to L.D. White, it is limited to the specific steps taken to attract suitable conditions to apply for examinations. In the words of J.D. Kingsley, "Public recruitment may be defined as that process through which suitable candidates are induced to compete for appointments to the Public Service". For a common man recruitment means picking up persons for filling up vacant jobs in an office. Technically however, recruitment means not only making appointments but selecting proper and suitable candidates. Thus for a job there can be many candidates but no recruitment may be made. In the words of D. Waldo, "Public recruitment may be defined as that process through which suitable candidates are induced to compete for appointment to the public service. " It is an effort to attract honest and qualified person with a tact for serving the people. Recruitment system may be both negative and positive. The basic elements of a positive recruitment policy according to Stahal are:

1. The discovery and cultivation of the employment market for different posts in the public service.
2. Use and publicity of attractive recruitment literature.
3. Adoption of scientific tests for determining the abilities of candidates.
4. Investigation of capable candidates from within the services.
5. Effective placement programmes and
6. An efficient follow-up probationary programme.

The increasingly technical nature of public service and growth of democratic ideas and institutions have made the problem of recruitment and selection much more important today than ever before. No aspect of public personnel administration is more important than recruiting, for unless the basic material is reasonably good, no amount of in-service training, supervision, service-rating, classification, or research will be able to provide an adequate staff of public employees. In short, recruitment is the first step in the employment programme and it is regarded everywhere as the core of the personnel process.

The Process

Recruitment of personnel for the civil services is one of the most crucial tasks of government. The increasing diversification of the nature of civil service functions and growth of democratic and equalitarian principles have largely determined the normative context of personnel recruitment in democratic countries. J.D. Kingsley says, "Public recruitment may be defined as that process through which suitable candidates are included to compete for appointments to the public service. It is thus an integral part of a more inclusive process-selection which also includes the process of examination and certification " According to Pfiffner and Presthus, "Personnel recruitment for the second half of the twentieth century will have to be geared to a nuclear physical world in which the solutions of human problems will demand the utmost in human competence. The emphasis will be not only on finding, but on building men who are capable of performing the complex task of co-ordinating institutions growing even more complex. "

The process of recruitment includes number of different steps which are as follows:

1. Announcement of examinations, through newspapers, journals and other media.

2. Holding of examination for testing or determining the abilities of the recruits.

3. Certification is the process of sending for an appointment.

4. Selection is the act of choosing from eligible candidates.

5. Appointment is made by the competent authorities of selected recruits. Appointment may be permanent, temporary, provisional.

6. Placement refers to the putting of recruited persons in the right jobs.

Various Methods

Recruitment from Within or by Promotion versus Recruitment from Without or Direct Recruitment. When the recruitment to the higher posts is made form among those who are already working in the lower grades, it is called recruitment from within. But when the persons for higher jobs are recruited by open competition and those considered as the best picked up, the system is called, that of the system from without. The former is called the system of recruitment by promotion whereas the latter is called that of direct recruitment. Each system has its own advantages and disadvantages.

Merit Promotion System

The method of recruitment, in which employees already in the service are promoted to higher post has certain merits:

1. Personnel have got experience of the government job, and this past experience helps them in performing new duties.

2. This method of recruitment provides ample opportunities for advancement to the employees. It is a great incentive to the employees to work efficiently.

3. In the promotion system another advantage is that there is already a personnel relationship between the officer

and subordinate but in case of merit appointment there is no such thing.

4. The very expectation of promotion as a reward for faithful and zealous service is of immeasurable value for the working morale of the service.

5. The personnel are already trained and therefore they can be entrusted with the new job without any risk or difficulty.

Defects of Promotion System

1. Under this system only those who are comparatively old and have lost much of their vigour and energy are provided an opportunity to hold high responsible offices.

2. Since it is a closed door system therefore it does not provide for fresh entry of the people in the service.

3. It narrows down the area of selection because recruitment is confined only to those who are already in the service. It is likely that less capable persons may be recruited. It leads to stagnation because there is no injection of new blood into service.

Direct Recruitment System

The principles of equality of opportunity is best served by the method of direct recruitment. Under the system the area of selection considerably widened and selection board get an opportunity to select the most capable and competent available persons in the market. The system is also in accordance with democratic principles which stands for equal opportunities for all. In the system stress is laid on written examination and interviews.

Qualifications of the Candidates

This factor is of enormous importance, for the efficiency of the service depends upon its qualifications required General/ Special.

General Qualifications

Civil Status : Since the growth of nation—states it has become a universal practice to recruit only citizens.

Residence : The domicile qualification is generally laid down in public services in countries with federal systems. In India domicile rules were prevalent till 1957 and have been discarded now.

Sex : Previously public services were the monopoly of men, but not now. India, Article 116(1) of the Constitution lays down that "There shall be equality of opportunity for all citizens in matters relating to employment of appointment to any office under the State."

Age : Two practices are generally followed. Some countries like India and Britain prefer young people while the U.S.A. employs more mature people. In India, young men, women in 16-28 age group enter the services.

Special Qualifications

Education : In India every university graduates can sit for the civil service competitive examination and the subject are so broad based at to include the wide range of university subjects.

Technical Experience : This is an essential to fill up technical posts in public administration by professionals like doctors, engineers and technicians etc.

Written Examination

Written test may be either essay-type or objective types in forms. In India the purpose of these examinations is to know the general intelligence or superior mind of the candidates. The examinations are held in the subjects; Which are taught in the Universities and Colleges. Essay type are meant to examine the power and clarity of expression and the standard of logical thinking of the candidates. The objective type of usually employed to test the general knowledge and speed of thinking, written test fall under the following main categories :

The Ability Tests : The main objective of this tests is to know the general mental ability of the candidates.

Aptitude Test : These tests used for recruitment in defence and other technical services.

Personality Tests : These are highly complex psychiatric devices meant to test hidden traits of human personality.

Oral Test or Interview

Oral interviews are resorted to measure the personal characteristics of the candidates by a competent Board. Such tests are quite frequently held in India for making selection of candidates both by the departmental heads as well as public service commissions both in the states and at the Centre. The oral tests can be individual as well as in group.

Forms of Recruitment

There are three main forms of Civil Service Recruitment. They are as follows:

Cadet System : Under this system recruitment is made at a young age, usually between 16 and 20 years, followed by a long period institutional training.

General Mental Ability : Under this system the government seeks to recruit young men and women after graduation in the liberal arts of basic science between the age group of 21 and 28 years for broad educational attainments and mental ability. It is based on the concept of career civil service.

Expertise : The government recruits people with specific qualifications, technical knowledge or experience suited for the recruitment to various posts. This system has the same objectives as the 'Lateral entry system', under which a certain quota is fixed for recruitment to the senior service posts. The age scale of recruitment varies from 18 to 45 years. The 'lateral entry system' may be followed in recruitment on the basis of general mental ability.

Administrative Machinery

Direct Recruitment to administrative and most of executive services is made on the basis of a competitive examination conducted by the UPSC. The scheme of examination is combination of three different views about what qualities need to be tested for entry into the administrative services. These are :

1. Belief in the transferability of academic talent to government work.
2. Object of selection is the assessment of the entire personality of the applicant and matching the selected one with the type of work in the Civil Services.
3. To select persons possessing intellectual ability and training, but whose intellectual training has been in subjects which provide the essential background, and knowledge, required for work in the civil service.

The problem of recruitment involves a number of elements as follows:

Location of the Recruitment Authority

There are two views on the subject. On the elective system. This system provides that:

1. The recruitment power should vest in the electorates.
2. All important officers of the government should be elected.
3. These officers should be elected for shorter period.

The system is open to criticism, (a) when it comes to election of a large number of officials, the electorate may not make a wise choice. (b) The electorate is likely to be swayed by personal considerations. (c) only a limited number of officials who have policy-determining functions need be under political control, not all of them.

Two, only the chief executive and the members of the legislature should be elected and all other officials be appointed by a system of recruitment.

Major Problems

Increase in the Number of Posts and Applicants. It is becoming very difficult for the Public Service Commissions to cope with such increasing work judiciously and meticulously. It is suggested that the commissions should concentrate more on policy formation like the U.K. and U.S. while the execution of the policy may be decentralized to the specially appointed officers.

Ineffective Probation System : It is not possible to guarantee the suitability of candidates through recruitment as there is possibility of some unfit candidates entering the services. Therefore, the appointment should be in the first instance on probation. The object of the probationary period is to give the appointing authority sufficient opportunity to observe and evaluate the ability, capacity and fitness of the employees to perform the duties satisfactorily. The probation period should be considered as an opportunity for the appointing authority to complete selection process. The new appointees should be carefully supervised and critical observation made of the work during the period of probation.

Recruitment Operations are Protected and Need Stream Lining : It takes a very long time between the advertisement of the job and the appointment. This creates great deal of inconvenience and harassment to the potential candidates as they cannot take up temporary employment for fear of not being relieved in time. On the other hand, the government suffers from lack of competent people. There is need to cut short delays by modifying and streamlining the recruitment procedures.

Ineffective Publicity : At present, recruiting authorities only fulfil the formality of advertising the posts and never try to get the best persons to fulfil the job. So there is need of positive publicity to attract the best talent.

Absence of Recruitment Rules: Absence of such rules result in corruption, favouritism and nepotism. There is need to ensure laying down recruitment rules for every cadre of service and post.

Proper Placements : An employee can give his best to the service only when he gets the proper opportunity to use his knowledge, skills and abilities. Maximum utilisation of employees energy is possible only if the placement are made according to the capacities, aptitudes, inclinations and capabilities of the employees, so some efforts must be made in this direction.

Recruitment Reforms

Any serious study of the problem reveals that drawing up a long-term recruitment plan is not merely a matter of statistical forecasting. In fact, the adoption of any such plan entails laying down very precise standards and more important, choosing a personnel policy. We shall now consider the long term programmes of (i) Statistical Forecasting, (ii) Standard, (iii) the Choice of a policy.

Statistical Forecasting : The objective of a long-term recruitment plan is to determine for a given period, several years in advance, the number and type of posts to be filled by recruitment. These requirements must be determined as precisely as possible with a view to formulating a recruitment policy. More specially, it is necessary to ascertain, in addition to the number of posts, the grade levels and to corresponding type of occupation. A number of objections may arise with regard to the feasibility forecasting. The number and type of new posts will be created and the number and type of resignations and deaths.

Standards : The idea of long-term planning is incompatible with any vogue system. The purpose of such planning is to determine what staff need to be recruited, by what date, with what qualifications, at what age, and in what type of appointment. A precise system for calculation and classifications is therefore required. The setting of the above objectives call for the number of posts to be filled by external recruitment.

The Choice of a Policy : All the foregoing remarks point to the conclusion that recruitment to posts which are reserved in principle for filling by promotion should logically take place increasingly at the junior level. Posts to be filled by direct external recruitment at middle level should be increasingly reserved for expert possessing special qualification. Lastly, it seems necessary to note that preparation of a long term recruitment plan should have two additional advantages that are by no means negligible.

From the technical point of view, the preparation of detailed programme of the recruitment operations should make it possible to eliminate almost all the time lag which occurs between the occurrence of a vacancy and the appointment of a new staff member to fill it.

From the policy point of view, a knowledge, grade by grade, of the number of separations (retirements, expiry of appointments, etc.) may make it possible to calculate in advance the changes which will be made in the years ahead.

Administrative Reforms Commission Recommended Following:

1. For all services advance projections should be made of the requirements of personnel for five years at a time. Mid term appraisal also should be made if circumstances warrant it and necessary correction made on the basis of the appraisal.
2. Such projections should be made by cadre management committee.
3. The recruitment to Engineering posts should as far as possible, be made only through competitive examination, and the selection after a simple interview should

be restricted to cases where some prior experience or special qualifications other than the basic degree are required or where new projects are to be undertaken at a short notice.

4. A committee should be set up to go into the questions of devising speedier methods of recruitment, in general of bringing down the proportion of candidates to posts, of reducing the expenditure on publicity, and revising the syllabus of the examinations for the higher services.
5. The total number of chances a candidate can take for the technical as well as the non—technical services should be restricted to two.
6. A special competitive examination for non—technical class I services may be held for first class graduates who have an aggregate of not less than 60 percent marks either at the first degree or the Master's degree.
7. In order to provide greater opportunities for the advancement of talented persons who are not already in class-I.

(a) The quota of vacancies in class I to be filled by promotion may be increased upto maximum of 40 percent where the existing quota falls short of that percentage.

(b) Everyone who has completed 6 years of service in Govt. and is less than 35 years of age may be given one and only one chance to sit for the open competitive examination for class I non—technical services, irrespective of the chances already taken, provided that he fulfils conditions relating to educational qualification.

8. Provision should be made for appointment to technical posts at the senior level of persons of proved competence from universities and industrial and commercial concerns etc. if the capabilities and expertise possessed by them are needed and are not available within the

ranks of the civil service. Care should be taken to regulate the seniority of lateral entrants.

9. Direct recruitment to class II posts of section officers may be stopped and these posts may be filled by promotion of assistants.

10. Direct recruitment to class II posts whose incumbents perform duties similar to those allotted to junior class I officers may be abolished. Such posts may be filled entirely by promotion.

11. For recruitment to clerical and repetitive jobs not calling for any special skill, simple objective tests may be devised and adopted in place of the essay type of examination or where no examinations are held at present.

12. There should be a provision for recruiting from the personnel of the state Governments for Central posts in organisations like the Secretariat and the Department of agriculture and education etc.

The Arguments

The plea for an All-India Service is ostensibly based on three grounds. The All India Service is considered to be a bulwark of national integration as its members possess an all India outlook. Secondly, being recruitment on an All-India basis it tends to attract the best talent in the country so vital for the accomplishment of national tasks. Thirdly, it reinforces the sense of independence and impartiality of its members by affording protection against local pressures and influences.

Broadly, the arguments against the All-India Services are as follows. Firstly the State ought to enjoy the right to recruit and control the civil service for the performance of tasks which have been allotted to them under the constitution. An All-India Service restricts the degree and sphere of their autonomy and patronage.

Secondly, in order to attract people from all over the country, and also to enable them to serve efficiently even in parts of the country, the pay scale of the All State Civil Services. This imposes heavier financial burden on the states, leaving them with correspondingly less resources for development task. Thirdly, the All India Services keep the members of the state services alienated and thus have a demoralising effect on the totality of civil service.

Besides, the All-India Services have to encounter from now onward practical difficulties which may render them increasing by unworkable. The recruitment to these services through the medium of regional languages makes maintenance of a common standard in the candidates highly improbable. A person selected to an All-India Service may not know the language of the state to which he has been posted. He may be sure, acquire working familiarity with the regional language of the adopted state but may not become fully proficient in it. Besides a member of the All-India Service also comes to the Central Government from time to time for a tour of duty. As the language in vogue in the Central Government is English, he may not prove to be effective in it. Indeed a member of the All-India Service is likely to be effective only at one level because of the language itself. As a result there is the risk of a person's remaining 'frozen' into ineffectiveness if he does know the language of the Central Government as well as that of the state to which he has been posted.

The foregoing analysis suggests that the All India Service as an institution is unlikely to remain unscathed in the foreseeable future. Statemanship lies in starting a meaningful dialogue with the states on the question. A suggestion has been made that, apropos the working of Article 312 of the Constitution, an All-India Services need be constituted only after its specific endorsement by the States formally signified through a resolution of their legislatures. This would give it political legitimacy. It may even be that a politically acceptable solution would lie in entrusting the Central Government with the recruitment and initial training of personnel and the State Government with complete control over them.

Recruitment Agencies

Sound recruitment policies and fair recruitment methods are of basic importance to personnel administration. The determination of recruitment authority is one of the essential features of the personnel system. In order to eliminate the pressure of recruiting authorities being subjected to pressure by those in possession of executive power, the constitution of India provides for the setting up of Public Service Commission independent of the executive, at the Union and State levels.

The growth of Public Service Commission as independent body to advise the executive in service matters, like recruitment, discipline, promotion, etc., is of comparatively recent origin. The Government of India, Act, 1919 prescribed that a Public Service Commission shall be established in India to discharge, in regard to recruitment and control of the Public Services such functions as may be assigned to it by the Secretary of State- in-council. The Public Service Commission came into existence for the first time in 1926 when the Central Public Service Commission was established under the Government of India Act, 1919. It was renamed as the Federal Public Service Commission after the Ist April, 1937, on the introduction of the Government of India Act 1935. This Act had also made a provision for the creation of Provincial Public Service Commissions. The Federal Public Service Commission Continued as such till 1950, when with the Constitution coming into force, it was designated "The Union Public Service Commission". The Public Service Commissions in India have a constitutional status and are in a stronger position than the Civil Service Commissions in the U.S.A. and Britain.

The U.S. Civil Service Commission was set up under a statute passed by the Congress in 1883, but was recently abolished, and replaced by the office of Personnel Management. The Civil Service Commission of United kingdom owes itself to an order-in-council, and thus does not have even a statutory base; what is more, it has been made a part of the Civil Service Department and thus does not function as a separate body.

In the Indian Constitution, Article 315 provides for the establishment of a Union Public Service Commission and State Public Service Commission but it also provides that if the legislatures of two or more states authorise the parliament by resolution, it may establish a Joint Commission for those states. Moreover, the Union Public Service Commission may also, if requested by the Governor of a State, agree with the approval of the President to perform the work of the State Commission.

Public Service Commission

The number of members constituting the Union Public Service Commission or a Joint Public Service Commission and conditions of their service are determined by the President of India and in the case of State Public Service Commission by the Governor of the State concerned by regulations. The Constitution has not fixed the number of the members of the Union or State Public Service Commissions but has left the matter to the discretion of the President or the Governor as the case may be. It has been decided that there shall be seven to eight members of the Union Public Service Commission. The members of UPSC and Joint PCS's are appointed by the President and those of State Public Service Commission by the Governor. It has been further provided that one half of the members of the Commission, Union or State, must have held office for at least ten years either under the Government of India or the Government of a State.

A member holds office for six years or until he attains, in case of the UPSC, the age of 65 years and in the case of State Commission, the age of 60 years whichever is earlier. A member can be removed from office only by an order of the President on the ground of insolvency, infirmity of mind or body or engagement in paid employment outside the duties of his office. He may also be removed on the ground of misbehaviour, if, following a reference to an enquiry by the Supreme Court, the Court has upheld the cause of removal.

The Constitution further provides that any concern or interest in any contract or agreement made by the Government of India or participation in any way in the profits these will be sufficient proof of misbehaviour. The other conditions of service of the members are determined by the President, but those cannot be changed to the disadvantage of the members during their terms of office. The entire expenses of the Commission, including the salaries of members, are charged to the Consolidated Fund of India. This means that they are not required to be submitted to the vote of Parliament.

In order to ensure the impartiality and independence of the members, the Constitution provides that, the incumbent will be ineligible for any further appointment in the same office or in any office under the Government except a higher appointment in the same commission. The President of India determines the salary and other conditions of service of the members of the Commission through regulations. The Chairman and members of the Commissions are paid the salary equivalent to the judges of Supreme Court in case of UPSC and judge of High Court in case of State PSC.

It is matter for concern that the procedure for the appointment of members has led to complaints that some State Governments have appointed as members, persons who are not competent. The Law Commission in its 1958 report, has also gone on record, saying that in the States, appointments to the membership of the Public Service Commission have sometimes been made on grounds of party and political affiliations and not considerations of merit.

In Britain, the Civil Service Commission consists of Commissioners (one of them designated as First Commissioner) appointed by the crown and holding office during good behaviour. Their number varied from time to time. Originally in 1953 there were six of them of whom two were part time. In Britain there are no special safeguards provided to protect the security or independence of the Civil Service Commissions, but long tradition and public opinion have done what elsewhere such safeguards are intended to achieve and the British Civil Service Commissions have world-wide reputation for their impartiality and independence.

In the U.S.A. the Federal Civil Service Commission consists of three commissions appointed by the President with the advice and consent of the senate for an indefinite term. The law requires the commission to be partisan which means that all its members cannot belong to the same political party. In practice of its three members, two belong to one political party and one to the other, the President is empowered to remove a commissioner at any time, but the vacancy must be filled with the concurrence of senate as usual. In its administrative work the commissioner is assisted by an Executive Director and Chief Examiner under whom there is a large staff to carry out the detailed work in connection with the Commission's activities. The U.S. Civil Service Commission also enjoys a high reputation for integrity and fairness. States have their own Civil Service Commissions organized on similar lines.

The U.S.A. is a big country and its federal personnel is much larger than that of other federal countries like India where much of the federal work is entrusted for performance to state offices.

Also, as will appear presently, the U.S. Civil Service Commission has to perform many more duties in connection with classification, hearing of appeals, etc., that belong to their opposite numbers in U.K. and India. The U.S. Civil Service Commission has, therefore, been obliged to develop a field organisation and to decentralise its work through it. Outside its mission has, therefore, been obliged to develop a field organisation headquarters at Washington, it has 13 district offices in the more important cities, 5,000 local examining boards and about 150 rating boards. Each district office is under a district manager who supervises the activities of the local examination boards and rating boards in his area. The local boards consist of certain federal employees serving in the field offices of the various departments. They act as representative of the commission in their respective areas and conduct examination and others connecting activities in that area.

The rating boards are established at centres which need a supply of skilled tradesman and mechanics and their function is to recruit and select these classes of employees. The supervision and check of the Commission over these bodies is maintained through the district manager who is an employee of its own. Same way, the classification work has been decentralised to departmental personnel agencies. The commission's own staff lays down the standard and detailed specification or classification. The departmental agency does the classification. The departmental agency conformity with them is later tested by post audit or check.

The functions and duties of civil service commissions vary widely in different countries. Broadly speaking we may classify these functions into three classes : (1) the selection of candidates for appointment and duties incidental thereto, e.g., checking up health and character of successful candidates, their assignment to the different departments and sometimes confirmation of appointment after the probationary period; (2) promotion disciplinary cases and hearing appeals and (3) fixing of salaries and wages, classification of posts, conditions of service, negotiations with service associations, organisations and methods, and training and research into personnel problem.

Functions of the Public Service Commission : The function of the Commission as prescribed in article 320 of the Constitution fall into two categories.

(a) Administrative. (b) Advisor.

The administrative functions relate to recruitment to all India Civil Service and posts under the Union Government or the State Government by written examination, or, and by interview. The advisory functions relate to advising the Government on all matters.

1. To advise the Government, on all matters relating to the method of recruitment and principles to be followed in making appointment to civil services either directly or by promotion.
2. To conduct examinations for appointment to the All India and Union Services. Some of the important of

these examinations are—The combined examination for the ITS, IAS, IPS, I.R.S. and other central services, the Joint Services Wing examination, the Engineering Services examinations and the Ministerial Services examination. For the various examinations conducted by it in 2000-2001, there was a total of some 2,49,000 candidates, of those the Commission interviewed some 17656.

3. To interview candidates for recruitment.

4. To advice the government on the suitability of candidates for promotion and transfer. Recommendation for such promotions are made by the concerned department and the Commission is requested to rectify them. On the average the Commission handles about 4000 cases annually.

5. The Commission is also consulted on matters like temporary appointments for periods exceeding one year but not exceeding three years, grant of extension of service and re- employment of certain retired servants. About 1,000 such cases came up every year.

6. To advise the government on disciplinary matters affecting civil servants. In 1998, the number of cases relating to promotion, disciplinary matters, seniority etc., was 31,509. On an average the disciplinary cases were 300 in a year.

7. The Commission is also consulted on matters like regularization of appointments, claims for awards of pension, claims for reimbursement of legal expenses incurred by government servants, in defending legal proceeding instituted against them in respect of acts done in the execution of their official duties, claims for pension of compensation in respect of injuries sustained while on duty.

8. To advise the government on any other matter specifically referred to it by the President.

Moreover, under article 321 there is a provision in the Constitution authorizing Parliament to extend the functions of the Commission.

Though it is obligatory on the part of the government to consult the Commission on these matters, however, failure to do so will not render the action invalid. The President has the authority to exclude posts, services and matters from the purview of the Commission. But all such regulations have to be laid down by him before each house of Parliament, as soon as possible, if not in session or repeal these regulations.

Annual Report : The Constitution provides that it is the duty of the UPSC and SPSC to present annually to the President or the Governor, as the case may be, report of its work. Immediately after the receipt of such report the President or the Governor is required to lay before each of Parliament or State Legislature together with memorandum of the cases where the advice of the commission was not accepted and reasons for such non—acceptance. It must be remembered, however, that the Commission is only an advisory body and its recommendations are not binding on the government. Yet it must be mentioned that by and large, the Commission's recommendations are accepted by the Government.

The working of the Union Public Service Commission as well as of the State Public Service Commission is increasing every year. Historically, the Public Service Commission emerged with a negative role-namely to keep the 'rascals' out. It is only after the 'rascals' have been kept out that a more positive role came to be gradually evolved. Talent-hunting marks the second stage in the history of Public Service Commissions in the world. In India the Public Service Commissions designed as to function in the first stage, for the Constitution does not envisage any wider or vital role for the Commission in personnel administration. It is par excellence a recruiting sergeant with purely advisory role, consulted also in certain disciplinary and other matters.

The ARC report on personnel administration had made some recommendations with respect to the appointment of members of the UPSC/ SPSCs on a uniform pattern. Welcoming the idea behind the suggestion of the study team on centre-state relationship that as far as possible one third of the members of SPSCs should consist of members belonging to another state, it recommended that it could be sufficient if provision was made for the appointment of at least one member of a State PSC from outside the state. It also recommended : (a) in making appointment to a State PSC, the Governor should consult the Chairman of the UPSC and the Chairman of State PSC. The latter may be consulted also with regard to the appointment of his own successor (b) in making appointment to the UPSC the Chairman of UPSC should invariably be consulted (even with regard to the appointment of his own successor). And (c) not less than two thirds of the membership of the UPSC should be drawn from among the Chairman and members of state PSCs.

It can be seen that these recommendations, besides maintaining uniform standards in the appointment of the members of the Commission, do at the same time, aim at a better coordination of their activities. This also implies that UPSC should have an integrative role in more vis-a-vis the lower courts in the states. Another of its recommendations with respect to the creation of a research cell in each of the PSC, where all the relevant date regarding candidates, etc. may be assembled, collected and interpreted is an attempt of sponsoring research activities in a vital sphere on a coordinated and cooperative basis. Another recommendation of ARC is that the minimum academic qualification for membership of a commission should be a university degree.

The formal contracts between the UPSC and SPSC will be useful is a fact which hardly needs justification. There has been considerable criticism of the manner in which many State PSCs have functioned. It has been alleged that the functioning of some of the State PSCs has reflected the "factionalism" and the "groupism.', prevailing in the ruling party in these states. It has also been very often charged that some members appointed to

State Commissions had neither requisite training nor the background for discharging properly the functions of an impartial and judicial organisation. The result is that while the prestige of the UPSC has remained fairly high, the prestige of some of the SPSC has fluctuated. It cannot also be denied that the relationship between the governments and the Public Service Commission in some states has not been very cordial and that some often than not the State Governments have gone against the advice tendered by their Public Service Commissions.

Another suggestion worth serious consideration is that the UPSC should be entrusted with the power of some kind of supervision over the State Commissions. For example, it might be given the power to review the various recruitment rules or service principles to ensure that they are in consonance with the standards governing service in the Central Government. This would also ensure that the civil servants in different states are not subjected to varying standards of treatment with regard to their rights and privileges, and eventually, in respect of emoluments as well. In the context of the peculiar social, economic and political factors in India, it is inevitable that a healthy relationship should obtain between UPSC and SPSC in order to ensure uniformity of standards in recruitment, service conditions and personnel practices relating to the Central and State Government employees.

Staff Selection Commission

The Union Public Service Commission is the recruitment agency for the higher civil service (i.e., Group A and Group B) in the Central Government. Till 1975, there was no centralized agency in government to make recruitment to the group 'C' posts. As more than fifty per cent of the civil servants fall in group C, an absence of a body to undertake recruitment to this class becomes a serious weakness in the personnel system of the country. On November 4, 1975, therefore the Central Government set up under an executive resolution, a subordinate services commission, latter renamed as Staff Selection Commission (SSC). The SSC has been made responsible for recruiting personnel to non-technical group C (i.e., class III) posts in the secretariat, the attached official and the subordinate offices in the Central Government. Like the UPSC, it is a recommendatory body, the acceptance of its recommendations are acted upon by the ministries.

The Commission consists of a Chairman, a Member and a Secretary-cum-Comptroller of examinations, all appointed by one government. The resolution setting up the Commission is silent about the tenure of its members, thus making their term of office department on the sweet will of the executive. The Commission has been given the status of an attached office of the Department of Personnel and Administrative Reforms.

17

Personnel Training

After the selection of the personnel for the various categories of jobs, the next function of the management is to arrange training for them, for a person, however capable, cannot do his best at a job without adequate training. Formerly it was presumed that the training of personnel was unnecessary on the ground that the new employee gradually picks up all the technicalities of doing the job. However, now as the processes and techniques of production, finance, marketing etc. have become more and more complicated, it is realised that the employee is essential. Training function, in fact, has become the cornerstone of sound management. Therefore, no organisation today, can choose between training and no training to its employees. Training has becomes a vital function of management as with this only the employees in an organisation can be developed.

The object of training is to improve employee's knowledge, skill, attitude and efficiency. An organisation gains by training employees through increased efficiency on the Job, reduction in absenteeism, waste, accident and employees turnover and improved morale. People in the organisation gain by acquiring new knowledge, better techniques and new skills which may make them eligible for advancement in terms of better job status and pay. Training also improves human relations in the organisation by developing better understanding of human nature, perceptions and motivation. There are different methods of training. However, employees will get their training mainly in employment itself. While the education in schools and colleges is considered formal education, the training is work oriented and occurs in a work organisation. Training is important not only to new recruits but also for existing employees. It is to be noted that training is a continuous process i.e., it is imparted to the employee throughout his stay in the organisation. It has been rightly said that "Training is not something that is done once to new employees, it is used continuously in every well-run establishment. Every time you get someone to do work the way you want it done, you are training. Every time you give direction of discuss procedure you are training.

Training enables the employee to improve his knowledge, skill and ability to perform specific jobs. A trained person reduces the cost of production and avoids all types of wastes. Thus the expenditure incurred on training is not a waste and is an investment on human capital which will enable the organisation function effectively.

The following are the advantage of a systematic training programmes:

(i) It helps in improving the quality and quantity of output.

(ii) It increases skill, and ability of the employee, and by this his productivity is increased.

(iii) It enables the employee to make more economical use of the materials and equipments This reduces the, cost of production.

(iv) A trained employees will not commit mistakes while engaged in doing a job.

(v) A trained employees avoid mistakes, much supervision is not necessary and the management can devote its attention on proper planning of the work.

(vi) Training enables the employees to use their tools and implements in the best possible manner.

(vii) Training creates a sense of satisfaction in the employees and make them feel that they are being properly cared for. It improves workers morale and also the relation between the management and the employees.

(viii) Training helps in reducing considerably the rate of employee turnover and absenteeism.

(ix) A trained employee requires less learning time to reach acceptable performance.

(x) Employees acquires knowledge on latest technology and techniques and in this they are developed and the organisation may fill up senior positions from amongst the existing employees.

Steps in Training Programme

Training programmes are needed, for employees at all levels. In large organisations separate training division is set up to plan and organise training for managers, supervisors and workmen. The steps involved in a training programme are:

Analysing the Organisation : Training aims at developing people to meet organisations goals more effectively. This objective be met only when organisational goals are clear and its problems are identified Organisational analysis, in 'terms' of review, organisations plans, environment practices and problems is, there, 'necessary for ascertaining training needs.

Identifying, Performance, Discrepancies and Problems : Periodical reports and performance approvals may reveal the discrepancies between planned and actual performance. The factors leading to such discrepancies may be 'studied and training programme may be designed to help people in overcoming the difficulties.

Choosing the Training Objectives and Techniques : Training objectives determine the type of training and techniques to be used, when, for instance, performance is poor due to lack of experience on-the-job training may be arranged. If the work in a particular department is not going smooth because of the supervisors inability to human-relations recommended.

Training Techniques

There are many number of training methods. The particular method to be selected depends on the factors such as the cost of training, time available, number of employees be trained, depth of knowledge required etc.

All the methods of training can be classified into two groups:

(i) On the basis of the subject matter of training.

(ii) On the basis of source of training.

The first group consists of :

(a) Induction training.

(b) Job training.

(c) Promotional training.

(d) Refresher

The second group consists of :

(a) On-the-job training.

(b) Vestibule training.

(c) Apprenticeship training.

(d) Internship training.

Induction Training

Induction refers to initial orientation or training provided to the employees when they are admitted to an organisation.

The subject of induction is to introduce the employee to the organisation and the existing policies, rules and procedures of the organisation. The employees under such training may be given a general idea about the history of the organisation, the job, the products being manufactured or services being rendered by the organisation, conditions of service, personnel policies, disciplinary rules etc. This knowledge will be very helpful to the employees in understanding the details of the goods produced, processes and techniques of production etc., and also in developing an interest in their organisation.

Job-Training

The object of job training is to increase the knowledge of the employee about the job with which he is concerned so that his efficiency and skill are improved.

Under this type of training, the employees are enable to learn the correct method of

(i) Handling the machines and equipment.

(ii) Removing bottlenecks.

(iii) Safety measures.

Promotional Training

Many organisations follow a policy of filling some of the vacancies at the higher level by promoting the existing employees. This policy increases the morale of the employees and they try to put up maximum efforts so that they may be considered for promotion.

When the existing employees are promoted to the senior positions in the organisation, they are required to shoulder new responsibilities, for this training has to be imparted to them so that they may not experience any difficulty to take up new positions.

Refresher Training

At the time of initial appointment of employees they are formally trained for their jobs. But with the passage of time, the employees may forget some of the methods or they may become outdated because of technological developments, and the improved techniques of management. Hence, refresher courses are arranged for existing employees, in order to provide them an opportunity to revive and also to improve their knowledge.

Vestibule Training

This method involves the creation of separate training centre within the organisation itself for the purpose of providing training to the new employee. An experienced instructor may be incharge of the training programme. Machines, tools and equipment are also arranged in the training centre so as to create such working conditions which are similar to the actual conditions in the factory. After the completion of training under such conditions, the trained employee will be assigned similar jobs in the actual workshop. This method avoids the initial hesitation and nervousness of the employee and also the inconvenience on the job training. Further, while training is being imparted there is no interference with regular production or flow of work. However, this method is relatively costly and adds nothing to production during the training period of the employee.

Apprenticeship Training

This method of training is meant to give the training sufficient knowledge and skill in those trades and crafts in which a long period of training is required for gaining complete proficiency. Generally, the trainee work as apprentice to the experts for long periods, say, two to four years. This programme consists of providing actual work experience on the actual job as well as imparting theoretical knowledge through class room lectures which may be arranged either in the plant or in the institution attached to the concern. Before accepting a person as an apprentice, an agreement is made between employer and the trainees stating the terms and conditions of the training. This method of training enables the trainees to become all round craftsmen. But this method is no guarantee that a trained worker will continue to work in the same concern after the training is completed.

Internship Training

This method of training is generally provided to the skilled and technical personnel. This method involves a joint programme of training in which enterprises and the vocational and training institutions cooperate. The object of this type of training is to bring about a balance between theoretical and practical knowledge. This training equips the students with such knowledge both in theory and practice which would enable them to undertake a certain profession with full confidence and responsibility. Under this type of training, the students of technical institutions with theoretical knowledge are sent to business enterprises to enable them to gain actual work experience. Similarly, the employees of business enterprises are sent to the technical institutions to enable them to gain the latest theoretical knowledge on the subject.

On-the-Job and Off-the-Job Training

Another way of classifying the methods of training is on-the-job and off-the-job training.

On the job training aims at improving employees' knowledge and skill about the job.

Off-the-job training aims to helping employee in acquisition of new skill improving decision-making ability and interpersonal relations etc.

On-the-Job Training : This training method is popular in industry since ages. In India the craftsmanship is inherited in the same way as property and other belongings of parents. Children belonging to the families of carpet and saree weavers, blacksmith, goldsmiths and other skilled crafts, learn manufacturing techniques from early childhood by observing and working with the elder members of the family.

Large organisations, today have vestibule schools to train workmen in different crafts. Training in workshops is also a popular method. The senior workers supervise the new employees and help them in learning the job.

In unskilled and semiskilled operations, on-the-job training is most popular. The jobs requiring high degree of skill in operation, the employee may begin as trainee and not as operator or producer.

On-the-job training helps in developing employees in accordance with the requirements of the organisation. They are better equipped to work on the plant on which they are trained. Before they are asked to start operating machine themselves, they learn the operational problems and techniques. The system is economical as well, since the employees may be producing also while learning.

The older employee's however, are burdened with additional responsibility when the freshers are placed on-the-job training as they have to look after the latter's work along with their own. Some wastage may also occur during training on-the-job.

Off-the-Job Training : This method lets the trainees away from the pressure of the job and daily routines so that they may concentrate on learning. It is an important means of developing supervisors and managers.

Some of the popular training methods under this category are:

(i) Lectures

(ii) Conferences and Seminars

(iii) Role-playing

(iv) Simulation

(v) Programmed learning

(vi) Sensitivity Laboratory of (T-Group Training)

Lectures : Lectures are the most widely used method because they are inexpensive and simple. A large number of participants can be trained at a time. The training instructor may present some concepts, facts and ideas and a number of participants can be trained at a time. The training instructor may present some concepts, facts and ideas and invite participants to ask for clarifications and comments. If listeners are motivated and the lecture is well prepared and delivered effectively, it is advantageous.

Conferences and Seminars : This method emphasises on group discussion, exchange of ideas and recollection of experiences of the trainers and the participants. It helps in developing communication abilities and broadening the outlook. The trainers must give good feedback to the participants to make them learn something positive. Conference may include buzz sessions that divide it into small groups of four or five for intensive discussion and reporting back with its recommendations to the whole conference. Seminars provide good opportunity of discussion case, problems or certain concepts.

Role-playing : This is one of the most effective methods of training. The participants are assigned certain roles to play. For instance, a case of dispute between supervisor and the workman may be acted out. One of the participants may act as supervisor and the other as worker. Some participants may be of reverse roles also. This helps trainees in understanding different view-points perceptions and attitudes and improving inter-personnel relations. It may be a little time consuming process but it does help develop leadership qualities in the participants.

Simulation : The method helps development of problem solving and decision-making skills. Business game is a popular stimulation exercise. It involves several teams each of which is given a firm to operate for a number of periods. In each period, each team makes decisions on such matter as what price charge, how much to produce and what amount to spend on advertising etc. Since the teams are completing with each other, each firm's decisions affects the results of all other. All the firm's decisions are fed into a computer which is programmed to behave like real market. At the end of each period the computer reports back how well each firm has done. The winner is the firm which accumulates largest profit by the end of the game. The participants thus get opportunity under this method to analyse facts and figures and choose from among various alternatives available.

Programmed Learning : It consists of presenting questions facts problems to the learner, allowing him to respond and providing feed back on the accuracy of his answers. The trainee learns while going through the material supplied at his convenience. The training time is considerably reduced in this method but the cost of preparing and printing the material may be very high.

Sensitivity, Laboratory : It is one of the highly published development method which focuses on individual and individual group problems.

Sensitivity refers to self and self-other relationship. T-Group training is a group experience designed to provide maximum possible opportunity for individuals to expose their behaviour, give and receive feed back, experiment with the new behaviour, and develop awareness of self and others.

A typical T-Group programme consists of 10 to 15, participants melting away from the job, without a planned agenda. The group under the direction of a trainer engages in a dialogue. Some trainees may try to impose some structure on the discussion for example, by developing agendas. T-Group is, therefore, highly instructed. The participants are encouraged to let each other 'know how they are coming across to each other in the group rather than in terms of past behaviour.

The Feedback process is important in T-Group as the trainees have to feel secure enough to inform each other truthfully about how the behaviour is being seen, and to interpret the kind of feelings it produces.

The advantage of T-Group training is that trainees become more sensitive to others, and more open after going through the programme.

'Researchers have found that this training results in the increase in company's performance and profits.

Yet it is still a very controversial technique. It is criticised because it creates stress situations for their own sake, its goals may be inconsistent with business goals. It results into 'unjustified innovation of privacy'.

18

The Promotion

Promotion literally means to move forward to advance from a lower to higher; to elevate; to further the progress; to exalt in station, rank or honour. Promotion is the advancement in rank and status, usually accompanied by an increase in emoluments. Promotion generally means allotting a person highest duties or higher responsibilities. This term has been well defined by Charlesworth, who remarks, "A promotion is a movement from a position or a status on a lower level of responsibility to a position or status on a higher level of responsibility" . L.D. White has defined it differently from another angle. In his words, "It is one the means of holding in government services the best qualified men and women who enter the lower grades and thus is an important phase of a career services. " Willoughby has defined promotion from his own point of view. To him, "To the employees, promotion is of direct significance as a reward or possible reward. Actual promotion is a reward while the opportunity for promotion is a possible reward. "

Promotion essentially means giving a person higher duties and responsibilities. The term finds its origin in the Latin word, 'Promovers' which means moving forward. It also means exalting a person in rank and to elevate him. Charles Worth says that "A promotion is a movement from a position or status of a lower level of responsibility to some higher level. " Promotion should not be confused with annual increase of salary of the employee. Every employee starts on a basic salary of the employee. Every employee starts on a basic salary, and gets on annual increment, till he reaches the maximum of his pay scale. Thus annual increment may be automatic or conditional, but in no case it is promotion. Real promotion means rise to a higher grade. The change in duties and responsibilities is the essential characteristic of the promotion process.

Why Promotion ? Unless there is a regular and scientific promotion system the organisation may fall to attract competent persons and also may lose those who have already joined the service. The rationale of promotion spring from various factors. An organisation gets its personnel through recruitment; but it retains its personnel through promotion. Promotion is as much a need of the organisation as of the employee. It enables the organisation to fill its higher post with trained personnel who have acquired the required expertise through learned by doing. Without proper promotional avenues there is bound to be dismay and low morality.

Thus a regular system of promotion is not only in the interest of the employees but also that of the employer and also in the overall interests of the organisation. In brief, the need of a sound promotion system cannot be over emphasised the absence of it breeds discontent among the employees, thus having its ill—effects on the working environment of the organisation.

Promotion Policy : Promotion policy is significant from the point of view of bringing efficiency and effectiveness in the organisations. A well-developed promotion policy is very essential for the efficiency of the employees. Promotion is a continuous incentive to efficient working on the part of the employee. The basic idea of a promotion policy are as follows:

1. Efficiency in the working environment in the organisation.
2. Rewards for efficient service.

3. To attract more qualified and efficient people.
4. Increase the capacity of work.
5. Brings self-discipline among the employees.
6. A sound promotion policy fosters a sense of belongingness of the organisation, assures continuity of politics and practices and help to build up traditions.

An unsound promotion policy would be pushing ahead unqualified or inexperienced hands breed discontent, impair incentive and demoralise the public service. It would worn off talent away from public service, drive out competence from the administrative field. A sound promotion policy is therefore, the foundation of rational personnel administration.

Essentials of Sound Promotion Policy : Recruitment to public service the world over is based one or other on these methods:

(i) Wholly by direct recruitment, (ii) A given proportion by direct recruitment and balance by promotion from lower cadres. (iii) Exclusively by promotion from the lower grades. (iv) Any of the above confined with deputation from other departments. Promotion follow the various levels of promotion and are confined to the personnel of each service of department. They are made according to the cadre and recruitment rules. The requisites of a proper promotion policy have been described by several other authors also.

The name of Willioughby may be mentioned in this respect. He has given six essentials of sound promotion policy. Firstly, he is in favour of setting standard specifications in which the qualification required for all promotions in the organisation. Secondly, he is of the opinion that all the promotions should be classified into distinct classes, grades and services. Thirdly, this type of classification should include all promotions except certain posts having practical.work. Fourthly, for higher posts the persons should be recruited from within. Fifthly, all the promotions should be based on merit policy. Sixthly, there should be adequate means to judge the merit of the personnel.

Promotion must be determined according to some principles. Promotion is essential for the efficiency of the Public Personnel, but only capable and fit men should be promoted. A wrong promotion system demoralises the whole working environment. The principles of any promotion system should be equality, justice and fair play.

Principles of Promotion

Seniority System : Public Personnel are, for obvious reasons, staunch advocates of the principle of seniority as the basis of promotion. Seniority means the length of service of an employee in a particular grade. It is a system in which promotion, from the lower to the higher position is on the basis of period of service put in by an employee in the department. The advantages of the system is that the organisation gets experienced persons and is not required to pay for the training of the employees working on the lower jobs. Further, it keeps the employees satisfied and provides an incentive to put in more labour. According to Dr. Finer, "It is automatic and avoids the need for making invidious distinctions between one person and another of placing young over the old, of measuring the responsibility for the result of promotion." Seniority principle is based on the following principles:

1. Simple Process.
2. Automatic in operation.
3. Equality and justice.
4. Attract capable persons.
5. Minimise political influence.
6. More promotional chances.

But seniority is not without its critics. This system has its own disadvantages. According to Brain Champan, "The trouble with the seniority system is that it is so subjective that it fails to take any account of personal merit. As a system it is fair to every official except the best one; an official has nothing to win or lose provided he does not actually become so inefficient that disciplinary action has to be taken against him. Thus although it is fair but it is heavy burden on the public and a great strain on the efficient handling of public business."

It has also been said that the system is based on certain wrong presumptions. It believes that all persons are fit for promotion which is not correct. It also presumes that all borne on seniority list will have a chance for promotion which again is not correct. There is also a danger of incompetent people being to man higher jobs the reputation and efficiency of the organisation will seriously suffer. E.N. Gladden says that the principles of seniority is based on the following wrong assumptions.

1. It assumes that all members of the grade one fit for promotion.
2. It assumes that seniority list is arranged in an order more or less coincident, with the ages of the staff, so that all in due turn shall obtain an opportunity to serve in a higher post.
3. It assumes that the percentage of higher post to lower is high, so every one shall get a chance.
4. It assumes that vacancies are arising in a reasonable flow.

Further, there is no guarantee of senior man being more efficient. So seniority alone will not necessarily result in the promotion of the most competent. According to Pfiffner, "A system of promotion by seniority will frequently result in raising to supervisory and directing positions who have rank complexes." Similarly Dr. White says, "Consistent application of the rule of seniority up to the scale of supervisory and administrative position would in itself cause the resignation of better man and thus invite progressive deterioration in the higher grades where special competence is particularly needed. "Hence it is generally stressed that only seniority should not be taken as criterion for promotion in the organisation.

Merit System : The principle of merit requires that promotion should be made on the basis of qualification and achievements of the public personnel. The methods generally employed, to assess suitability for promotion is on the basis of record, or a competitive examination or a competitive test. As against seniority system it is the merit system of promotion. Under this scheme it is not seniority alone which matters but there are several other considerations as well.

There should be some objective tests of merit. The first objective method of testing a candidate's ability is through promotional examinations. The second method to test merit is through service records or efficiency ratings. The judgement of the Head of the Department or Promotion Board is the third method of judging the merit of the candidate for promotion.

Examination System : Competitive examination method is another criterion of judging fitness for promotion in the organisation. Such an examination besides being an objective test of merit, eliminates extraneous consideration like bias, and favouritism and facilitates selection of the really fit. Those successful of the written examination may be called for an interview for the purpose of a personality test. It is said that under this system chances of grudge and grumble are reduced to the minimum and all keep their knowledge most up-to-date so that they can compete with others in the examination.

Further, promotion on the basis of written examination eliminates chances of corruption, favouritisations and arbitrariness. However, this system of promotion is also not without defects. The system of written examination is not considered to be a sure of one's ability and quality. Due to these defects the system of written examination is not considered to be a sure of one's ability and quality. Due to these defects found in the examination system alternative methods of determining merit have been sought and the general trend is towards the adoption of a system of formalised reports by which each eligible employee is regularly assessed on a standard basis. According to Prof. L.D. White, 'A third type promotional test is to pass' examination in which an individual is promoted by the departmental head, subject to proof on minimum qualifications either by examination or submission of experience and education credentials."

Discretion of the Head

The most important factor in promotion is the personal opinion and judgement of the higher officials of the Department concerned. This system has great advantages, because the Head knows about each and everybody's efficiency and conduct in the organisation. The judgement based on personnel association is more valuable than any other system of judging the qualities of the employee. The importance and utility of the personal judgement of the Head of the Department will depend on three factors:

1. The capacity to make good judgements.
2. The freedom of action.
3. Intention.

But the system has to be criticised. It is said that it is likely to encourage favouritism and nepotism. The employees opposed to this method of promotion, they feel that promotions are based on favouritism and the system is undependable because the concept of quality and efficiency always differs from man to man.

The above mentioned defects can be removed by consisting Departmental Promotion Boards. These Boards should consist of chief official of the Department and on the basis of seniority service records, etc. They should recommend promotions. The competence of the Promotion Boards will be judged by the general efficiency of the organisation. All these various tests are employed to secure a sound policy of promotion in the organisation.

Efficiency Rating : It is the system under which efficiency of an employee rated. This system is the product of Scientific Management movement. This system is in vogue in U.S.A. There are three major system by efficiency rating:

1. Production Record System
2. Graphic Rating Scale System
3. Personality Invention System

The first type is helpful in case of mechanical type of work in which work can be evaluated. The second type includes finding out many types of qualities in an employee. Third type i.e. Personality Inventory system is the "Probationary System" devised by J.B. Probst Chief examiner for the city of St. Paul in 1927. But the system of efficiency rating has also been criticised. It said that it is likely to encourage favouritism, nepotism and is undependable because of the concept of quality and efficiency. Thus, the efficiency rating cannot be made the exclusive factor in determining promotion. They are helpful as aids to the judgement of the promoting authority.

To make efficiency ratings useful training and supervision of the rating officers is essential. The rating officers should be thoroughly trained in the art of evaluating employees. Individual employees should also be given right to appeal if they feel that efficiency rating are wrong.

Promotion Machinery

The Indian Constitution provides that the Union Public Service Commission shall be consulted on the principles to be followed in making promotion from one service to another, and on the suitability of candidates for such promotions. The various departments have framed promotion rules, or issued order, for the services under their control; and in the criteria they laid down for promotion, they diverge considerably. This generally provides for:

1. Promotion by merit or
2. Promotion by merit-cum seniority or seniority-cum-merit
3. Promotion on the basis of seniority, subjects to the rejection of the unfit

Promotions are made by the Union and State Governments generally on the recommendations of the Heads of Departments, and sometimes with the aid of the advice of the concerned Public Service Commission confidential reports; which are filled up every six months, are the basis for promotion. Such promotions are usually made in accordance with the principle of seniority. Promotions are made by a Departmental Promotion Committee or other selecting authority which first divides the field of choice i.e., the number of eligible officers awaiting promotion who should be considered for inclusion in the 'select list' provided, however, that an officer of outstanding merit may be included in the list of eligible even when he is outside the normal field of choice. Promotions are normally made from this 'select list' in order in which the names are finally arranged. The 'select list' is periodically reviewed.

Promotion Procedure

The promotion procedure is impartial and fair. The vacancies to be filled by promotion are duly notified in advance for the information of the employees. The Selection List is based not on the judgement of single individual but of the Committee as a whole which takes all aspect into consideration and the UPSC/SPSC are associated at every stage in the process of selection. There are duly constituted Departmental Promotion Committees (DPC) which assess the suitability and merit of the candidates for promotion to Selection Posts' other than the Head of Departments and Secretaries to the government. Government's decision on promotion to Gazetted posts in the State Public Service Commission is final.

Reforms in Promotion System

The existence of a proper promotion system is vital for attracting talented persons to public service and preventing them from migrating private ones. Lack of promotion system has a marked retroactive effect on all the process of personnel administration. A good promotion system keeps the employees interested in the job and works as continuously effective incentive to them. To the employees, promotion is of direct significance a reward, or possible reward. Actual promotion is a reward, while the opportunity for promotion is a possible reward.

A proper promotion system helps in retaining the services of the most capable amongst its employees and also in giving them an impetus to improve their capacities and qualifications. In view of the great importance of promotion system it is essential that it must be based on sound lines. The inference of a good promotion system is all pervasive. It is an influence phase of a career service.

Promotion System in U.S.A.

Higher Administrative Officers, and Departmental Heads make the promotions on the basis of seniority, examinations and efficiency records. In U.S.A. maximum use is made of "efficiency rating system" but the employees are not satisfied even there with it because the system is very complicated. The Hover Commission found that the efficiency rating system was too complicated, and the Commission also criticised its use a basis for both rewards and penalties. In America a promotion scheme was devised by the Civil Service Commission under an Executive Order of 1938. Under this scheme the Departments are charged with the responsibility of developing and administering competitive promotion test and procedures.

Promotion System in England

In England promotions are made on the basis of annual reports which are maintained by supervising officers. But significant feature of the system is that one single individual is not given powers to decide promotion cases. Promotion Boards exist in each Department. They include the chief officials of the Department. This arrangement has been made with a view to avoiding the chances of corruption and nepotism. The Board may also interview the candidates recommended for promotion. Any aggrieved employee has a right to appeal against the decision of the Promotion Board.

Promotion System in India

In India promotion system has its own history. The principle of seniority was announced in 1669. On taking over administrative functions in 1771, the East India Company modified seniority in favour of merit in the interest of integrity and competence. But the Charter Act of 1793 sanctified the principle of seniority. It remained in force till its repeal by the India Service Act of 1861. As long as India is concerned, there was no well developed personnel system, there was no well knit promotion system as well. In fact till 1919, when all high jobs were denied to Indians, there was no question of any system of promotion for natives. After 1919 Indians were given limited chances of promotion which were virtually on the recommendations of the head of the department. It was after the independence of the country when the question of higher jobs and promotion to the Indians came to the forefront. Normally promotions are made by three methods as (a) promotion by open competition (b) Seniority-cum-merit or fitness-cum-seniority and (c) by Selection.

Technically speaking the promotion making authority in India is the Government or the Head of the Department concerned, but promotions to higher posts are generally made in consultation with Public Service Commission both at Centre and in the States. It is provided in our Constitution that the Public Service Commission may be consulted on the principles to be followed in making promotions, transfers from one service to another and on the suitability of the candidates for such appointments, promotions and transfers. The promotions to the highest administrative posts viz., Secretary, Joint Secretary, Deputy Secretary are made form a "Pool" which consists of such candidates as have been selected by a Selection Committee appointed by the Government in consultation with Public Service Commission.

Sometimes, selection for promotion from State Civil Service to the IAS is also made. It is done by a Special Committee for each State which consists of a Chairman or a member of the UPSC and some IAS senior most officers of the State as members. The promotion system in India has its own problems. It has been criticised both by the services themselves and by the public in general. The following are the basic defects in promotion system in India:

Firstly, it is argued that the Head of the Department has given too much direction in recommending names out of which selection is to be made.

Secondly, the system of evaluating the efficiency of employees is also not satisfactory. The entries made in their immediate offices are not shown to them except adverse remarks.

Thirdly, promotion Cards or Committees do not exist in every administrative department and in the absence of such a machinery, promotions are haphazard and arbitrary.

Fourthly, promotions are made within classes and often within cadres of a class which makes higher public service more or less a closed shop.

Fifthly, there is no effective policy of the government regarding the basis on which regular promotions are to be made. Sometimes, promotions are made by the departments on the basis of length of service or seniority, sometimes, on the basis of merit as adjudged by a departmental committee and at other times, through selection by the Public Service Commission.

In India, the First Pay Commission (1947) recommended a judicious blend of both direct recruitment and promotion. It argued strongly for promotion because the civil service in India attracts over qualified staff. The commission recommended that at the higher level merit should be the basis whereas at the lower level the basis for promotion should be seniority-cum-fitness. Examination method should be adopted for technical jobs only. The Commission, while endorsing seniority-cum-merit demurred to the view that seniority shall prevail unless a person is declared unfit. The object of promotion is not primarily to give him more pay but to give him more responsible position with more extensive authority. System of limited competitive examination should also be encouraged. Confidential report should indicate general assessment and potentialities of an employees and that confidential reports should be scrutinised at efficiently high levels.

The Second Pay Commission (1957-59) made several recommendations or performance appraisal and promotions are follows:

1. The annul confidential reports are not always objective assessments based on careful observation.

2. The Commission would prefer that the general grading is done at a higher level, preferable at the level where a whole cadre is considered for promotion in the interests of uniformity in the final assessments and that the reports received at the higher levels should, after scrutiny, be returned to the Reporting Officers for rectification, amplification or explanations whether called for.
3. There should be a system of promotion by a special limited competitive examination to provide young officers in class IInd and IIIrd services and additional opportunity to enter any of the class Ist or class IInd services to which there is direct recruitment by a competitive examination.

The Estimate Committee on Public Services (1965-66) endorsed this suggestion that 10% of the vacancies in the All India and Central Services Class Ist be reserved to be filled through a limited competitive examination. This would give talented candidates an incentive for better and more developed service. The written examination may be supplemented by an interview.

Recommendations of A.R.C.

The Administrative Reforms Commission (ARC) recommended significant reforms in the promotion system in India as follows:

1. They emphasised the importance of merit over seniority in promotion and suggested the elimination of the subjective element in determining merit of the eligible candidates for promotion.

2. They suggested the replacement of the existing system of confidential reports by that of Performance Records.

Administrative Reforms Commission also went through the present system of report writing of the employees. The procedure for preparing the Performance Records of each employee generally suggested is as follows :

1. At the end of each year, the official reported upon should submit a brief resume not exceeding 300 words of the work done by him bringing out any special achievement of his. While assessing the reporting officer should take due note of the resume and after making his own comments and assessments submit the entire record to the next higher officers, the receiving officer.

2. There should be three grading for the purpose of the assessment, viz. (a) fit for promotion out of turn, (b) fit for promotion and (c) not yet fit for promotion. Both the reporting officer and receiving officer should assess the official according to these grades.

3. The grading "Fit for Promotion out of turn" should be supported by specific mention of outstanding work that has been done.

4. Good work done during the year should receive prompt appreciation either on the file or in a tour or inspection note the officer concerned should quote this in his resume.

5. Where merit is equal, seniority should be decisive for promotion.

Estimate Committee's Recommendations

The Estimate Committee in its 9th report, 1953-54, made the following suggestions in regard to promotion in the country:

1. Promotion should be solely on the basis of merit regardless of the seniority of the persons concerned in service.

2. Persons should be judged for promotion by the people who have watched their work and conduct over a period.

3. Promotions should be made on the recommendations of a Committee consisting of not less than 3 officers, one of whom at least is acquainted with the work of the persons concerned.

4. In judging the person on the basis of the Confidential Report on him, it should be seen that he was warned in time of the defects noticed in his work and conduct and that if he did not show improvement he was warned again.
5. If no warning has been given to a person, it should not be presumed that the reports on him are so good as to justify his promotion.

Policy Implications

1. The system followed in the confidential reports an employee's performance should be remodelled to facilitate assessment of performance, Personnel qualities of employees and identification of the trueability of the employees with as much objectivity as possible.
2. The system is now too heavy loaded in favour of seniority than merit system.
3. Promotion should be linked to training and professional expertise and should ensure opportunities for development in career.
4. To avoid any kind of subjectivity, Promotion Boards should be established and take recourse to a system of appeals where necessary.

Adequacy of Recruitment Practice in All India Service Recruitment Reforms : A remarkable feature of the administrative system in federally governed India is the deliberate retention of the All India Services. The broad categories of Services are three : (i) All India Services (ii) Central Services (iii) State Services. The All India Services are changeable between the Central and the State Governments. Of the All India Services as provided in constitution are Indian Administrative Service and Indian Police Service the successor of services to the Indian Civil Services (ICS) and Indian Police Services (IPS). The All India Services constitute an administrative device peculiar to India and to Pakistan which was a part of the sub-continent prior to partition. Dr. Ambedkar, while explaining reasons for making this extraordinary provision for the creation of All India Services remarked, "The Indian Administration through a dual polity, will have dual Services."

There shall be an All India Service recruited on all India basis with common qualifications, with uniform scale of pay and members of which alone could be appointed to these strategic posts throughout the Union.

Historically, the All India Services, then known as the Secretary of States services, were formed when India had a unitary centralised system of government. They were ideally suited to the requirements of that times as their members acquired experience in both the Central Government and with local and provincial levels. Recruitment by the Secretary of State for India and the control over conditions of service of the personnel who could be employed in any part of the country were the essential attributes of the All India Services.

Such a power was thought to hold the key to the exercise of British control over the country, because it guaranteed control over the whole administration. The British Government wanted only British officers in key positions in India, and as these officers were neither willing, nor was it expedient to compel them, to serve under Indian Control, recruitment to and control over the top services by the Secretary of State was considered to be essential. The All India Services as an institution had strategic control of the framework law and order, which the imperial rule considered necessary for its survival. The dependence of the imperial government on them became steady more obvious as the popular desire for fully responsible government become more vocal and assertive.

The All India Services were not at all created at the same time. The oldest was the famous Indian Civil Services which owes its origin to the Macaulay Report submitted in 1854. The last to be added to the list was the Indian Agricultural Service Constituted in 1906. Before 1947 many times continuance of All India Services was opposed but at the time of independence a conference was held on October 21-22, 1946 under the Chairmanship of Vallabhbhai Patel, the home member in the interim Government, made a strong plea for an 'All India Administrative System'. The arguments advanced for this were the obvious reasons for maintaining the highest possible standard of administration. The civil service experience, at the case of efficiency and administrative experience of the service as a liaison between the provinces and the centre and of introducing both in the provinces and the centre, a progressive and wide outlook and freshness and vigour of administration. The provinces generally made a distinction between recruitment and control; while a majority of them were in favour of recruitment of personnel on All India basis. There was a general inclination to favour retention of provincial control over such personnel. A Consensus, however, appeared in favour of an All India Administrative Service. All this was a magnificent victory for the centre and more truly, a personal triumph for Vallabhbhai Patel may rightly be acknowledged as the father of All India Services.

The drafting committee of the Indian Constituent Assembly did not originally provide a constitutional base to the All India Services. The draft constitution accordingly makes no mention of the All-India Services. Yet the constitution which finally emerged from the Constituent Assembly not only embodies reference to it but also includes provision for the creation of new All-India Services.

Recruitment of All-India Services, i.e., Indian Administrative Services, Indian Police Service and other Central Services is made by the Union Public Service Commission on the basis of a competitive written examination supplemented by a viva voce test. To appear at the examination, a candidate must be between the age of 21 and 28. Till recently, the upper age for entry into public services was 26 but in 1989 it was raised to 28. Only a University graduate (one holding B.A. or B.Sc., or an equivalent degree) can appear at the examination. Engineering graduates are allowed to compete, and now medical graduates have been not included in the competitive examination. The examination test by the Union Public Service Commission in the form of a personal interview. The former aims at judging the level of intelligence and academic learning and the latter attempts to take a measure of the qualities of personality and character. The examination system is modelled on the British 'general' type rather than the American 'specialised' type.

Till 1978, there used to be single competitive examination for the higher civil service and there was no screening test, whatever to judge that only those who showed some intellectual promise were to be allowed to write it. In the absence of any screening, a large number of candidates were being let loose on the written examination. By mid seventies nearly 40,000 candidates were thus, taking the main tests whereas the number of posts to be filled did exceed 400. It was senseless to administer a competitive examination to such large numbers.

Kothari Committee on Recruitment Policy and Selection Methods : A realization like this induced the Union Public Service Commission to set up a Committee to examine the system of recruitment to the all India and central services and to recommend such changes in the scheme of examinations and in the selection methods as would give adequate emphasis to knowledge, skills and qualities appropriate to the role and functions of the services in the context of tasks of national development. This Committee was set up in 1975 under the chairmanship of D.S. Kothari and it submitted its report in 1976.

The Kothari Committee recommended that for recruitment to the IAS and other class I Central Services there should be a preliminary screening examination and a post-training test besides the main civil services examination (plus, an interview worth 30 marks). The suggestions for a preliminary objective test was to weed out candidates who are not competent enough to write. The main examination is unexceptionable. The Union Public Service Commission is at present more a rejecting body than a recruiting one. The screening test should be an objective type so that it is easy to identify those who have the requisite range and depth of knowledge.

The basic policy governing recruitment to civil service was first laid down in the year 1854, thanks to the Report on the Indian Civil Services, submitted by Macaulay and his colleagues. Even after over 140 years, Macaulay continues to dominate the system of public recruitment in India. Thus, viewed, the Kothari

Committee Report may look more like a revised edition of the Macaulay Report reflecting the latter's spiritual philosophy but updating it, primarily to take care of the vast numbers who now offer themselves for public employment.

The Kothari Committee is a useful report but it must not be used to divert the nation's attention from the range of reforms necessary in the face of contemporary challenges. The Committee had limited terms of reference, and it did not, or could not, call into question the existing civil service system of the country. Outside the ambit of the Committee lie many basic questions demanding resolution. Is the existing structure of the Civil Service rational and functional? Are civil servants given the type of institutional and on the job training which in harmony with the nations' professed goals? Are the performance appraisal and promotion system fair and objective? Is the machinery for redressal of public grievances 'and complaints against mal—administrations adequate? This is only an illustrative list, personnel administration includes many more facets and personnel reform is necessarily to be broadly conceived, designed and executed.

In December 1978, the Central Government accepted the scheme of examinations as recommended by the Kothari Committee and, thus the competitive examination held by the Union Public Service Commission since 1979 marks a significant departure from the pattern hitherto followed. In other words, the competitive examination for the higher Civil Service held in 1979 and onward is based on the new scheme.

The civil Services Competitive examination comprises two stages:

1. Civil Services Preliminary Examination (Objective Type) for the selection of candidates for main examination; and
2. Civil Services Main Examination (Written and Interview) for the selection of candidates for the various services. The Preliminary Examination is held annually in May/June and the Main Examination in November/December.

The Preliminary Examination consists of two papers of objective type (multiple choice questions) and carry a maximum of 450 marks. This examination is meant to serve as a screening test only. The marks obtained in the Preliminary Examination by the candidates who are declared qualified for admission to the Main Examination will not be counted for determining their final orders of merit. The number of candidates to be admitted to the Main Examination will be about twelve to thirteen times the total approximate number of vacancies to be filled in the year in the various services and posts. Only those candidates who are declared by the Commission to have qualified in the Preliminary examination in a year will be eligible for admission to the Main Examination of that year.

The Main Examination consists of a written examination and an interview test. The written examination will consist of 8 papers of conventional essay type each carrying 300 marks and one paper of essay of 200 marks.

Candidates who obtain such minimum qualifying marks in the written part of the Main Examination as may be fixed by the Commission shall be summoned for an interview for a personality test. However, the papers on Indian language and English will be qualifying nature. The marks obtained in these papers will not be counted for ranking. The number of candidates to be summoned for interview will be about twice the number of vacancies to be filled. The interview will carry 250 marks (with no minimum qualifying marks).

Marks thus obtained by the candidates in the main examination (written part as well as interview) would determine their final ranking. Candidates allotted to the various Services keeping in view their ranks in the examination and the preference expressed by them for the various services.

The Preliminary Examination consists of two papers one in general studies and the second in an optional subject which students study at the graduate level. Both the papers are of objective type. The paper in General Studies carries 150 marks, and the paper in optional subject 300 marks. Only those who qualify in the Preliminary Examination are allowed to appear at the Main Examination. The Main Examination consists of two parts-the written examination and the interview.

Paper I	One of the Indian language be selected by the candidates from the languages included in the Eighth Schedule of the constitution.	(300 Marks)
Paper II	English	(300 Marks)
Paper III, IV	General Studies(300 Marks for each paper)	
Paper V, VI, VII and VIII	Any two subjects to be selected from the list of optional subjects. Each subject will have two papers.	(300 Marks for each paper)
Paper IX Essays		(200 Marks)

The paper of Indian language and English is of Matriculation or equivalent standard and of qualifying nature. Certain combinations of various papers have been disallowed. Each paper is of three hours duration.

A major change in the medium of examination to be offered by the candidates has been that they now have the option to answer all the question papers, except the language papers viz., Paper I and 11 above, in any of the language in the eighth schedule to the constitution or English.

The question papers other than language papers are set both in Hindi and English.

Interview Test : Candidates who obtained such minimum qualifying marks in the written part of the main examination as may be fixed by the Commission for their discretion are called by them for an interview for a Personality Test. The interview carries 250 marks with no minimum qualifying marks.

The interview test is intended to judge the mental calibre of a candidate e.g. balance of judgement variety and depth of interest, ability for social cohesion and leadership, intellectual and moral integrity. The marks obtained by candidates in the main examination, i.e. both the written part and the interview, are added to determine the final ranking. Candidates are allotted to the various services keeping in view their ranks in the examination and the preference expressed by them for the various services and posts.

The candidates are allowed three chances for the civil service examination. The Scheduled Caste and Scheduled Tribe candidates are, however, allowed to take the examination without any restriction on the number of chances, of course, subject to the prescribed age limits.

Such a system of examination has come in for a great deal of criticism. In the first place, doubts have been expressed as to the reliability of marks awarded at viva voce, and it has to be admitted that there is considerable scope here for the elements of chance and luck. Much depends on the personnel of the interviewing Board, the passing for marks of examiners, the difference in the nature of questions put to different candidates, and so on. It is legitimately open to question whether 15 to 20 minutes desultory conversation on Subject matters can lead to a correct assessment of the qualities sought for in candidates and for that matter, a comparative different candidates. However, this kind of drawback is by no means peculiar to India. One candidate put first by one Board was put 20th by another, and so on.

Suggesting the replacement of the existing interview system in India by psychological tests, A.D. Gorwalla points out: "The importance of psychological tests must be realised and they must gradually replace the viva voce. A fifteen minutes conversation with laymen, although possessing the wide experience of the public service commissions, can be no substitute for an expert psychological examination designed to give a scientific insight into the candidates mental and emotional make-up. The holding of such tests will, of course cost more, but if there by the services get better material and there is no reasons to suppose that they will not, extra money will have been well spent in India, so far the British 'House Party' or 'week end' type of interview (which includes a series of tests extended over a period of about forty eight hours) has not yet been adopted except for the selection of officers in the defence forces."

The written examination has also not escaped criticism. Pointing out the weakness of written examination Gorwala says, There are also often complaints about the low standard of some of the papers set optional subjects, and it is felt that candidates taking those subject have unfair advantage. This is inevitable from time to time, but in order to give as equal a chance as possible, that part of the examination which is common to all candidates must form a larger proportion of the whole that at present enabling relative merit to be more properly judged.

Commenting on the general inadequacy of the system of recruitment, Appleby remarks:

"The criteria by which personnel are selected by the Public Service Commissions are not up to date and examining and appraising techniques are far from modern selection tends to be by one type of person, which naturally perpetuates its own type. Recruitment is too much in terms of academic records and appraisal by experienced academic examiners, too little in terms of other considerations as are highly important in public administration too little attention in selection is given any but the most subjective and incidental attention to capacity for growth."

19

Pay and Service Conditions

In our modern set-up public and private sectors are working side by side. Both have a very difficult but important role to play, which they can do with efficient personnel system. Public servants are expected to be politically neutral and to satisfy themselves with the usual rates of increment. They cannot be benefited in their economic enterprises to the extent to which a businessman is benefited. This has given rise to the problem of compensation.

What is Compensation? Compensation may conveniently be defined as reward for certain facilities or privileges denied to one class as against the other. In personnel administration compensation plan aims at impartiality making up deficiency and rewarding a person for efficiently and honestly doing his allotted duties without any temptations for any rewards from outside. This is done by giving good salaries, leave, pension and other facilities. This has become still more essential because many citizens adopt public service as a career.

Salaries : In each country there is a regular salary structure. Several considerations are paid while deciding this structure. One such principle is that public sector should pay at least that much which is paid in the private sector. This, however, has its own difficulties. Firstly, because the state is a model employer and must be above all other employers. Secondly, in private sector there are not many comparable posts as those which exist in the public sector. A question has been posed as to who is model employer? According to some thinkers such an employer is one who is ahead of other employer in providing facilities to the employees ; while according to others it should be first hand employers ; while still others feel that it means responsibility of state towards its employees.

First viewpoint has, however, been found more acceptable than the other views. Then another principle for consideration is that the organisation should pay sufficient attention to his employees so that it can attract the best available people and also retain them. It is also said that salary structure should be related to the cost of living but this system is very inconvenient and undependable. Then another principle suggested is that as far as possible it should be based on the democratic principle of equality. About salary structure it has also been said that it should be comparable to the per capita income of the country. Still another principle which has been suggested is that there should be equal pay for equal work. In the interest of work it is essential that all these principles should be taken into consideration and treated as complementary and not contradictory to each other.

Methods of Deciding Salaries

Salaries can be fixed either by the legislature or by the executive government under instructions from the legislature or by mutual adjustment between the employers and the employees. Salaries can also be fixed by wage board or can be decided in an ad hoc manner. In most of the cases there are, however, standing commissions or ad hoc commissions which are appointed from time to time for the purpose. Their terms of reference are decided at a time when the Commission is being constituted.

Uniform Salary and Graded Salary System : A uniform salary system is one in which there are uniform rates on the basis of equal pay for equal work. On the other hand, graded salary is one in which there is certain minimum and maximum of pay scale with a rate of annual increment. Usually graded salary is preferred over uniform salary because in the latter there are more chances of incentive for good and meritorious work and the system is also conducive for efficiency. The system also makes a distinction between the old and the new entrants and gives stability to administration. It also recognises that as an employee gains experience with that he should be paid more than what he should get as a learner or raw hand.

Pay Structure in India

In the past, usually there was no salary structure and the employees were paid very low salaries or wages. They were thus usually forced to be corrupt and accept bribes. There was also no consideration or system for rise in the salaries for meeting the dearness in living. It was in 1940 that Grain Compensation scheme was introduced though that did not work well with the result that in 1942 the scheme of dearness allowance was introduced. In 1946, Central Pay Commission was appointed which reported in 1947 about salary structure in India. Under the scheme I.A.S. officers were graded Junior (Rs. 400-1000), Senior (Rs. 900-1800) and Selection Grades of pay (Rs. 1800-2000). The highest post carried a pay scale of Rs. 2000 to Rs. 3000. Central Services were also graded as Class II to IV.

The Commission also recommended payment of some other allowances to the employees. Since then efforts are being made to keep our pay structure up-to date and government ensures that its employees are not put to any financial hardship. Today our salary structures are being governed on the recommendations of Pay Commission. One of the most significant recommendations of the Commission is that it has merged dearness allowances with the pay and also provide that twice in a year. The employees should be paid dearness allowance depending on the rise of price index. It has increased higher rates of annual increments and reduced the number of pay grades by merging some grades.

The system of pension payment has been very much simplified. House Rent Allowance has been fixed and will be paid without production of rent receipt.

Systems of Compensation : Each public servant is supposed to get some pay for the post which he holds. In addition to this he can also get additional pay when an employee holds charge of another post and performs duties of that post, in addition to his own normal duties. When an employee performs some work of special nature, he becomes entitled to Special Pay. In certain circumstances he gets Personal Pay to compensate him financially from possible financial loss. When a government servant is required to go out of his place of duty be becomes entitled to Compensatory Pay. When some special work is done by an employee he is paid some honorarium as well.

Other Methods of Compensation : In addition to pay each public servant is compensated by other methods as well. Each employee is paid House Rent Allowance, if the government fails to provide him residential accommodation. In a city like Delhi this allowance was 15% of the basic pay. Now he is entitled to get fixed amount depending on his salary slab. In addition to this, certain categories of employees are paid Children's Education Allowance by way of reimbursement of tuition fee, etc. In major cities, where public servants population is concentrated, there is a provision for medical facility. There are Central Government Health Service Scheme Dispensaries where the employees get almost free medical aid. There is also the system of reimbursement where such dispensaries exist. Public Servants are also paid travelling allowances whensoever required to go out on tour and uniform allowance when the servants are expected to put on a particular uniform.

The state also ensures that its employees have regular hours of work and in case they are detained beyond working hours, they are paid overtime allowance or compensatory allowance. They are provided with decent working conditions and an atmosphere in which they can give what is best in them. Similarly, the employer helps in running recreation clubs, games, cultural activities, etc.

But one of the major methods of compensation is that of leave which is of various kinds. A central government employee earns one month leave in a year, can accumulate his earned leave upto 240 days. In addition to this each employee gets 12 days casual leave in addition to two days restricted leave. When an employee is sick and has exhausted his earned leave, etc., he becomes entitled to medical leave. He can also get special leave, which is allowed for special reasons and study leave, when government servant is allowed to study while in service. When a government servant becomes disabled in an accident, etc., he gets disability leave. Maternity leave is allowed to female employees during their family days. When an employee is suffering from some contageous disease he can be allowed S/C to have some -half pay and leave without pay also.

A government servant is entitled to LTC (Leave Travel Concession) once in four years. He can then go to any part of the country and his employer will pay him travel cost.

It will thus be observed that compensation is not only essential but also inevitable if the government wants to have able and efficient people in its service. Without payment of proper compensation the state shall not be in a position to attract the best brains and efficient people. That is one of the reasons which compels personnel administrators to think in terms of providing more amenities and facilities to the employees.

The Fourth Central Pay Commission was set up *vide* resolution dated July 29, 1983 with Mr. justice P. N. Shinghal, Chairman.

The Commission came into existence on September 1, 1983.

The Commission was required to examine the structure of emoluments etc. of all Central government employees, including those of Union territories, officers belonging to All-India Services and Armed forces personnel.

The Commission received about 8500 memoranda of which more than 2000 were from unions and associations of government employees.

The number of government employees, including armed forces personnel, covered by the recommendations of the commission was about 52 lakhs.

There were 153 scales of pay for civilian employees at the time of setting up of the commission. The number of pay scales has now been reduced to 36, which is a reduction of about 76 percent.

The 36 scales of pay recommended by the commission for the civilian employees are :

(1) Rs. 750-940 (2) Rs. 775-1025 (3) Rs. 800-1150 (4) Rs. 825-1200 (5) Rs. 950-1400 (6) Rs. 950-1500 (7) Rs. 975-1540 (8) Rs. 975-1660 (9) Rs. 1150-1500 (10) Rs. 1200-1800 (11) Rs. 1200-2040 (12) Rs. 1320-2040 (13) Rs. 1350-2200 (14) Rs. 1400-2300 (15) Rs. 1400-2600 (16) Rs. 1600-2660 (17) Rs. 1640-2900 (18) Rs. 2000-3200 (19) Rs. 2000-2120 (20) Rs. 2000-3500 (21) Rs. 2375-3500 (22) Rs. 2200-4000 (23) Rs. 3000-4500 (24) Rs. 3000-5000 (25) Rs. 3700-5000 (26) Rs. 4100-5300 (27) Rs. 4500-5700 (28) Rs. 5100-5700 (29) Rs. 5100-6700 (30) Rs. 5100-6700 (31) Rs. 5900-7300 (32) Rs. 7300/-(Fixed) (33) Rs. 7300-8000 (34) Rs. 7600-(Fixed) (35) Rs. 8000/-(Fixed) (36) Rs. 9000/(Fixed).

The scales of pay for some categories of employees in the proposed pay structure are given by way of illustration.

(1) Peon, Sweeper, Chowkidar, Mali, Khalasi, Messenger-Rs. 750-940.

(2) Postman, Lineman in P&T, Police Constable-Rs. 825-1200.

(3) Lower Division Clerk, Ticket Collector, Staff Car Driver-Rs. 950-1500.

(4) Commercial Clerks in Railways-Rs. 975-1540.

(5) Postal Assistant Telephone Operator in Telecommunication-Rs. 975-1660.

(6) Upper Division Clerk, Travelling Ticket Examiner in railways-Rs. 1200-2240.

(7) Assistants and Stenographers in Secretariat-Rs. 1400-2600.

(8) Inspectors in Income Tax, Excise & Customs and Police-Rs. 1640-2900.

(9) Section Officers in Secretariat, Asst. Engineer, Dy. Superintendent of Police,-Rs. 2000-2500.

(10) Junior Time scale in Group 'A' Services-Rs. 2200-4000.

(11) Junior Administrative Grade, Deputy Secretary in Secretariat-Rs. 4700-5000.

(12) Director in Secretariat, D.I.G. Conservator of Forests-Rs. 3500-5700.

(13) Scientist Grade 'G'-Rs. 5100-6700.

(14) Joint Secretary in Secretariat, Senior Administrative Grade in Group 'A' Services, IG police-Rs. 5900-6700.

(15) Additional Secretary in Secretariat- Rs. 7300/-(Fixed).

(16) General Manager in Railways, member in P&T Boards, Member in C.B.E.C. and C.B.D.T-Rs. 7300-8000.

(17) Secretary to the Government of India, Chief Secretary, D.G.H.S., D.G (Works), Member Railway Board-Rs.9000/-(Fixed).

(18) Cabinet Secretary, Chairman Atomic Energy Commission - Rs.9000/-(Fixed).

The lowest basic pay recommended for Central Government employees is Rs. 750/-p.m. and the highest pay recommended is Rs. 9000/p.m. The pay of Rs. 9000- p.m. is for the Cabinet Secretary, the three Services Chiefs, and Chairman of the Atomic Energy Commission. The ratio between the lowest pay (Rs. 750/-) and the highest pay (Rs. 9000/-) will between the lowest pay (Rs 750/-) and the highest pay (Rs. 9000/-) will be 1 : 12 (pre-tax). The ratio after necessary tax deductions will come to 1 : 9.15.

Relationship between Political and Permanent Executives

The civil servants have to come into contact with the politicians, legislators and others directly or through the Ministers. The ministers in charge of various departments are responsible and accountable for the good and the honest administration of their departments, and for this they need good conduct of civil servants in their Ministry, initially for the formulation of policy and then its sincere implementation. In the 'Mundhra deal" Mr. M.C. Chagla, Chief Justice of the Bombay High Court, as a one man Commission stated: "It is clear that constitutionally the Minister is responsible for the action. Taken by his Secretary with regard to this transaction. It is clear that a Minister must take the responsibility for action done by his subordinates. He cannot take shelter behind them, nor can he disown their actions. The doctrine of ministerial responsibility has two facets. The Minister has complete autonomy within his sphere of activity. As a necessary corollary, he must take full' responsibility or the actions of his servants.

It is true that this may throw a very great burden on the minister, because it is impossible to expect that in highly complicated system of administration which we have evolved, the Minister could possibly know, leave alone, give his consent to every action taken by his subordinates. But it is assumed that once the policy is laid down by the Ministers, his subordinates must reflect that policy and must loyally carry out that policy. If any subordinate fails to do so, he may be punished or dismissed, but however variously, the responsibility of his action must be assumed by the Minister. In its conclusion, the Commission added "The Minister must take full responsibility for the acts of his subordinates. He cannot be permitted to say that his subordinates did not reflect his policy or acted contrary to his wishes or directions.

Public Representatives

The political bosses are the representatives of the public and hence responsible for the good and efficient management of public affairs. Being responsible, they are obliged to see that the public will, reflected in the legislative mandate, is properly executed by the administrative agencies, or by the civil servants. Any member of the Legislature can ask any question from the Minister, move adjournment motions, table resolutions for the purpose of getting redressed the grievances of the people against inefficiency or high handedness. The conduct of the Minister may be censured for any act of omission or commission of his civil servants. During question hour, the members of the legislature draw attention of the minister to the failure and the abuses of the administrative authority and the Minister has got to be ready to answer any criticism.

The Question hour is regarded as important for legislatures as it acts as a searchlight on the activities of administration. Anybody who has worked in a civil service department, said Hugh Gaitskell, "would agree with me that, if there is one major thing which loads civil servants to be excessively cautious, timid and careful to keep records which outside the civil service would be regarded as unnecessary, it is the fear of parliamentary questions."

In addition to the indirect contacts of the civil servants with the legislature, they sometimes, come in direct contact with the politician and the public. Many a time, the heads or other officials of the departments have to appear before the committees of the legislature to explain things, or answer certain administrative objections. In parliamentary countries like India the best examples of such committees are the Estimates and the Public Accounts Committees. The enquiring jurisdiction of these committees is practically all pervasive and unlimited. These Committees in India can summon public officials of a Ministry to furnish such information as they may ask for. The civil servants or the public officials have to satisfy the committee that it is being frank and full information and that no attempt is being made to confuse the issues. The public officials appearing before these Committees have, therefore, to be well prepared with their answers and show courtesy and patience in rendering information. They have also to carry the records of the office with them if the Committee asks for that.

In the U.S.A., civil servants have to appear on behalf of various administrative agencies before a large number of committees, the Appropriation Committee and its sub-committees, the Ways and Means Committee, the various subject matter committees like those of Foreign Affairs or Armed Services, and the Standing Committees on Government Operations. Before the Appropriation Committee and its Sub-committees and the Ways and Means Committee, the civil servants (on behalf of the administrative agencies) have to justify and defend and budget proposals of their agency; before the Subject Matter Committees, they have to present their legislative needs, and before the Committees on Government Operations they have to answer for any act or policy of their agency which may come up for investigation or inquiry before the Committee.

In addition to the above, there are enquiries, complaints, or requests from individual members of the legislature to be attended to by the civil servants. In dealing with the members of Parliament, the civil servants have got to the very careful. Any enquiry or request by the members of parliament should be attended to by the head of the department personally and immediately. Even where the reply cannot be immediately given due to certain reasons, an acknowledgment of the receipt of enquiry or complaint must be despatched within 24 hours. The reply to the questions should be courteous, reasonable, accurate and adequate. It should be neither too little nor too much. As regards request for doing something, it should be done as promptly as possible, provided in conceding to it no infringement of the law, the rules and the consideration of propriety is involved. If the request made not within the legal competence of the civil servant to concede to, it should be politely but frankly refused.

The Politician/Minister on his part should also avoid undue interference in the day-to-day working of the civil servants as well understood by the advanced opinion in most of the democracies. As Herman Finer put it "We do not mean that political bosses have, pretend to have, or ought to have, the power of continuous intervention in administration and positive participation in the execution of law. They do not in fact do more than act as the Judge and corrector of Cabinet as its administrative assistants. We could show further that it is almost impossible to do more than this (take, as an example, their financial power) and that where they confine themselves to this alone the result of joint work of the Minister and the civil servants is better than where the Minister attempts to interfere more positively.

However, in practice, there is a growing volume of evidence to support that politicians in power infiltrate into the boundaries which do not belong to them. They create confusion and affect official decisions and actions by their every occasional meeting with the higher civil servants. They 'drive' a wedge in the chain of the administrative responsibility, invoke through partisan devices, morale destroying ministerial interventions, and promote partisan and individual interests even at times to the detriment of public welfare".

The Ministerial prejudices against civil servants often become obstructions in the way of mutual understanding between them. The legislators have no soft corner for the civil servants who have sometimes their individual judgement on issues and the result is unhealthy relations between the two. It is sometimes the prejudiced view of the Higher Civil Service and had logic which are responsible for the gap that yawns between the administrative class and the legislators. Hence the need for an enlightened comprehension by the legislators of the creative role of Higher Civil Service in a welfare state context.

It is important that the civil servant not only keeps on reurnishing his own intellectual equipment but also takes pains to see that the intellectual and emotional gears of his boss or political master mesh with his own. It is only then that alive and virile relationship will be established between the political boss and the bureaucrat and that alone will ensure the emergence of a sound policy and its proper implementation.

Elected Representatives

Equally important is the question of attitudes of the elected representatives of the panchayati raj institutions. Having committed to socialistic democracy, our State and the Union governments have to function through appointed officials as partners in the responsibility of modernising the country along with the elected representatives. In view of the involvement of the officials in all fields of development of the people, it is essential that the approach and outlook of the elected representatives towards the officials is properly oriented to get the maximum and quick results. The elected representatives should appreciate that already there is a significant departure in the outlook of the officials from their purely conservative approach in response to the new demands. There is also a positive aspect to his role that consists of telling the civil servant what the public wants how much and at what cost. It is this area between 'What the public wants' and 'what it shall not stand' that is demarcated by a politician and is then entrusted to civil servants as his sanction and frame of reference.

Ultimately, therefore, all decisions have to be political decisions or as least subjected to political considerations. In the nature of things, civil servant tends to defy rules and regulations and worships the cult of file, forgetting that a file contains a human case and rules and regulations are intended to achieve a given social objective and not to frustrate any goals. Such an outlook has its own validity and has a rightful role to play in decision-making. However, there is another body of people who, by their instinct and training, are able to see what the civil servant is prone to overlook and that is the overall, ultimate, human or, if you will, political implications of a decision. The officials are on longer entirely the watch-dogs of the government over the people's representatives but are functioning as partners in these institutions. In the present context, it is almost impossible either for the official or for the elected representative to work in water-tight compartments. The official, whether he likes it or not will be involved in the political developments and, similarly, the elected representatives will have to play some part as administrators.

It is time we demolished the popular, rather vulgar, notion which puts politicians and bureaucrats in different, even hostile categories, who live, think and function in absolutely water-tight compartments and who, willy nilly, co-exist because they have to suffer each other. This conception of their bellicose separateness seems to have originated during the struggle for freedom when the British-Indian bureaucracy was under instructions from an alien government to crush a national movement led by politicians. Over the years this feeling has, no doubt, diminished considerably but still there is a feeling of separateness of identity which deserves to be played down. In a welfare state, a degree of commitment to national goals is called for not only from politicians but also from civil servants. A welfare state cannot be brought into being merely by enacting a Constitution which enshrines pious inspirations to that effect; it has to be structured, bit by bit, step by step, by concerted action directed at translating the ideals of welfare state into tangible terms. This is the task of bureaucracy.

Emerson once said that the difference between an ordinary person and a great man is that whereas an ordinary man sees a patch of land, a great man imagines the number of houses that can be built upon it. It is the 'vision' which characterise or should characterise a real political leader. On the other land, it is the ability to plan and construct the houses which is the hallmark of a civil servant.

The Administrative Reforms Committee has also recommended that, in the present situation there should be maximum delegation of authority and that executive centralisation based on distrust would be ruinous to development.

The three important qualities essential for the success of panchayati raj both for the official and the elected representative are: (a) impartiality i.e., the ability to project and assess the merits in terms of public interest; (b) high sense of discipline i.e., be fully conversant with rules and procedures so as to ensure proper utilisation of resources to secure the maximum and quick results for the benefit of the people; and (c) good disposition i.e., they should have good and cordial relationship with all the people so that they could secure fullest participation of the people in all developmental progammes. They should adopt action-motivated and problem-solving approach and should not be prisoners of indecision.

Panchayati Raj is participating democracy where the people, through their elected representatives, have to involve themselves in the process of development along with the officials. Although the relationship between the officials and elected representatives has been generally satisfactory, according to the recent surveys conducted. There are two important sources of misunderstanding and strained relations.

1. Lack of clear demarcation of the functions and responsibilites of the two functionaries. The elected representative, as the chief of the institution interferes in the day-to-day administration of the office as a result of which

there will be scope for indiscipline in the office staff. Similarly, the official's interference also is there to influence the elected representative in policy matters such as selection of programmes and works.

2. Utilisation of the block vehicles by the elected representatives and the officials.

Clear-cut Distinction

Although it is necessary to have a clear-cut distinction in the functions of the elected representatives and the officials of panchayati raj, it is difficult to enforce it through government Acts or rules particularly at the panchayat samiti level. "Development Administration", it has been aptly said, "is one of those few sophisticated silhouettes of administrative concepts whose broad shadow outlines are widely recognised though its inner details admit of no ready and precise identification." At the national and state levels, such neat distinction between the legislature and executive is possible. The relations at the lower level are primarily personal and their roles are complementary and supplementary to one another.

The relationship between the two functionaries is, therefore, mainly personal. Basically their problem is a problem of temperamental adjustment which is a long and slow process. It should be basically understood by each that their spheres of activity are well-defined. The political boss is the policy making agency, while the official is the person to execute these policies. There should not be any inroads into the jurisdiction of the one by the other. Once these inroads take place, the conflict sets in. It must be realised both by the official and the non-official that the success of panchayati raj will mainly depend upon the cordial relationship between these two functionaries which can be ensured only when there is mutual regard, trust and respect for each other. The two functionaries should be motivated and actuated by the missionary zeal to make this programme a complete success.

Panchayati Raj has been criticised severely not because of the incompetence of or the dis-interestedness on the part of the non-officials but because of lack of wholehearted support, both financial and otherwise, extended to them by government. The central and the state governments should have the fullest confidence and faith in the people and their representatives.

Jawaharlal Nehru once observed: "In the new experiment, people would commit mistakes in their enthusiasm but they will get over this difficulty gradually as they gain experience. Having empowered them with full authority, there should not be official interference. The officials should function as advisers and partners but not as bosses." Democracy can lead to development only when it is associated with the deepening of understanding.

20

Indian Training System

Indian system of the training of civil servants is largely conditioned on the British pattern. At the higher levels the emphasis is on a University degree. The principle of 'catch the young' results in recruitment of persons who have no education or training of public administration. They are usually brilliant young men and women with a background of liberal University education. Before giving them new administrative responsibilities, they need a systematic training in the skills and techniques of administration and in the total ethos of modern democratic administration.

Therefore, new entrants to the All India Services and higher Class I Central and State Services are provided with well planned institutional training in India. But systematic arrangements for the training at middle levels of class II, Class III and subordinate services do not exist in the country. They are largely expected to learn by experience on the job. A few departments have their own staff colleges or training institutes, e.g., Railways, Central Excise, Post and Telegraph etc. The Institutions like Central Secretariat organisation, Institution of Economic Growth etc., provide practical job- related training to the middle and subordinate level staff.

However, for most of the services, at middle and lower levels, the training there is on the job training under expert supervision. There is too much emphasis on the higher civil services in India. The initial post-entry training is imparted in two different ways:

1. Institutional training (for Administrative, Police, Audit and Accounts, Income Tax etc.)
2. Departmental Training under the guidance of senior and experienced officers (for Defence, Accounts, Customes, Posts etc.)

Probationers of the All India Services like I.A.S., I.P.S., I.F.S. and Central Services Class I are given the institutional training in two phases:

1. Foundation Course, and
2. Professional Course

Foundation Course : It is a combined course for the new entrants of the All India Services like I.A.S., I.P.S., I.F.S., etc. and Central Services Class 1. The foundational course is of five months' duration conducted by the Lal Bahadur Shastri National Academy of Administration of Mussoorie. In the foundational course emphasis is laid on the teaching of the subjects like Public Administration, Economics, Planning, Law, Political Theory, Indian Constitution, Cultural History of India, the National Movement etc. For those entrants who cannot read and write Hindi, special lessons are also given in Hindi.

The idea behind the foundational course is that the officers of the higher services in India should live together for five months and develop a spirit of belongingness to common public service; a feeling of comradeship and a broad common outlook. At the same time the officers of higher services acquire an understanding of the constitutional economic, social, political and historical context within which the administrators have to function. The foundational course removes the barriers between various services. It can be called as a 'National Course' of training of higher services in India.

Professional Course : After the completion of the foundational course of five months at the National Academy, the second phase of training in professional course is given to the probationers. Those who belong to the I.A.S. continue to stay at the National Academy and a further professional training is given to them for a period of about two to three months. During this spell of professional training, they study in more detail the problems of public administration, district administration, revenue administration, development administration, Indian Penal Code, Criminal Procedure Code, Legal and Constitutional System, economic theory and economic planning etc. After completion of the first spell of professional training, the I.A.S. probationers are sent to the State to which he/she has been allotted, for practical on the job training for one year. At the end of this year, I.A.S., probationers again come to the Academy for the second spell of problem oriented 'professional' training. Emphasis is placed on the discussion of particular administrative problems.

Case-analysis, and conference method of training is adopted. At the end of the second spell of training at the Academy, the I.A.S., probationers appear at an examination conducted by the U.P.S.C. For the training of the probationers of other All India Services (like I.P.S., I.F.S.) and Central Services, the specialized and professional training institutions have been established. After the completion of the foundational course at the National Academy, they are sent to various specialized training institutions for further professional training. The I.P.S. probationers go to National Police Academy at Hyderabad to receive professional training in drill, handling of weapon, crime and criminology, law, combating techniques etc. The probationers of Indian Audit and Accounts Service receive professional training at I.A.S. Training School at Shimla.

Similarly Income Tax Training School at (Nagpur), Railway Staff College (Baroda), Institute of Secretariat Training and Management (New Delhi), National Forest Research Centre (Dehra Dun) etc. provide specialized professional training to the newly recruited personnel in the various services. The duration of professional training range from one to two years.

Various Methods

Four types of methods are involved in the entry point training of the foundational and professional courses at the various training institutions described above.

1. Lectures on the subject matter of the course.
2. Assignments given to the trainees.
3. Case-analysis method.
4. Apprenticeship i.e., on the job training.

Refresher Courses

Apart from the foundational and professional courses conducted by the various training institutions for the new entrants to the various higher services, the refresher courses have also assumed great importance in the country. These refresher courses are short term trained courses of the duration ranging from one week to four weeks. The senior and experienced civil servants are given the refresher courses-two to three times in their career. For the purpose of conducting these short-term training programmes, there are many institutions in the country.

For the I.A.S. officers apart from the intensive entry-point training of two years as discussed earlier, there are two new types of training programmes started in 1985-86.

Four Week's Training Programme : In general management and administration arranged two to four times in the career of the employees.

One Week Compulsory Refresher Programme for Every I.A.S. Officer Every Year : Apart from I.A.S. officers, other officers of higher civil services like I.P.S., I.F.S., Income Tax, Railways etc. also are given refresher training career. These refresher courses are conducted by the National Academy of Administration, or other institutions like (1) Indian Institute of Public Administration, New Delhi; (2) Administrative Staff College, Hyderabad,

(3) National Police Training College, Mount Abu, (4) National Institute of Rural Development, Hyderabad and (5) Indian Institute of Management, Ahmedabad etc. Various professional institutions in the field of various services like Police, Income-tax, Audit and Accounts, Railways, Tele-communication, Foreign Trade, Forests etc., also conduct the refresher courses for the senior offices of their respective services. A majority of state government have also established state training institutions in their respective states providing post-entry and in-service training to their employees. Besides, many University Departments of Public administration and Public Enterprises etc., also provide short-term training courses for the higher and middle level civil servants.

Prominent Institutions

Compared to most of the developing countries, India has a long tradition of civil service training. Ever since the days of East India Company, institutional training has been provided to the higher civil servants. After Independence, the social economic and political changes resulted into tremendous expansion in the government machinery and its functions. In order to meet the requirements of the rapid post- independence changes, the need for systematic and up-to-date training of the civil servants was felt urgently. Training needs were emphasized by all efforts of the administrative reforms in the country. Today training of civil servants has become an integral part of the personnel policy of the Centrai as well as State Governments.

A number of new training institutions have been set-up by the institutions providing both general and professional training to the civil servants at the entry-point and also during their career. The number of the training institutions is very large. Some of the most important institutions of civil service training are described below, in brief

Lal Bahadur Shastri National Academy of (Mussorie) U.A.: It was established in 1959, the academy is the most important training institution in the country. It provides the following :

1. Combined Foundational Course for all the probationers of the All India Services like I.A.S., I.F.S., I.P.S. and of the Central Services Class I.
2. Professional and problem oriented training for the new entrants of Indian Administrative service.
3. Refresher Courses of four weeks for the senior I.A.S. Officers.
4. One week training programme for the I.A.S. Officers.

Central Police Training College Mount Abu (Rajasthan) : Upto 1975-76 it provided entry point professional training for the new entrants to the Indian Police Service (It is now given at the national Police Academy Hyderabad). Now this College provides refresher training and in-service courses to the middle and higher level senior police officers of both I.P.S. and of the State Police Service.

National Police Academy, Hyderabad (Est. 1976-77) : It provides professional training for the new entrants to the I.P.S. It also conducts refresher courses for the senior I.P.S. Officers.

Administrative Staff College, Hyderabad (Est. 1957) : It was established in 1957 on the model of the Administrative Staff College Henley (England). It provides 4 months advance level training for the highly placed senior administrators and experienced executives drawn from government, public sector, and private business and industries. Exchange of experiences and ideas in group discussions, syndicates and panels is the method emphasized for the training.

National Institute of Rural Development, Hyderabad (Established in 1955) : It organises regular orientation course for the higher and middle level civil servants engaged in the field of rural development administration. It is also engaged in research in the area of rural development.

Indian Institute of Public Administration New Delhi (Established in 1953) : Apart from research in Public Administration the IIPA organises short-term orientation and refresher courses for the senior and middle level servants of the central/ state governments. Here courses are regularly conducted for the benefit of senior and middle rank officials. These specialized professional courses heavily rely upon lectures by senior officers and experts in the subject. At the same time exchange of ideas and experiences in the group discussions and field visits are also arranged. The IIPA also organises a nine-month educational programme for the senior and middle level civil servants. This is the only course of its kind in the whole country.

Many of the central services also have set up their own training institutions, where institutional training of professional nature is provided for their respective civil servants. Some of the leading training institutions are listed below.

1. Indian Institute of Management, Ahmedabad.
2. Income-Tax Training School, Nagpur.
3. Railway Staff College, Baroda.
4. Institute of Secretariat Training and Management, New Delhi.
5. National Forest Research Institute, Dehra Dun.
6. Central Audit and Accounts Training School, Shimla.
7. All India Institute of Local Self-government, Bombay.

Most of the State Governments have also set up state training institutions in their respective states for providing post-entry and in-service training to their employees. Many Universities have Department of Public Administration, where short-term training is organized for the civil servants in addition to regular teaching and research in public Administration.

The Evaluation

Training of civil servants has assumed a great importance after Independence. It has become an integral part of the Government's personnel policy. A number of new training institutions have been set up in the country to provide both general and specialized training programmes. A large number of employees are benefited by these training arrangements in the country. In spite of this boon, the training system has not been able to fulfil the expectations of it. There have been many weaknesses of the Indian system of training.

First, in the light of the vastness of the country and rapidly expanding sphere of the Government functions, the training arrangements are not adequate to meet our requirements. Only a small number of civil servants (one out of five) benefit from the present training facilities.

Second, too much emphasis is laid on entry-point and in service training of the higher civil services like All-India Services and Central and State Class I Services. The training needs of the middle and lower level personnel is neglected. Up-to-date in-service training and Refresher Courses for lower level staff are not adequately planned. As a result of this neglect, a vast majority of civil servants (80 to 90%) have an opportunity of training.

Third, there is a general lack of seriousness on the part of the Government in the matter of civil service training in the country. Many wrong types of training programme is planned and wrong methods are adopted. Selection of the trainees is not done carefully. An 'unwanted', 'separable' or 'favourable' person is selected in place of a right and appropriate person. In most of the organizations, bureaucratic politics and patronage play an important role in the selection of trainees. If at all right person gets, by chance, selected, he may be sent to a training course which has no direct relation with his job. Serious thought is not given to utilize the training opportunity after a trainee returns to his organization.

Fourth, the contents of the training programmes are not always relevant and meaningful for the trainees. There is no relationship between the training contents and actual placement of the trainees. Many training agencies do not have co-ordination between the training programmes and needs of systematic career development. Most training courses do not fulfil the requirements of democratic policy and development administration.

Fifth, in most cases the training institutes follow traditional lecture-methods of training. Up-to-date and modern methods of training are not easily adopted. Lecture-method occupy almost 80% of the training in most institutions.

Final, training system is not linked with the education and research in the country and systematic evaluation of the training results and follow up of the effects of training on the efficiency in administration are not attempted.

Suggestions for Improvement

There is a lot of scope for the improvement of the Indian system of training in the years to come. Some of the suggestions to improve it are discussed below

Clear Objectives : The objectives of civil service training at all levels, must be clearly laid down by the Government. These objectives must include the following:

(a) Developing social economic and political awareness of employees;

(b) Developing functional and technical competence of the employees;

(c) Developing capacities to deal with the people and their problems at all levels;

(d) Making the employees democratic, responsive and development oriented;

(e) Making them aware of their moral and public responsibilities;

(f) Developing a secular and national outlook among the employees.

Clear Policy : Government must lay down a clear and comprehensive training policy for its employees. It should become an integral part of the personnel management of the government. Needs of various services and functions must be examined and various types and methods of training must be related to these needs of the services.

New Techniques and Methods : The training system must adopt and absorb new and modern techniques of training from time to time. Traditional methods must be replaced by modern methods at regular intervals. It is necessary to maintain contact with well-known national and international training agencies for knowing the latest developments in the field of training. Prevailing training methods and their effectiveness in the light of the results must be evaluated and examined from time to time and necessary changes must be incorporated in the light of the earlier experiences.

Link with the Educational System : The training system must have a co-ordination with the University and educational system of the country. This will avoid a lot of unnecessary and unrealistic wastage of money and energy on the present training system in the country. Job requirements, training contents and the educational system must be co-ordinated in such a way that together they provide the best administrators for the country.

In modern times training of civil service has become an integral part of personnel management. As the functions of the governments have increased the administration has become a complicated, complex and technical activity requiring specialized knowledge and skills. Systematic and coherent training of civil servants has, therefore, become absolutely necessary. In almost all the countries today elaborate training arrangements have been made and appropriate training institutions have been set up to provide suitable and effective training for the civil servants. India is not exception to this. In post-independence period training of higher civil services has received very careful attention in the country. Both pre-entry or entry-point training as well as in-service training courses has been systematically planned and innumerable general and specialized training institutions have been set up in the country. An increasing number of civil servants are now receiving some kind of training at some point during their career.

In spite of this both in the field of civil service training and proliferation of the training institutions in the country, the Indian system of training has not been able to fulfil the desired expectations from it. There are many weaknesses in it and a lot remained to be done to improve the Indian system of civil service training in the days to come.

Historical Background

I.A.S. Staff College, Shimla : Apart from the entry point training provided to the I.A.S. Probationers by the I.A.S. Training School New Delhi. It was realized that after a gap of four or five years, the senior officers of the I.A.S. also need some kind of orientation or refresher courses, during their career. The Government therefore, established I.A.S. Staff College at Shimla. This staff college arranged for the short-term, in-service training of the senior I.A.S. officers who put in 6 to 10 years service. It also organizes training courses for the senior officers of other All India Services and Central Services.

National Academy of Administration : In 1959, the two sister organisations i.e., I.A.S. Training School, New Delhi and I.A.S. Staff College, Shimla, were amalgamated and a National Academy of Administration came into existence at Mussoorie on 1st September 1959. It was named in 1972 as Lal Bahadur Shastri National Academy of Administration. There were many reasons for the establishment of the N.A.A.

Firstly, the number of I.A.S. recruits increased from 33 in 1949 to 120-130 in 1957 per year.

Secondly, there was a growth of interservice tensions and conflicts among the various higher civil services in India. Therefore, it was felt necessary to start a 'co-ordinated' general courses for the entrants to various All India Services.

Thirdly, the facilities at the I.A.S. Training School were not enough to meet the needs of the increasing number of the recruits to the I.A.S.

Fourthly, there was a need to provide refresher courses or orientation training to the senior I.A.S. officers after completing ten to fifteen years of service. This was necessary to make them aware of the up-to-date and latest development in the country and abroad.

Objectives of the N.A.A. : Originally, the Academy was established to provide the following courses :

1. A 'Foundational Course' for direct recruits of the I.A.S. and other All India Service (like I.F.S., I.P.S.) and Central Class Service (like Audit and Accounts, Income Tax, Post, Railways, Defence Accounts, Customs and Excise etc.) for five months.
2. Professional Course to the direct recruits of the I.A.S for seven months.
3. Refresher, orientation, re-orientation courses of short duration for I.A.S. officers with 6 to 10 years of service.
4. Short-term courses, seminars, conference etc. for the benefit of senior officers.

The National Academy of Administration has become the most important national institution of Civil Service Training in the country. Now it provides the following courses :

1. A combined foundational course for five months duration for the entrants of all the All India Services and the Central Service Class-I.
2. Professional Course in two spell for the directly recruited I.A.S. probationers for a period of one year (divided in two spells of six months).
3. A four to six week Refresher Course for the I.A.S. officers of the seniority of 10 to 15 years.
4. One week compulsory Refresher Courses for the I.A.S. officers every year.
5. Short-term Refresher Courses for the senior officers of other All India Services, Central and State Service.

6. Courses, seminars, conferences etc., for the senior civil servants of the All India Central and State Service.

The N.A.A. is located at Mussoorie, a hill station in Uttaranchal geographically isolated from the rest of the country. Attempts to shift into Delhi have not been successful and it continues to function at Mussoorie itself. It has a director and other teaching facility and non-teaching staff etc.

Training System for the I.A.S.

After selection through the All India Competition all the new I.A.S. recruits, who are called as the Probationers, have to undergo a compulsory training course at Lal Bahadur Shastri National Academy of Administration at Mussoorie. This is in fact entry point training of the I.A.S. probationers for a duration of two years. It is called as 'Sandwich' course of training.

'Sandwich' Course of Training for the I.A.S. : The training programme for the I.A.S. has undergone a change since 1969. In 1969 the Central Government introduced what is called as 'Sandwich' course of training for the newly recruited members of the I.A.S. They are required to undergo two spells of training, with an interval of one year's in-service training in the states.

First Stage : The first spell consists of the foundational course and professional training for the duration of six months. This is conducted at the National Academy of Administration. In the foundational course, the I.A.S. probationers join with all the probationers of the other all India Services and the direct recruits to the Central Services Class 1. This course is for the duration of five months. After the completion of the foundational course, an examination is held in which all the probationers have to appear in it and all are expected to pass. After this is over, the probationers of central services and all other All India Services like I.F.S., I.P.S. are sent to their respective specialized/professional training centres for their further professional training. But the I.A.S. probationers stay at the Academy for further professional training. The first spell of training thus includes

(i) Foundational Course and

(ii) Professional Course.

These methods have been discussed in detail in the preceding pages.

Second Stage : *In the States :* The second stage of training begins when the first spell for the training at N.A.A. is over. The I.A.S. probationers go to their allotted states for one year's field training. The second stage of training is mainly divided into two phases :

1. a purely 'on the job' training where they learn practical administration by doing;
2. And a mixture of institutional and practical on the job training.

The condition of this second stage of training mostly depends upon the State Government. Many States have established regional training institutes but the overall situation is not satisfactory. The training arrangements varies from State to State. The field training is absolutely essential and relevant to the actual work during the first five years of the service of the I.A.S. officers. There is no substitute to this kind of field training. It is absolutely necessary. But this stage of practical training seems to be taken less seriously by the State Governments. The senior officers, with whom the probationers are posted, are either indifferent or too busy to give them sufficient time and attention. Some of them are not competent enough to train the young probationers. The Administrative Reforms Commission, therefore, recommended that, "during their training in the states the I.A.S. probationers should be assigned to carefully chosen senior Collectors, who are known for their interest in training and whose methods of work are considered worthy of emulation".

The practical training of the I.A.S. probationers in the States does not have a nationally accepted common pattern. Each and every State has adopted a pattern suitable to its own local conditions. However, the second stage of training in the States, normally, consists of the following (with some variations)

1. A short period in the State Government:
2. Work with a District Collector;
3. Work in treasury and Accounts;
4. Work in Development departments like, Agriculture, Cooperation, Irrigation, Community Development, Panchayats etc.
5. Magisterial and Judicial work.
6. Work in sub-divisional office.

Many State Governments have their own training schools/ institutes. The I.A.S. Probationers are sent to these institutes for a period of two/ three months for imparting them training in the revenue administration of the state concerned. The probationers are also expected to study the organisation and working of the various departments of the State Government, discuss with the concerned officers about the broad features of the State departments, study some important files and cases of the concerned department and set and observe the functioning of the interdepartmental committees and meetings. All the minute details are to be noted down by the probationers.

1. Work relating to Land Records and Settlements.
2. Work relating to Panchayati Raj Bodies.
3. Work in Police Office.

During I.A.S. probationer's training in the States, they are in constant touch with a tutor at the N.A.A. who guides him, sets specific tasks, exercises and writing of reports etc. The probationers have to keep diaries, which are scrutinized by the Collector. Periodical reports are sent to the Academy by the probationers through the Collector. They are, in some states, expected to work as B.D.O., V.L.W. or Patwari also. Such experience gives reality to the already acquired theoretical knowledge of the probationers. At this stage more emphasis is on field training in the work of Sub-divisional Office and District Collector. More attention is given on specific cases arising in the routine of district administration. At the end of this second stage of field training in the state, the I.A.S. probationers go back to the National Academy for the second spell of the professional training. Each and every probationer has to submit a detailed report of his one year's on the job training to the Director. The report should contain details of his practical training, his experience, his reactions to the methods of training and his suggestions, if any, for improvement.

Third Stage, Second Spell of Professional Training at the N.A.A. : In the third stage of the 'Sandwich' training programme, the I.A.S. probationers come back to the National Academy after gaining one year's practical on the job field experience of the working of administration in the States. The Academy arranges a second spell of more problem oriented professional training for a period of about six months. During this period of training emphasis is not on theoretical aspect of public administration but on practical/applied aspect of public administration. The experiences already gained by the probationers during their field training for one year in the States has to be fruitfully related with their theoretical knowledge to solve the problems of administration. In fact, training during this period is entirely problem oriented training. More and more emphasis is laid on discussing the specific cases arising out of the real administrative situations in the districts. Case studies are taken up. The syndicate method is employed and group discussion takes place in the light of the field experience gained by the participants.

This stage of training rely more on discussions, presentation of individual views and on participation of each and every probationers in the training. Everybody is provided with ample of opportunities to purposefully express his opinions upon the various aspects of his training in the districts, and upon the assignments prepared by him and also upon the information gathered by him during the course of training. Exchange of views, opinions and experience through open discussion and free participation is the essence of training at this stage in the National Academy.

At the end of this final phase of the training the I.A.S. probationers have to appear in the Probationer's final examination. The Academy conducts the examination in accordance with the I.A.S. (Probationer's Final Examination) Regulation of 1955 (amended from time to time)

Language problem is solved by requiring every I.A.S. probationer to pass an examination in the language of the state to which he is allotted and Hindi language.

The 'sandwich' course of I.A.S. probationers, as described above has been borrowed from the French system of training. The trainees of the highest civil services in France, spend three years at the National School of Administration in Paris. During the first year they are attached to the Office of a Perfect district/ departmental officer) to get practical experience in administration. In the second year they return to Ecole Nationale (i.e., National School) at Paris for general academic training. In the third year they are given training in specialized/professional course related to the Ministry to which they are assigned. The introduction of the 'Sandwich' course for the I.A.S. has made the entire training system more realistic and action-oriented.

Since its adoption in 1969, many significant and useful changes have been introduced, on the recommendations of the various Committees, especially on the basis of the recommendations of the Administrative Reforms Commission to improve the system of I.A.S. training at the National Academy.

Further Training of I.A.S. Officers : After the second spell of professional training at the National Academy, the I.A.S. probationers are sent back to their respective State for posting. They are posted in charge of sub-divisions to begin with. In order to enrich and diversify the administrative experience of an I.A.S. officer, he is transferred from district to district after every two years' stay. He is also sent to work in the State Secretariat as Under-Secretary, for nearly eighteen months. All this is, to prepare him to be posted as a District Collector. This, therefore, a type of in-service training of the concerned officer, to give him a variety of experience before he becomes perfectly ready for a senior post after about six or seven years of service. I.A.S. cadre is primarily meant to provide senior level officers. Their appointment on junior positions is basically intended to train them for higher positions. But his in-service training of young I.A.S. officers is not uniform in different States and leaves much scope for improvement. It has to be taken more seriously.

Refresher Courses for I.A.S. Officers

The rapidly changing field of administration, requires continuous changes in the ideas, attitudes and temperament of administrators. The world of knowledge is expanding so fast that every existing skill and knowledge becomes out-dated after a few years. The Civil Servants, therefore, need a continuous doze of in-services training, refresher or orientation courses to be periodically provided formally or informally.

After a spell of five to seven years of service it is absolutely necessary for the officers to get together to exchange views and experiences on various issues of administration. It is also vital for them to keep abreast and up-to-date about the latest thinking on various problems facing the administration with the type of dynamic administration, democratic polity and socio-economic problems we have. It is still more necessary that senior and responsible officers should come together and acquire fresh understanding of the problems and new ways to solve them. Refresher or orientation training also becomes necessary for securing a balance between democratic process and responsive administration on the one hand and modern management techniques and administrative efficiency on the other. The expansion of the activities of the State has thrown up a lot of new social, economic and human problems before the administration, and posed new challenges before the administrators. The role of

I.A.S. Officers in this situation does assume a sensitive and critical dimension. The country needs a new administrative culture, high quality of services and result-oriented techniques to ensure an effective delivery system to suit the policies of the Government and aspirations of the people.

Apart from the intensive entry-point training for two years, imparted to the I.A.S. probationers at the National Academy, there are several Refreshers or Orientation courses for the senior I.A.S. officers. These courses are of the duration ranging from one weak to six or eight weeks. On an average, it is expected that each and every I.A.S. officer receives some kind of Refreshers/Orientation course at least three to four times during his career. These courses are conducted by various training institutions or even Universities.

One Week—Compulsory refresher course for all the I.A.S. officers every year with virtual participation in which junior, middle level and senior officers would attend the same course.

Four Weeks—Orientation training in general management, and administration, arranged in three stages viz., 6 to 9 years service, 10 to 16 years service and 17 to 20 years of service. Subject like development administration, project programming, decision-making, management techniques, problems solving skills, organisational performance and policy planning and analysis are included in the four-weeks refresher courses.

The Government has identified 43 training institutes for imparting the above mentioned one week refresher course and four weeks training to the I.A.S. Officers. They include a central institute, 18 national training institutes, 13 state training centres and other centres, (Universities etc.). These institutions have already started conducting these courses for the senior and experienced I.A.S. officers in the country.

Morale and Job Satisfaction

An administrative system does not exist without employees, workers or state hired servants civil or military. An administrative system having employees, workers or servants is meaningful, if it is progressively working for the improvement in its efficiency. Administration when put to test or is subjected to some evaluative criterion has to qualify some condition. Administrative system when subjected to an evaluative criterion can be thus judged as good or bad. An administrative system, similarly can be classified on the basis of ranking provided. It is subjected to the evaluative criteria where on a "developmental scale", its rate of growth could be measured.

Ordinarily, an administrative system can be classified or ranked according to the evaluative criterion as given below:

Efficiency : as input output ratio.

Economy : rate of growth of profits or ratio of profit to the capital invested.

Responsiveness : the time taken in for quicker disposal of a request made in a government department.

Effectiveness: the ratio of goal achieved to goal announced.

Democratic: representativeness degree of people's participation in final policy making process.

For progressive improvement in the "efficiency" in an administrative system, morale of the employees, civil military servants has to kept high. We are encouraged to propound a hypothetical statement:

"The higher the level of morale of employees, servants (civil or military) the higher shall be degree of performance".

The morale of the public personnel constitutes an important factor in the efficiency of an administration.

What is difficult is to foster and to maintain continuously as state of high degree morals among all ranks of the public employees. In order to achieve sustained and comprehensive efforts are needed in this regard to achieve success.

Alexander Leighton defined morale in these words:

"The capacity of a group of people to pull together persistently and consistently in pursuit of a common purpose. "

It is an inner possession of an individual as well as of a group, each interacting upon the other........it refers to a sense of belonging, and a sense of unity of purpose which may prevail among the employees of an organisation.

At Indian Institute of Public Administration New Delhi, one of the most important conference was held under the leadership of Professor V.K.N. Menon the then director of the Institute of "Morale in Public Service" (January 3-4, 1959) in which stalwarts like R.C. Dutt (I.C.S.), Durga Das (Journalist) N.V. Gadgil (the then Governor of Punjab), B.N. Jha (I C.S.) S.S. Khanna (I.C.S.) , Prof. Kali Prasad (Psychology University of Lucknow), L.P. Singh (I.C.S.) Prof. N.K. Siduanta (Vice Chancellor of University of Calcutta) and Prof. V.C.N. Menon were activity associated. The Indian Institute of Public Administration crows for an assembly of such a galaxy of Administration and intellectuals. Now-a-days "gatherings" are of course, "arranged" like, formal chit-chat get-to-gether where seminars are not held but "dramatised." The down grading of the Institution is because of ordinary men occupying executive, managerial as well as academic positions.

In this conference, it was highlighted that morale is affected by a number of factors which may be summed up as:

A. Recruitment and training policies, terms of employment and working conditions.

B. Internal relationship, communications and human relations in an organisation.

C. The nature of relations between the public employees on one hand and the legislators and ministers on the other.

D. Attitude of the people towards the public servants.

The intangibility of the concept of morale is worldly known. Pt. Gobind Ballabh Pant—the then Home Minister of India had made the following striking revelations about Indian Administrative System and the Indian Administrators:

1. Our system of administration still continues to be based on the old framework.
2. The administrators and those connected with administration have to develop an outlook in tune with the changing social and economic objectives.
3. The success of our efforts and the achievement of our objectives will necessarily depend to a large extent on the services, their morale, efficiency and quality.
4. .... the art of administration can not be defined in terms of rules and regulations of the trade, the concept of morale is still more intangible, it nevertheless encompasses almost the entire field and every aspects of administration. It is affected by and in turn affects every aspect of administration.
5. We are all engaged in a common task and guided by a common purpose to raise the level of life in the country.
6. We have to promote and strengthen a positive attitude to work in every office and administrative unit.
7. There has to be a greater degree of "communication" between those at the top and those below them so that this feelings of partnership and sense of purpose may be transmitted to the lowest in the hierarchy.
8. It has also to be borne in mind that our efficiency is rather low in terms of quality and quantity.
9. If there is efficiency and a feeling of adequacy then, morale will be high.
10. Morale is essentially related more to the attitude of mind than with other externals.

Morale, is a matter of spirit the quality of outlook, the way one approaches one's job. A high standard of morale is reflected in a high standard of efficiency, integrity and responsiveness. It may also mean that public servants may function honestly, efficiently and impartially. A complete support between services and the general public is a definite indicator of high degree of morale.

Recruitment, Training, Terms of Employment and Working Condition

"When fair play and merit are the guiding principles in the recruitment of staff, employees will have confidence in the management and this will be conducive to their morale".

The statement above raises the fundamental question i.e. how far our present methods of recruitment in their different aspects are satisfactory?

ARC's Recommendation on Recruitment

1. For all services, advance projections should be made of the requirements of personnel for five years at a time.
2. For the Indian Administrative Service Indian Foreign Service and other non-technical class-I services, recruitment should be made only through a single competitive examination.
3. Subjects to be offered at the combined competitive examination for non-technical services may include Engineering subjects as well as subjects relevant to a medical degree.

The ARC had unwillingly suggested medical as well as engineering subject for I.A.S. because these subjects create a bias towards technical subjects and students offering humanities are at great disadvantage because these subjects do not fetch marks as compared to science and medical or engineering group of subject.

Training of Government Employees

"The objective of training to public servants is not only of inculcation of skill or occupational knowledge but development of administrative leadership and making the rank and file of the employees conscious of the purpose of the organization as well as the place which it occupies in the community as a whole."

1. I.I.P.A. Conference Report on Moràle in Public Services (Jan. 3-4, 1959) New Delhi, mention that such projections should be made by a Cadre Management Committee.

2. ARC Report on Personnel Administration op. ci. p. 44. Such a discussion about nature of training to government servants takes us to a point where one question the nature and content of Indian training courses in Lal Bahadur National Academy of Public Administration Mussorie (Uttaranchal) It thus raises the question as to what sort of orientation is that the nation provides to a new probationer (I.A.S. recruit) and whether such training courses really develop in the young officers the much needed executive leadership.

ARC Recommendation with Regard to Training

1. Government should formulate a clear-cut and far sighted national policy on civil service training by setting out objectives and priorities and guidelines for preparation of training plans.

2. Expenditure on training should be 1 per cent of the total wage bill whereas it was hardly 0.4 per cent (in 1980).

3. Central Training Division should be located in the new department of personnel.

4. Each Ministry/Department with sizeable training programme should have a separate training cell located in its Chief Personnel Office manned by a Training Coordinator.

Terms of Employment and Conditions of Service

"Inadequate salaries and retirement benefits create financial worries in the minds of employees in regard to the present as well as the future. These worries will have a depressing effect upon the morale of employees which, in turn, will injure the administrative efficiency."

Similarly insecurity of tenure of job produces uncertainty in the minds of employees about their future. Security of tenure always foster loyalty to the organisation which will raise morale.

The provision of adequate incentives can go a long way towards the stimulation of morale among employees. Regular consultation of employees through the institution of Whiteley Councils regarding the conditions of work and promotion of staff welfare, increases sense of belongingness and participation which is bound to have a positive impact on the morale of the employees.

The physical environment in which work is carried out also affects morale. Clean surroundings and absence of physical stresses and strains is conducive to the maintenance of enthusiasm and improves morale.

The conditions of services and other related matters include the following:

1. Working hours
2. Holiday
3. Over time allowance
4. Retirement and pensions
5. Transfers
6. Medical care
7. Incentives/Rewards
8. Residential accommodation
9. Equal opportunity for employment under government

10. Methods of work procedure
11. Proliferation of personnel.

ARC's Recommendation about Conditions of Services

1. The system of restricted religious holidays may be dispensed with by adding two more days to the present 12 days casual leave quantum.
2. Superseded servants may be allowed to voluntarily retire if they have put in at least 10 years' service.
3. Unsuitable or inefficient civil servants may be allowed to retire at the age of 50 or after the completion of 25 years.
4. Contributory Health scheme should be extended to all government servants.

21

Training of Civil Servants

Aims and Objectives

Training of civil servants has become an integral part of the modern personnel management programmes in all the countries of the world. Here we are going to study various aspects of training. After studying this lesson you will be able to

1. Describe the importance of the employee's skills.
2. Describe the meaning and objective of training; and
3. Make an overall assessment of the various types and methods of training in different countries.

In most of the countries, only well-educated, qualified and meritorious persons are recruited in the civil services. Most of them are graduates, post-graduates and degree/diploma holders. They have already obtained the minimum educational qualification required for entering the Government service. Their education is normally completed before they enter the civil service but the process of education continues even afterwards. However, they need a different type of education, which will help them in their daily work, and improve their skills and efficiency in administration. This new type of work-education is called as "training in the civil service".

In modern times, the administration has become more and more complex and complicated. It requires special knowledge and technical skills. Normal college and university education does not fulfil these requirements of modern administration. Therefore, there is an increasing need of training for the civil servants. Training now has become an integral part of the modern personnel management. In almost all the countries including India, elaborate arrangements are made to provide suitable and effective training to their civil servants. Here we are going to study and examine the importance of training for the development of employee's skills, objectives, needs, meaning, types and techniques of training.

The Importance

All over the world, training of civil servants has become an important aspect of modern personnel management. It has been recognized by all the modern Governments that suitable and effective training programme for their civil servants is absolutely necessary for efficient and up-to-date administration. On the one hand, the functions of the Government has increased and expanded rapidly and on the other, administration has become more and more complex, specialized and technical.

It is true that the recruitment policies and programmes based on 'merit system' try to select the best qualified and competent persons for the civil service most of the selected degree or diploma holders but the University degree or diploma is not enough to make them best administrators. It is necessary to have some knowledge and skill required for doing the actual work of administration. This practical knowledge is imparted through training. Training prepares an employee for the new administrative tasks. Training improves his skill and efficiency. Training prepares him for higher and higher responsibilities. In fact, the very induction of an employee in an organisation needs training. An employee must know about the goals and objects of his organization; the nature of work he is expected to perform in the organisation; and the techniques plus skills and methods of doing his new administrative work. All the required knowledge and skills can be imparted only through a systematic and coherent training programme.

Similarly, with the passage of time, the knowledge and skill acquired by an employee become out-dated. He needs new and up-to-date knowledge and skill. This up-dating of knowledge and skill is possible only through his training and orientation. We can therefore, say that training is a continuous activity. Although the formal education of an employee is normally completed before he enters the civil service, but the process of education, in the form of training, continues even afterwards. Training is thus, necessary before entering the civil service and even afterwards. Like education training is also a life long process. But training has narrow and specific objectives as compared to education. Education is much wider than training. Education influences the entire process of the upbringing of an individual from the childhood, the formation of his personality, characters, habits, manners, attitudes, mental and physical capabilities etc. Education in general aims at broadening the mind. But training aims at improving the specific skill and knowledge required for some particular kind of work or profession. However, both education and training are closely related to each other and many times they overlap each other.

Development Skills

When a brilliant young graduate from the University enters the civil service after successfully passing the written and oral examinations he does not know much of the practical administration. Nor does he have any knowledge of the actual work he is expected to perform in administration. At this entry-point itself an employee needs a pre-entry training. It is essential for the very induction of the new employee into the new organization. Unless he is given the essential information about the organization, its objectives, his own role in the organization and the methods of performing his own role effectively, he will not be able to make any real contribution and participate in the organization's performance. Without effective individual participation the organisational efficiency cannot increase. At the same time, an employee cannot effectively participate unless he thoroughly knows the techniques and skills necessary for the performance of his task. These technical skills can be acquired by the employee through training.

Training aims at continuous and systematic development, among all the levels of civil servants, of that knowledge and those skills and attitudes which are necessary for their own advancement and for increasing the efficiency of administration. Training imparts that knowledge of facts which is essential for specialized and professional work of administration. It also teaches the techniques and skills necessary for doing the administrative work. It also helps in formation of good mental and physical habits and attitudes necessary to be a successful administrator.

Ultimately we can say that the main objectives of civil service training are development of employee's skills, improvement of his individual performance, and overall efficiency of his administrative organisation. In the achievement of these objectives following training should be provided:

The Functions

1. Training helps the employee to understand the goals of his organization and his own role in it.
2. It helps him in acquiring the personal ability, physical tools and mental capacity required to promote these goals.
3. It helps him in acquiring the specialized and technical knowledge and professional skills required to perform his role effectively in the organisation.
4. It helps him to know the most suitable and up-to-date methods and procedures of work.
5. It helps him to attain precision and clarity in his individual work.
6. It helps him in effectively dealing with the fellow workers and with general public.
7. It helps in making adjustments with the changing work conditions and in adopting new outlook and new methods to new needs of new times.
8. It not only helps him to suitably adjust himself with the present work in his organisation and also prepare him

for the future higher duties and responsibilities in the administration.

9. It helps him in keeping a high morale and gives him emotional lift by increasing his pride in his work.
10. It helps him in equipping himself with necessary capacities to perform his role as development administrators in a satisfactory manner.

The importance of civil service training has been recognized by most countries, including India. They have devised suitable training programmes for their civil servants and established many training institutions for implementing these programmes. However, these arrangements are inadequate and a greater need of training is felt in many countries.

Training in Developing Countries

Training of civil servants is of basic importance in all countries but the need and importance of training is more urgently felt in developing countries. There are many factors responsible for this urgent need of training in developing countries. These are as follows :—

1. There is generally a shortage of trained and qualified persons in most developing countries;
2. Training facilities and training institutions are inadequate in these countries;
3. Functions of the Government have increased rapidly. They are called upon to perform many new functions, which require highly skilled and technically trained personnel;
4. Administration has complex, technical and specialized functions;
5. Socio-economic conditions, in these countries are rapidly changing. In order to meet the challenge of these rapid changes, there is a need of innovation in administration;

6. There is public pressure on the Governments to implement the development programmes with extraordinary speed and efficiency.

Because of the above mentioned factors, the need for civil service training is more urgently felt in developing countries. In fact we can say that in these countries, the entire success of the development policies depends upon chalking out systematic and suitable training programme and its timely implementation through the appropriate training institutions.

The Meaning

The dictionary meaning of training is "imparting instruction in a particular profession re-occupation". In public administration, training means conscious mode to improve the skill, powers and intelligence of an employee and to develop his attitudes and value-system in a desired direction. In broad and general term, training is a life long phenomenon. From early childhood we are trained in our life informally and unconsciously. But in the narrow and specialized sense, training of civil servants is a deliberate effort, directed to increase the specific skill and vocational competence of the civil servants in their routine work. William Torpey (Public Personnel Management, New York, 1953), defined training as "the process of developing skills, habits, knowledge and aptitudes in employees for the purpose of increasing the effectiveness of the employees in their present government positions as well as preparing the employees for future government position". In order to understand the meaning of training we can say that :

1. Training is a conscious, deliberate and planned effort;
2. Training is specific and limited;
3. It means imparting instructions about a particular work or profession;
4. Its purpose is to improve the skill, knowledge and effectiveness of the employees in their task;
5. It also aims at preparing an employee for higher responsibilities.

Sometimes we confuse training with education. Distinction between training and eduction must be very clearly understood. Education is a broader concept which aims at broadening of mind, and influences the total life, personality, habits and attitudes of an individual. Training is a narrow concept. Its aim is limited and specific. It imparts specific vocational skills and knowledge to improve the efficiency and effectiveness of a civil servant in carrying out his routine office work.

The Objectives

Following are some of the most important objectives of training of civil servants :

First, the training improves the efficiency of the administration.

Second, training improves the occupational skill and knowledge of the employees, so that they can do their work effectively.

Third, training in-acts a new employee into the organisation and gives him knowledge of the goals and objects of the organization, his own role in the organisation and techniques and methods of carrying out his duties. Consequently the employees can best contribute in the attainment of organisational goals.

Fourth, because their constant change in the goals and techniques of the organisations, training adjust the employees with the new organisational changes.

Fifth, training makes up the differences of the newly recruited persons. Fresh University graduates are given necessary training to shape and mould them into the desired direction and make them suitable for the work of administration of the Government.

Sixth, training helps the employee informal about the latest developments in his special field and thus, keep his knowledge up-to-date.

Seventh, training improves the integrity and morale of the employees. The very existence of the training process gives the trainees an added sense of the dignity and pride of their work and office.

Eight, training develops a sense of community service and belongingness in the employees. They realize that their work is an essential part of the organisation and the community. Therefore, they put more efforts in their work. This gives the employees a sense of pride and self-fulfilment in their work. It is, therefore, said that everybody in the civil service must get an opportunity of training of one kind or other.

Ninth, training makes the employees public oriented. It inculcates a basic principle in them that they are public servants and not masters.

Tenth, training prepares the employees for higher positions and greater responsibilities.

Final, training fosters homogeneity of outlook and broadens the vision and outlook of the employees.

Various Types

There are different types of training employed in different countries. Some of the major varieties of training are as following:

1. Formal and Informal training.
2. Short-term and Long-term training.
3. Pre-entry and post-entry training.
4. Centralized and Departmental training.
5. Skill training and background training.
6. Orientation training.

Formal and Informal Training

Informal training is training by experience, which an employee acquires during the course of his actual routine work in his organisation. No special efforts are necessary for informal training. This is a routine organisational activity. It does not require planned training programme, specialist/trainers or some training institutes. This kind of informal training neither prescribes a specific time period, nor a group of trainees is especially selected for it. This has been the traditional method of training in public administration and is preferred even now by practical administrators. But this process is a very hard way of learning and require a lot of persistence and patience on the part of the employee. It is slow, ineffective and frustrating. Formal training is free from these defects. That is why informal training is not very popular amongst most of the countries.

Formal training is that kind of training which is carefully planned, arranged and conducted under the expert supervision and guidance. Specialist trainers in a training institute or under the auspices of the Departmental training programme impart the formal training to a specially selected group of trainees during a specific time period. It consists of an actually course of study, with lectures, seminars, workshops, group discussions, conferences, work projects and written reports etc. It may lead to an award of a professional degree or a certificate of satisfactory completion of the training. It may be imparted before the entry into the service or during the probationary period of the career service. It may be full-time or part-time. It may be orientation course or it may be a course of general nature. The formal training has carefully defined objectives, predetermined courses or topics, planned course of action and systematically chosen methods of techniques. It inculcates necessary administrative skills through well-defined courses conducted at appropriate stages during the career-service. As the need of improving the administrative efficiency is felt urgently every where, the system of the formal training is becoming more and more popular. In fact, the best way is to supplement informal training by formal training programmes. Both must be combined to give best results but the various training programme adopted in different countries like pre-entry training, post-entry training, orientation training etc., normally rely on formal techniques of training only.

Short-term and Long-term Training : These two types of training depend upon the duration of the training course. The duration of training depends upon the subject-matter of training course; the nature of the service; and the needs of the Government. If the training course is completed in a few weeks or month or two it may be called as short-term training compared to the long-term training programmes conducted for a period ranging from six months to one year or two.

Pre-entry and Post-entry Training : It is clear from the above names itself that the training imparted before entering the civil service is pre-entry training whereas that which is given after a person enters the service is called as post-entry training. Pre-entry prepares future recruits for the services. The college and university education and professional or technical education can be called as pre-entry training. In recent times many training institution have been set up to provide training courses for administrative and managerial positions in the Government. Similarly there are many institution centres which provide training to the candidates appearing for competitive examinations. In some place practice of internship and apprenticeship is commonly employed for pre-entry training of the public potential recruits in the services. Practical administrative training is also provided in some Universities and Colleges. Comprehensive pre-entry training programmes are there in the U.S.A. and many western countries.

Post-entry training is given after a person joins the service. Post-entry training is very common in many countries. It is also called as inservice training. It may be a combination of formal or informal methods and it is imparted at all levels in the service. It helps in improving the efficiency and performance of the employees and makes them professionally more competent and able. Sometimes post-entry training is not directly concerned with the actual work of the employee but indirectly it is of much help to improve his general ability and organisational performance.

Centralized and Departmental Training : When training programme is made within a department or office, its aims are limited to improve the specific knowledge and skill relating to the department and it is conducted only for its own employees then it is called as Departmental training. Such training is imparted by experienced officers of the department itself. Police training college is an example of this type of training. But when training to the officers of many department is provided by a central training agency it is called as centralized training. The training programme of the Lal Bahadur Shastri Academy of Administration is an example of centralized training system in India.

Skill Training and Background Training : Background training is of general nature. It provides knowledge of such subjects which help the trainee to understand the social, economic, political, administrative and constitutional background and conditions prevailing in the country. The purpose is to broaden the mind and knowledge of the employees and to make them aware of the society and their own role in the society. But when it is intended to improve the skill of the employee in a particular kind of work, it is called as skill training. Still training aims at providing employees with the knowledge of special skills, techniques, procedures, methods, crafts or complicated systems etc., necessary to carry out his specialized kind of work. Craftsmanship training, or income-tax officers training are examples of the skill training whereas the I.A.S. entrant's training at Lal Bahadur Shastri National Academy of Administration at Mussoorie is example of background training.

Orientation Training : A new entrant must know about his organization, his work and his working situation and methods. He has to be introduced to his new organization. This is done through orientation training. Orientation training is planned effort to adjust an employee to his organization and his job. Basic objective of orientation training is to introduce an employee to the basic concept of his job, new work environment, aims and objects of his organization and his own place in the organization. Orientation training is also necessary to keep the civil servant up-to-date and attuned to the new developments in his field. Orientation training is becoming important in India in recent years.

Training of civil servants is of prime importance in all countries. In order to make civil service more efficient and effective, every where, suitable training programmes are chalked out. Training is necessary not only to the new entrants but also to those who are already in the service. It may be of any type formal or informal, short-term or long-term, pre-entry or post-entry. Training programme must be planned according to the requirements of different services keeping in view the socio-political and administrative conditions prevailing in the country. However, we can conclude that, whatever may be its type, training is a permanent need of public administration.

Various Methods

There are many techniques and methods of training followed in different countries. Some of the important methods are as follows:

Training by Experience on the Job : A person is posted on one job and allowed to learn from the experience gained by doing that job. Then he is posted to another section/ department to learn by experience about that new section. In this way an employee may be transferred from branch to branch, section to section or department to department and allowed to learn by the experience of doing a job. Senior and experienced officers help the trainee in this process of learning by giving necessary oral and written instruction and directions from time to time.

In order to give him wide experience of administration, a trainee is sometimes sent to work in an outside office or organisations. Short visits to other related offices, interdepartmental exchanges, study tours etc., are also arranged. This is like the method internship or apprenticeship commonly used in industrial management training. This method is cheap and simple. With the passage of time a person learns the techniques of administration and improves his performance as an administrator. But this method is slow and time consuming. Many times it does not have clearly defined objectives and specific time-limit. However, this method training is extensively adopted in most of the countries.

Training by Formal Instructions : In this method of training, formal instructions are given by the senior officers, to the trainees by arranging some lectures, or classes. Lectures of outside experts are also arranged. A specific course is planned and lectures, classes, group discussions, seminars, addresses or workshops etc. are arranged for imparting the necessary training to the employees. Head of the office/ department also addresses the employees and gives them necessary instructions. This is arranged through an agency or institute of training. Nowadays in most of the countries, this technique of training by formal instructions has been followed.

Selected group of trainees are given formal courses in specialized training institutes. At the time of the formal training, necessary written institutions, information, documents, rules and regulations etc., are also provided to the trainees. Films / Audiovisual aids and computers are also used for this type of formal training.

Conference Method of Training : This method of training has become very common now. A selected group of trainees from different departments are brought together to discuss various problems in a meeting or a conference. The trainees are the active participants in this method of training. Some specific cases are given for discussion in the conference. All the participants express their views and opinions based on their own experiences. This method, called as case-analysis method of training provides the opportunity to learn from the experiences of others.

In-lecture method of training, the trainer has an active role whereas in conference method the trainees have the active role. They learn from each other by exchange of experiences and ideas. The chairman of the conference plays the role of a guide and instructor. His role is only to put the discussion on the right track. In U.S.A. and many other countries the conference method has become very popular. In India also this method is used for senior level short-term training of higher civil servants like I.A.S. etc.

In conclusion we can say that all the Governments have to make training arrangements and establish suitable training organisations for the civil servants. While the broad objectives of training are decided by the Governments, it is the duty of the training organisations to plan the training programmes and adopt suitable methods of training. No one method is best. Different methods may be combined to suit the requirements of the jobs and of the training programmes. Lectures and talks of the senior departmental officers or experts may be arranged.

Seminars, conferences, workshops, group discussion, and field visits may be organized. Refresher or orientation courses may be conducted. Case-analysis method can be adopted. All these methods may be employed singly or in combination according to the needs and facilities available.

In modern times training of civil servants, has become an integral part of the personnel administration. With the tremendous increase in the functions of the Government, administration has became more and more complex, complicated and technical activity. It requires specialized knowledge and skills to run modern administration effectively. Systematic and coherent training of civil servant, therefore, has become absolutely necessary. In almost all the countries today elaborate training arrangements are made and appropriate training institutions have been set up to provide suitable and effective training for the Civil Servants. India is not exception to this.

Training Procedure in India

Civil Service Training is comparatively a new phenomenon in the modern world. In India, it began during the 18th Century British Raj itself. Today India is the leading developing country which has made an elaborate training arrangements and established a number of training institutions for the civil servants. Here we shall examine the Indian system of civil service training and make a critical evaluations of the civil servants. After studying this part you will be able to understand

1. Historical development of the concept of civil service training;
2. Evolution of Indian system of training;
3. The present system of training of civil servants in India and also about some important institutions of training in the country;
4. A critical evaluation of the Indian system of training; and
5. Suggestions to improve the present Indian system of training.

Training of military recruits has been a regular practice even since ancient times. Craftsmanship and professional training has also been given through apprenticeship for thousands of years. After industrial revolution, skill training of industrial workers became necessary. But civil service training is of comparatively recent origin. Only in the twentieth century civil service training had assumed a great significance in the personnel management.

Training to higher civil servants was started during the days of East India Company in the 18th century itself. I.C.S. officers were provided with extensive entry-point training in England before sending them to India. The system of training evolved during the pre-independence period has been modified to suit the changed requirements after independence. Today India is the leading developing country which has made elaborate training arrangements and established a number of general and professional training institutions which provide up-to-date training for its civil servants.

Evolution of the Concept

Although training of civil servants is comparatively a new phenomenon, the training of military personnel has been a regular feature of military administration for thousands of years. In ancient India, there was an institution called as Guru-Shisya Parampara (Teacher-pupil relationship) under which the student stayed away from his home in the Gurukul/Ashram, to learn the best of the knowledge skills and arts from the Guru. Rulers, artists, artisans and even administrators were perfectly trained under the Gurukul system But this arrangement was restricted to the upper strata of society. Ordinary citizen's profession was decided by his birth and caste and he used to get informal training of the family craft or profession from his family and caste group.

Since the middle ages in Europe the craftsmen were trained by formal apprenticeship with experienced craftsman. Conscious and systematic training began only after the industrial revolution in the field of private industry, business and management. Industrial expansion required skilled and expert workers to operate the intricate machines. Naturally the need of industrial and technical training of workers was felt urgently. In order to increase the efficiency and production of the industries they required trained managers and therefore the need of management training was also felt urgently. The training of employees, thus became necessary for the success of the industrial administration.

But in the field of civil administration training was not considered to be necessary because the functions of the Governments were limited and administration was a simple activity. Civil servants were expected to learn by experience through a process of trial and error. This method of the hard way of learning was continued for a long time.

In modern times the social and political conditions have changed. Modern State has become a welfare State. Functions of Governments have tremendously increased. All governments have to promote the welfare of the people plan for the socio-economic development and implement the development programmes efficiently. Scientific and technological developments have rapidly changed the lives of the people. After the Second World War many new states have come into existence. In many of them democratic governments have been established. All these changes have made administration a very complex activity.

We need highly skilled personnel to run modern administration. For this purpose the need of planned and purposeful training for the civil servants has been felt urgently everywhere in the world. More and more attention is now being given to civil service training in many countries. In almost every country a national academy or institute is established to provide some general kind of training to its civil servants. There are also specialized training institutions in every country.

Historical Background

History of civil service training in India can be traced back to the days of East India Company, which established Haileybury College in 1805 for the training of the young recruits to the covenanted civil services. The Indian Civil Service was manned by the products of the Haileybury College until 1855 when the first competitive examination was held. The successful I.C.S. candidates were required to spend 1 to 2 years in a British University and learn subjects like Indian law and Indian language etc.

During the Second World War a camp school was set up at Dehra Dun to impart training to the new entrants in the I.C.S. After

Independence the Indian Civil Service was converted into Indian Administrative Service and to impart institutional training to the new recruits. Indian Administrative Service Training School was set up in 1947 in New Delhi. In 1957 Indian Administrative Service Staff College was set up at Shimla to train senior officials and recruits other than direct recruits. Both these institutions were subsequently merged and the National Academy of Administration was set up in September 1959 at Moussorie. The academy is now named as Lal Bahadur Shastri National Academy of Administration, which is the most important central institution of training of the higher civil service including the All-India Services.

During the British Raj it was believed that the education received before joining civil service was sufficient to qualify a person for the job. After joining the service, he was generally left to learn by experience on the job. Formal training was not considered to be essential for the civil servants. Only the I.C.S. and technical personnel were provided with institutional training. Police, Telegraph/Railways, Income-tax, Accounts and Audit were the departments which required training arrangements for their technical personnel. However, in spite of all these arrangements, government relied more on training by experience on the job till independence.

The problem of civil service training has assumed special significance only after independence with the changes in the social, political and constitutional conditions. The nature of government work has changed the functions and machinery of the government has expanded and many new services have been constituted. As a result of all these rapid developments, it has become imperative for the Central and State Governments to plan and provide suitable training to their civil servants. Accordingly a number of National Central Training Institutions have been set up by the Central Government. Similarly in almost all the States there are state level training institutions like Administrative Staff Colleges and public training centres etc. Apart from these institutions many other academic bodies and Universities also provide training to civil servants.

Objectives in Indian Context

After Independence the Civil Service training assumed special significance in India. The Planning Commission observed as early in 1954 itself that "next to recruitment the training of personnel has considerable bearing on administrative efficiency. Each type of work in the government requires a programme of training suited to it. In general, in all branches of administration, it is necessary to provide for the training of personnel at the commencement of service as well as at appropriate intervals in later years". Following are the major goals of civil service training

First, and foremost goal of training is to improve the competence, skills and efficiency of the civil servants for the present job and also for the future.

Second, training should inculcate democratic attitude and respect for the civil servants. This is necessary because of the authoritarian character of the British Administration in the past.

Third, in a vast country like India, training should foster a national outlook amongst the administrators.

Fourth, training must fill up the gap between the civil servants and the public. It should make them realize that they are not masters of the people as in the past, but are essentially public servants.

Fifth, training of civil servants should aim to make them aware of the realities of rural India and give a rural-orientation to them in their work.

Sixth, India's development requires successful implementation of Five Year Plans. It is therefore, necessary that training of civil servants should make them good planners and development administrators.

Seventh, training of civil servants must make them aware of latest developments in their field, and enable them to acquire knowledge of latest techniques tools and skills, necessary for the successful administration.

22

Human Relations in Administration

In an administrative organisation, a superior has to direct and supervise a large number of subordinate employees. If the former does so invariably in an authoritarian fashion, morale will not tend to be stimulated to fear of authority and morale do not go well together. On the contrary of the administrator displays high qualities of leadership, morale among the employees will be encouraged. A sympathetic heart which cares for the welfare of the subordinates goes a long way to inspire personnel rather than dynamism broad vision and other similar qualities. Feeling of casteism, regionalism and parochialisation tends to obstruct the growth of the morale. Thus it is necessary in the interest of morale to remove emotion barriers between the various categories of employees in an administrative organisation.

In the field of morale, internal communications play most effective role. Both formal as well as informal internal communications have repercussions on the morale of the employees.

The following measures should be taken to develop morale among employees:

1. Develop humane administrative leadership.
2. Relationship between higher personnel and the rank and file should be fostered to such an extent that mutual confidence could be sufficiently built. It is essential between generalist super or and a technical subordinate.
3. As far as possible, the feeling of casteism, communalism and regionalism needs to be expelled.
4. Internal communication should be improved and information needs to be made available to all the employees at all levels.

Public Servants, Ministers, Legislators and the Public

In a parliamentary democracy there are three partners engaged in a common adventure i.e. the endless enterprise of administrating a wide variety of men, the legislators, ministers civil servants and the people. The success of partnership and also the parliamentary democracy depends upon a proper undertaking of their respective roles. Any mal-adjustment in this partnership will have adverse effect and bearing on the morale of the public personnel.

Some politicians try to exert political pulls and pressures directly upon a civil servant in order to get favourable treatment for one purpose or the other. They may go even to the extent of browbeating the latter. On the other hand, some civil servants do not show proper courtesy towards the representative of the people. Again inefficiency and delay on the part of civil servants can be an important cause of annoyance to the politicians. Any mal-adjustments in the relationship between the politicians and public servants will not only endanger political neutrality of the latter but will also have an adverse effect on administrative morale.

Ministers need to adopt realistic and constructive attitude in their criticism of the actions of the civil servants. Ministers should avoid political pulls and pressures of the public personnel.

A good equation needs to be developed between a minister, civil servants and the common man (Public).

Job Satisfaction

Work is a potent source of need gratification viz. physical, social, egoistic and personal, occupations are important source of need satisfaction in our culture (Roe). A man's work is a social device for his or her identification as an individual.

Blum has given a number of reason for studying job-satisfaction. A job grants some status, power, dignity and a feeling of achievement. The terms like "morale", "job-satisfaction" and "motivation" have been used interchangeably.

Robinson and Hoppock had collected the data and came with the conclusions that the medium figure was 18 per cent dissatisfied. A summary of many previous studies on Job-Satisfaction suggests that two-third of the studies reveals that less than one third of the workers were dissatisfied. In India, studies conducted by Gangul and Sharma have confirmed that the Indian workers are more concerned with such factors as pay and security of job thus the motivator-hygiene theory is only a partial explanation of the phenomenon of job satisfaction.

Human behaviour is caused by an individual's need structure. Secondly, human behaviour is goal directed, the goal being the satisfaction of the need. Need creates a sort of dissonance or tension in an individual motivate him to take action as will lead to need fulfilment. Needs are something which an individual lacks creating tension in him. These may be considered as internal demands that must be satisfied in order to achieve adjustment. Four categories of needs influence human behaviour :

1. Physical Needs
2. Security Needs
3. Social Needs
4. Ego Needs

The above mentioned classification has been made by Marlow.

An individual's behaviour or adjustment on the job is intimately related to the extent to which an individual's needs are satisfied both at work and outside it.

Thus occupational satisfaction can not be separated from the over all need satisfaction in life. An individual's work is only one area of human behaviour, and whatever social and psychological mechanism that operate to make an individual satisfied or dissatisfied in life, would also be effective on the job situation as well.

Some hypotheses have been formulated by people to validate or reject these through empirical studies:

1. The higher the occupational level, the greater would be the satisfaction of physical needs.
2. The higher the occupational level, the greater would be satisfaction of security needs, similarly the same hypothesis could be constructed by correlating higher occupational status and social as well as ego needs satisfaction.

Physical Needs and Job-Satisfaction : A significant and positive association exits between physical need satisfaction and job satisfaction in case of managers, workers and supervisors of Indian industries.

Security Needs and Job-Satisfaction : There is high and positive correlation between the above mentioned two variable for all the time categories of respondents. Lahiri too, had noted that managerial motivation was closely associated with the satisfaction of security needs.

Social Needs and Job-Satisfaction : Social participation is considered as an important index of social need. Social need satisfaction, too, is positively related to job-satisfaction is all the three groups of respondents e.g. managers, supervisors and workers.

Ego Needs Satisfaction and Job : Ego need satisfaction is positively correlated with job satisfaction.

Moral Satisfaction

This correlation was found to be very high among managers, foreman and workers studies by Dr. A.K. Srivastava (Punjab University, Chandigarh 1982-84), Srivastva had studied three other ego-related variable in relation to their association with job-satisfaction:

1. Occupational mobility
2. Putting efforts to improve career prospects
3. Success in achieving job ambitions

Srivastava had found a definite correlation between the above mentioned three ego-related variable and job satisfaction. We thus find that there is a definite correlation between need satisfaction and job-satisfaction. It was confirmed in Srivastava study (1982-84) that "total need satisfaction goes on decreasing with the decline in occupational level. Similarly job-satisfaction also goes on decreasing simultaneously. The more is the number of needs that are satisfied, the greater is the job-satisfaction. The problem of job-satisfaction can only be considered in relation to the individual who performs it. His motives, experiences and social interaction with his family, company and community are intricately and intimately linked with problem of job-satisfaction. When one is dissatisfied, he is dissatisfied all over. Empirical evidence also suggests that the universality of the concept of "motivator is not hrygienic" is a myth. They are situation and culture-bound.

What is intrinsic or extrinsic dependence upon the perception of the researchers. In Indian context, many of the hygiene factors are motivators both for workers and managers. This is a reality. Management should also try other old techniques to improve work-efficiency viz. work enrichment (job-enrichment), improving quality of life and make work more satisfying humane and enjoyable.

So long as the real basic needs of employees, workers, managers and administrators are not satisfied, the sophisticated techniques of administrative improvement will not provide them with any intrinsic satisfaction. Marlow and Herzberg's need Hierarchy is constantly at the helm of the affairs so far as employees job satisfaction is concerned. Discriminatory and exploitative organisational structure also does not prove job satisfaction conducive organisational motivational in India could result in heightened job satisfying conditions. Hoppock (1935) had written a monograph on Job-Satisfaction. Job-satisfaction, job attitudes and morale are typically measured by means of interviews or questionnaires. Job-satisfaction is a complex set of variable job and work-role variables which affect job-satisfaction These are the following:

1. Supervision
2. The Work Group
3. Job Content
4. Wages
5. Promotional Opportunities
6. Hours of Work

Problems of Generalists and Specialists

Who are the Generalists? **:** An administrator who gets into an organisation without having received education and/or training in only one area of human activity and its administration but gets into service because of his general intellectual excellence and academic superiority over others in the fields of general knowledge, a foreign language (in case of India English because Indians are still fooled of the English about superiority of their mother tongue) and one or two subjects out of a long list of subjects (not less than 56). Such a recruit is generalist, who has least knowledge of administration or management but must excel in two out of the fifty six or so odd subjects. This is how Indians initiate concept of generalist administrators from their old British masters even today, decades of independence, Indians are the best aping-genius of the whole world.

Who are the Specialists? **:** Specialists are those persons, who are recruited on the basis of their pre-entry qualifications to the services. By specialist, is generally meant a person, who has special knowledge or skill in a specific field. Specialized services are called functional services, which include a technical function for which pre-entry qualification is required. The specialists are supposed to know more and more about less and less.

The role of professional has remained largely subordinate to that of the administrator, he is regarded primarily as an adviser when it comes to responsibility for policy-determination.

Generalists in Great Britain **:** Generalists are those persons recruited on the basis of their general educational background, irrespective of the subjects studied in the universities. The generalists' services again fall into two groups. The first group consists of the generalist administrative services which do not have any well defined functional area, or in other words have to perform diverse types of functions. This category does not include any background experience of the field in which one is recruited. The second group consists of functional services. In this category, however, a person is appointed on the basis of general qualification as his functions are confined to some specific areas and each area has its own well defined functions.

Administrative Trainees belonging to the generalist services in U.K. advance in their career, by acquiring diverse nature of experience, a breadth of vision and outlook, a capacity to coordinate and synthesize mutually conflicting approaches and an understanding of socio-economic and political environment. Since the functional generalist services operate within their specialized areas, their roles in administration in many ways are comparable with that of the specialists, but, they can be distinguished from the latter on the basis of recruitment which is their pre-entry professional qualification.

Acceptability of Generalists among Public Administration Academia : There is, it appears, some acceptability among the academia of Public Administration "generalists". There is also a wide consensus on the concept of administrators as generalists rather than specialists. This concept is particularly applicable to the higher level administrators as generalists rather than specialists. This concept is particularly applicable to the higher level administrators, whose responsibilities usually include the coordination of the work of many specialists or experts. It may also be applied to other administrators as well-albeit in a more limited sense.

Generalists' acceptability generally depends upon social philosophy of a country or the mind i.e., the top intellectuals and their values and philosophy. It is seen that intellectuals in U.K. have not analysed in depth the damage which a generalist service is doing to their country. An intellectual generalist is not worse but at the same time it is not the best. It is time for the British intellectuals to heed to the advice of Fulton. Once the British discard generalist administrators, the Indian will also follow suit because Indian politicians and bureaucrates are habitually imitators.

In a Report on the Indian Civil Service submitted in 1854 by Lord Macaulay, Ashburton, Melvil, Sowett and Lefevre had advocated "gentlemen" type of civil service.

The duties of a civil servant of the East India Company are of so high nature that in his case it is peculiarly desirable that an excellent general education, which may enlarge and strengthen his understanding, should precede the special education which must qualify him to dispatch the business of his cutchery.

F. F. Ridley had edited a volume on generalists and specialists in which the role of public bureaucracies of U.K., Australia, France, West Germany, Sweden and United States were studied in relation to "professionals".

F. F. Ridley had noted that, none of the countries have any thing like air Administrative Class, generalists in functions and generalists in background. Recruitment to the higher Civil Service on the basis of an entirely non-vocational education is rare. It is true that in most continental European countries, there are administrators who are not specialists professionals in our sense and who in the European context, can be described as all-purpose administrators. In each case however they have legal training directed to their work (administration in Administrative Law Countries has a higher legal context than in Britain). They are no exception to the finding that higher civil servants are generally recruited for qualification and / or experience related in some way to their duties.

Most foreign civil servants would therefore be surprised at our pre-occupation with the rival merits of generalists and specialists. All of them can be regarded as specialists of one kind or another, their knowledge and training related to the kind of work they do.

The notion that a man who has done well at Cherokee is if so facts likely to make a good civil servant is not found elsewhere.

Even where the higher Civil Service contains generalists-jurists as well as specialist professionals, this reflects no theory about the organization of government work. There is no structural separation of specialist or advisory work from general administration (policy-making/ management). Indeed it is most unusual for any distinction to be drawn between the nature of the work involved in policy-making and in other. One rarely finds abroad the parallel hierarchies of administrators and specialists common to British Government Departments. If the work of a section requires specialized knowledge then, it is likely to be put charge of a professional official with the appropriate training and experience. He will take responsibility for whatever policy questions arise. Ministries are usually organized on the assumption that it is impossible to distinguish technical and advisory functions from general administration; they are not structured to separate advisory staff or advisory functions.

Indeed, there is difficulty abroad in understanding the importance of advisory posts in the British Scheme of things. It is generally assumed of men in senior positions that their specialized knowledge will not merely contribute to good administration but that it will also enable them to give the best advise to their political superiors.

The Most unfortunate aspect of British model which we dare call a "Fusion-Model" i.e., fusing generalist services with specialists could not be adapted by the Indians. Indian bureaucrats are known all the world over to be silent imitators but in so far as the sharing of bureaucratic power, they are niggardly miser and orthodox. Indian generalist services can not be reformed unless our political leader are sufficiently educated to be capable to understand after all what this Fusion-Model is and how does it operate in Great Britain, sooner they learn better it will be. It is political elite which has to encourage specialists' greater say in administration.

Specialists or Professionalists in Great Britain

Specialists, as we have already defined are those experts who have acquired special knowledge about specific category of tasks, functions or jobs, These professionals are scientists, technicians, auditors, computer specialists and other people like doctors, engineers etc.

About 25 per cent of the non-industrial civil servants are professional scientific or technical staff, who are generally known as specialists. The range of officials included within this term is extremely wide. Some are such as doctors, architects and lawyers, member of established professions which have their own regulatory bodies which control entry to the profession and enforce certain standards of conduct. Others such as economists and statisticians have high level qualifications but do not enjoy formal professional status.

Professionalists are now being consulted quite often in British Administration. The initial stages "specialists" were regarded as "outcast" by generalists, but now gradually, specialists' acceptability in British Administration has increased. Reason being the changing nature of modern administration. Generalists, is totally unsuitable for most of the modern state functions which are in continuous state of change. The more the man's or group's life becomes complex, the more becomes the functions of modern state different, cumbersonic and technical. In such state of affairs to cling to Macaulayan concept of generalist service is not only ridiculous but dangerously hazardous. As the British have understood need, necessity and desirability to impure performance of their administrative system by reforming the nature, character of their bureaucratic system we earnestly hope Indian mind would also accept the hard reality and absorb as quickly as possible the specialists and professionalists into the generalist cadres.

The latest developments in the character of Indian generalist service is interesting. We find many engineers and medicos are entering the competitive services. It is in no way a replica of Fusion Model of Britain, Indian Syllabus-makers of I.A.S. competitive examination have included as many as 27 different subjects which is too large a number. It is of no use to require a Statistician or a Mathematician to compete with a student of Sociology or Political Science, we find that students of engineering and medicines etc. which are highly scoring subjects do normally better as compared to students offering Social Science subjects. Indians should adopt French method and German technique to groom our future administrators.

In our opinion, some 16 to 18 specialized areas of administration needs to be carved out and entrance test in these 18 different subjects need to be conducted separately rather than a single test for all such pooled officers need to be appointed after training in their respective areas of specialization for first 20 years of service and then may enter the common pool by virtue of seniority of serve the Union Government nearing to 12 years of retirements.

Generalists in the Indian Administrative System

Generalist in India do not have to specialize in the disciplines of Public Administration, Policy-Making, or Budgeting. It is not essential for them term to be specialists in planning or project formulation etc. They are neither expected to qualify law, economics and politics, which is a necessary condition of service in some other countries. In India, the basic eligibility degree is simple graduation. The generalists on which the present structure of Civil Services is based was summed up by Lord Macaulay, which states that the personnel belonging to the generalist services are capable of performing all types of functions conferred on them. It is the "gifted amateur" theory on which the existing entrance examinations to the generalist class is still based. It advocates that a general qualification is more important to fit a man to understand the complex problems of the administration than the narrow training. It is the natural intellect and ability which counts in the performance of administrators rather than the technical expertise.

It may be correct to say that generalist when trained in specialized areas is better than a specialist develops who develops a narrow vision, outlook and opinion. Influenced by this gifted amateur theory the generalists are entrusted diverse types of important functions like policy making and execution as well as indulge in caution and advice to ministers.

The history of Indian Civil Services (pre-47 period) informs us that civil services were designed on British model, i.e., "generalist-type", where are leadership roles in administration at all levels of government were the reserve of I.C.S.

The existing structure of civil services is influenced by the Northcote-Trevelyan Report on the organisation of permanent Civil Services in Britain (1853-54). According to the report, the generalist services should be manned by the most promising young men, who are to be given the most important functions like policy-making and policy-execution.

After independence, the civil services somehow successfully won over the hearts of its bitterest possible critics in pre-independence days in J. L. Nehru and Sardar Patel. With their dedication, sense of purpose and in some cases "Loyalty", they turned their enemies into well-wishers. The old theory of generalists was not only continued but even strengthened further. The generalists were at the helm of the affairs, who held very important governmental positions as compared to specialists. In a nutshell, we can say that after independence the structure of civil service in India was not allowed by strong pressure group of I.A.S. Officers to be changed. It continued in its old form. The specialists clamoured at little later stage and now it appears the conflict between generalists and the specialists has become perhaps the "Knottiest internal problem of the day in the civil services".

Specialists in the Indian Administrative System

The specialists are grouped into sixteen civil services. Apart from these, some of the employees who are not grouped into an organized service are included in what is called the General Secretariat Service. The specialist services are the following :

1. Archaeological Service. 2. Botanical Survey of India. 3. Central Electrical Engineering Service. 4. Central Engineering Service. 5. Central Health Service. 6. Central Legal Service. 7. Central Revenue Service. 8. Geological Survey of India. 9. Indian Economic Service. 10. Industrial Metrological Service. 11. Indian Statistical Service. 12. Overseas Communication Service. 13. Survey of India. 14. Telegraph Traffic Service. 15. Telegraphy Engineering Service. 16. Zoological Survey of India.

Specialists are those who are recruited to the civil service on the basis of their specialist qualifications. The specialists services and non-technical civil services have joined hand against generalist service. In 1970, The All Indian Confederation of Central Government Officer's Association was form. This is the premier institution to spearhead the cause of specialists and non-technical civil services. Specialist services had represented to Second Pay Commission that they should be appointed to administrative and secretariat posts.

An empirical study was conducted by Miss Pratima Kapoor- a very diligent, industrious and trust worthy research student of the department of Public Administration (H.P. University) in 1989. The study was obviously, conducted about the relationship of specialists and generalists at district level—BILAS PUR—Himachal Pradesh.

Miss Pratima Kapoor's study of specialists and generalists (1989) of Bilaspur district (H.P.) inform without relationship between the two categories are cordial (86.65 per cent) and excellently cordial (6.66 per cent).

(Source : Relationship of Generalists with Specialists in District Bureaucracy in BILASPUR, H.P.—A dissertation presented by Miss Pratima Kapoor, 1989).

Union Public Service Commission's survey inform us that on 30 per cent of I.A.S. men had first class in their graduate courses. On the contrary, 80 per cent of persons belonging to the Engineering services had first class in their B.E. examination. Dhruba Jyoti Mhowmic also says the same thing. During the I.A.S. examination of 1960-65 there were only 46 per cent of the recruits who had secured first class in their M.A. examination whereas this figure was almost double in case of specialized services.

Comparing Generalists and Specialists in U.K. and India

Before Fulton, the administrative class or the top-bureaucrats in Great Britain were all "generalists" after the submission of Fulton Committee Report a new thinking had emerged that "for the performance of highly technical function even in matters, of policy-decisions requiring specialized knowledge of technical nature, a generalist-administrator, i.e., administrator recruited on the basis of general academic and highly incompetent"—Professor R. D. Sharma.

As stated above the Fulton message was clear, the competitive services could not perform the tasks of 20th Century England. The twentieth century's state had gone far ahead of Macaulays days when state had nothing short of a law and order state. Now-a-days state is more than a welfare state.

Fulton emphasised that the claim of generalist civil servant to be specialist in all fields of administration is hardly acceptable and tenable and the criticism of a specialist to be competent of a segmental part of administration whose utility is only confined to a restricted or limited area and hence of fractional utility is not acceptable and valid. In Great Britain, the Government has found a new method of making use of services of specialists and holding them responsible and accountable in case of posts requiring policy-decisions.

In U. K. conflict resolution was possible when in certain departments of technical nature specialists have now acquired credibility with the political administrators 'credibility and acceptability of specialists in policy-position is a great victory for specialists. This system is all discriminatory. It has not been accepted as a matter of "right'. Specialists even today, can't claim penalty of pay-scales as well as equal status in administrative hierarchy.

The position in India is even worst. Indians have not yet found it appropriate to associate "specialists" in policy-making position. The generalists-specialists controversy is at its peak these days. The I.A.S. is highly dominating. Even sometimes the top political executive becomes scarce of top heavy administration at the Union level. Indraji had once shaken the whole administrative superstructure out of its self-imposed "superiority" but not all Prime Ministers are Indira Gandhi. The political executive as well as the technocrats are both marked by much stronger I.A.S. lobby in Indian Administration both at the Union as well as at State governments.

23

Comparative Study

Civil services have become steel framework of modern administrative systems, particularly in countries which have parliamentary from of government. It is in these countries that the Ministers are not expert in the fields which they are required to supervise but are forced to largely depend on the civil servants for carrying out the administration. But today the task of a civil servant is very complex, manifold and difficult. Today he is required to work in a state which cannot rule the people with an iron hand. Concept of welfare state has replaced the old concept of police state. A civil servant is supposed to satisfy his political master i.e., the Minister on the one hand and the tax payer on the other. He cannot afford to displease either. He is supposed to be expert and efficient as well as duty conscious so that the nation is benefited by his wisdom and knowledge.

Significance of the Personnel Administration

We have hitherto been considering the principles of administration. Undoubtedly the planning is both essential and desirable but no principle can be a success unless that is properly manned.

For making it a success it is also essential that available resources should be properly utilised by honest and scrupulous persons. It is this need for utilisation of available resources which signifies the need and necessity of personnel administration.

Civil Service in England

Though England is one of the oldest countries with Parliament in the world, yet the Parliamentary form of government in that country is not the old. The people of England had to struggle hard against their monarch for getting their rights. It was after Glorious Revolution of 1688 that the monarchs accepted the supremacy of people. Before that, England was ruled despotically. Those who were to run the administration were the favourites of the King and appointed and dismissed according to his whims and wishes. In fact, upto 1853 there was no personnel administration or system of civil servants started in England. In 1854, a committee was appointed under Lord Macauley to report on the method of recruitment for civil services in that country which became a pattern for England. It was on the basis of this report that the system of patronage was abolished and that of open competitions upto a particular age started. The Report also recommended that a distinction be made between administrative and clerical grade services. It was in 1855 that a civil service commission was appointed in England for making recruitment to civil services.

Functions of Civil Servants in England : Like India, England also has parliamentary form of government. There also the ministries, who head their departments, are not the experts and therefore, supposed to depend on the civil servants. It is therefore, the duty and responsibility of civil servants to provide data, facts, figures and to guide the Ministers on the proper lines. They should assist the Minister in the formulation of policies and should not indulge in political game. They should be neutral in politics. They should most honestly enforce the laws passed by the Parliament. While enforcing the laws they should see that the method is not repulsive and blanks which have been left by Parliament are very reasonably filled. Not only this, but in our modern times, the system of delegated legislation has not only come to stay but is a powerful method of filling the gaps in the laws passed by the parliament. It is, therefore, very essential to ensure that the powers thus delegated, to the civil servants are not misused.

Organisation of Civil Service in England : In England there is a proper and reasonable organisation of civil services. First of all is Administrative Group which includes superior civil servants who are recruited on the basis of competitive examination and possess certain academic qualifications. Their posts are transferable. They help the Ministers in policy formulation and replying to Parliament questions. Then comes Executive Group. The personnel of this group are partially recruited on the basis of competitive examinations and partially by departmental promotion. The personnel of this group are usually required to perform internal executive job and provide preliminary data to the administrative group. Working class of the Administrative Service forms another group in civil services in England. This includes clerks but their appointment is also made on the basis of competitions. Then there are ancillary clerks, including shorthand writers and peons, etc. Each civil servant is supposed to work under the direction and control of the Minister who heads his Ministry but over all supervision and control is that of Secretary of the Treasury.

In the country non-industrial civil servants have been divided into three categories. In the first category falls free area of all varieties of public activity sort of the blatant violation of the public trust. In the second category is an intermediate group which is allowed to participate in all forms of political activities except contesting elections to the Parliament. In the third category falls all those who are denied all political rights excepts voting and active party membership.

The appointment to the services is made by Civil Service Commission which consists of Civil Servant Commissioners. The

Commissioners are appointed by the crown and hold office during good behaviour. The Commission is an independent body. Royal Administrative Staff College trains civil servants. The training is usually for a period of 6 week only. All promotions to the higher posts are made on merit basis by a Promotion Board. Civil Servants of all categories enjoy pensionary and leave benefits and also have some security of service. With good behaviour a civil servant usually goes upto the age of 65. His term of service can also be extended upto a period of 5 years at the most.

Civil Services in U.S.A.

The U.S.A. is not a Parliamentary but a Presidential form of government. In that country civil servants have to play a different role that the role which they are supposed to play in a country with Parliamentary form of government. Upto 1883 there was practically no permanent civil service in the technical sense of the term. The U.S.A. was then known for its spoil system. Under this system, with the change of the President, whole staff changed. It was presumed that the staff of a President belonged to the political party to which President belongs and that the President belonging to another political or another President belonging even of the same political party could not depend on that staff. The system however, did not work well and, with the passage of time it was realised that under this system there was disruption and over all dislocation in the administrative machinery.

It was only in 1883 that the Congress passed Pendelton Act which empowered the President to appoint a Service Commission for making recruitment to federal posts. Accordingly Civil Service Commission was set up in that year. The members belong to different political parties. The Service Commission is loaded with the responsibility of making recruitment, classifying positions, arranging for in-service training programme, enquiring into the allegation of participation in political activities by the civil servants and frame rules and regulations for conducting examination. The Commission is also responsible for making arrangements for providing training facilities to the persons recruited by it. In order to facilitate its work the Commission has divided itself into several divisions.

Appointment to civil services in the U.S.A. is now made on the basis of competitive examination. A merit list so maintained by the Commission and appointments are made out of the list of drawn. The promotions are made on the basis of efficiency and ability. Civil servants are categorised as 'Professional', 'Sub-Professional' 'Clerical' and 'Crafts Protective'. The civil services are now supposed to be impartial in politics and in fact this impartiality has now gone to the extent that one of the duties of the Service Commission is to enquire into the allegation of participation in political activities by the government servants. The civil servants in the U.S.A. enjoy same facilities as are enjoyed by their counterparts in other countries of the world.

Civil Service in France

Case of France is quite different than that of England and the U.S.A. Civil servant in France is much more powerful than his counterparts either in the U.S.A. or in U.K. That is primarily because as against the U.S.A. and England in France there is multi-party political system. Under this system there is no political stability and there are frequent ministerial changes. This ministerial and political instability has strengthened the hands of civil servants who are considered largely responsible for maintaining continuity. Unitary character of France, where there is much of centralisation of authority is also responsible for the strength of civil servants. Only those working in the Ministries proper are called civil servants. One of the peculiar characteristics of French civil service is that they are entitle to go on strike, particularly those who are in essential services. All others are not considered civil servants. Then another feature is that the civil servants in France are entitled to participate in politics and they can continue to hold their office as well as take part in politics. Not only this, but civil servants in that country can get leave for participating in political activities.

Recruitment to services is made on the basis of competitive examination. For that purpose there are four categories of services, namely, (a) Chief Administrators, (b) Secretaries of Administration, (c) Clerks, and (d) Manual workers. There are, however, different educational, qualifications for different posts. Civil servants are trained in France National School of Administration. It has organised itself into (a) general administration (b) economic and financial administration, (c) social administration, and (d) foreign affairs sections. The civil servants can get their grievances redressed through such organisations as Supreme Council of Public Service.

Civil servants in all the countries of the World are an integral part, of administration. These are provided with better service conditions and kept satisfied so that they can put in their maximum. It is today difficult to think of administration without civil servants.

Indian Perspective

While the evolution and development of personnel administration in UK, and U.S.A. was largely voluntary. In India personnel administration had to be provided along by governmental intervention and coercion. While in the West the pioneering work in the field of personnel management was motivated by the managerial preoccupation with the concept of welfare. In India a combination of the disquieting recruitment practices growing labour unrest resulting in strike and loss of production and consideration of numerous grievances initiated some interest in personnel management especially in the textile mills in the years prior to the Second World War.

The Indian Institute of Personnel Management summarises the evolution of Personnel Management in India as : "It will be seen that it was the interaction of Government policy and the initiative of the leading employers association in the textile industries that brought about the rapid development of personnel management in India just before and during the war. It is noticeable also that in textile industries personnel management developed rather a form of recruitment function and the consideration of grievances in other countries. It was the problem and the discontent to which the old system of recruitment though jobbers gave rise that led the Royal Commission on Labour to advocate the appointment of labour officers. Their function as industrial relations officers to handle grievances and to prevent disputes arising was stressed from the first. The labour officer was looked on as the friend and confidant of the workers, but he was clearly to be a member of management".

Personnel management in India owes its origin to legal compulsion. Prior to the recommendations of the Royal Commission of Labour in 1931, the area concerning the management of people in an organisation was either part of financial management or a necessary appendage to the operations of a business. Thus, personnel management in India has a short history of about four decades.